Psychology Revivals

Language Acquisition in the Blind Child

Originally published in 1983, the papers in this volume were first presented at an international symposium "The Development of Language and Communication in the Blind Child" held in 1981 in Germany. The topic although specialized, had importance within several disciplines. Contributions came from the fields of education and medicine as well as psychology and linguistics. In bringing these researchers together the aim was not only to pool results but to encourage inter-disciplinary cooperation, thus giving work in this area a broader and sounder theoretical basis.

Today it can be read in its historical context.

Language Acquisition in the Blind Child

Normal and Deficient

Edited by
Anne E. Mills

Routledge
Taylor & Francis Group
LONDON AND NEW YORK

First published in 1983
by Croom Helm Ltd

This edition first published in 2026 by Routledge
4 Park Square, Milton Park, Abingdon, Oxon, OX14 4RN

and by Routledge
605 Third Avenue, New York, NY 10158

Routledge is an imprint of the Taylor & Francis Group, an informa business

Publisher's Note
The publisher has gone to great lengths to ensure the quality of this reprint but points out that some imperfections in the original copies may be apparent.

Disclaimer
The publisher has made every effort to trace copyright holders and welcomes correspondence from those they have been unable to contact.

For Product Safety Concerns and Information please contact our EU representative GPSR@taylorandfrancis.com. Taylor & Francis Verlag GmbH, Kaufingerstraße 24, 80331 München, Germany

A Library of Congress record exists under ISBN: 9780933014893

ISBN: 978-1-041-19971-7 (hbk)
ISBN: 978-1-003-71441-5 (ebk)
ISBN: 978-1-041-19972-4 (pbk)

Book DOI 10.4324/9781003714415

Language Acquisition in the Blind Child

NORMAL AND DEFICIENT

Edited by
ANNE E. MILLS

CROOM HELM
London & Canberra

COLLEGE-HILL PRESS
San Diego

Croom Helm Ltd, Provident House, Burrell Row,
Beckenham, Kent BR3 1AT

British Library Cataloguing in Publication Data

Language acquisition in the blind child.
1. Children, Blind 2. Perception in children 3. Communication Psychological aspects.
I. Mills, Anne E.
362.7'95 HV1598

ISBN 0-7099-1768-6

COLLEGE-HILL PRESS, INC.
4580-E Alvarado Canyon Road
San Diego, California 92120

Library of Congress Cataloging in Publication Data
Main entry under title:

Language acquisition in the blind child.

Papers originally presented at an international symposium, held Sept. 1981 in Tübingen, Germany.
1. Children, Blind--Congresses. 2. Children, Blind--Education--Congresses. 3. Children--Language--Congresses. 4. Verbal learning--Congesses. 5. Language disorders in children--Congresses. I. Mills, Anne E.
HV1596.2.L36 1983 401'.9 83-1917
ISBN 0-933014-89-9

Printed and bound in Great Britain

CONTENTS

TABLES AND FIGURES

Tables

<u>Figures</u>

PREFACE

Anne E. Mills

The papers published in this volume were first presented at an international symposium[1] "The Development of Language and Communication in the Blind Child" held in September, 1981 in Tübingen, Germany. The topic may seem a specialized one, yet it is of importance within several disciplines. Contributions to the symposium came from the fields of education and medicine as well as psychology and linguistics. Such meetings are also rare and those who do research in this area are separated both by distance and by the academic frontiers of the disciplines involved. In bringing these researchers together the aim of the symposium was not only to pool results but to encourage inter-disciplinary cooperation, thus giving the work in this area a broader and sounder theoretical basis.

Some of the chapters are predominantly a report of results from work from blind children. These are of interest in themselves since so little is known about the early learning of blind children. Other chapters contain a more general discussion of the critical issues raised by such research and emphasize the relevance of findings from the blind to theories of language acquisition.

A general issue which recurs throughout this volume is the question why we should study the language of blind children at all. It is not enough to state merely that we want to know what happens in the language acquisition of a handicapped group; it is important to formulate a clear motivation.

Taking a theoretical perspective, we can use evidence from the blind child to evaluate the role of vision in the language acquisition of sighted children. This is the perspective predominant in the chapters by Mills and Mulford. Under the assumption that all other things are equal (which they are usually not, see the chapter by Elstner), the blind child faces the task of acquiring language with one missing source of information, the information gained through vision. In theories of language acquisition in sighted children, the role of vision is in fact more often implicit than explicit. The evidence from blind children is therefore of general interest since it helps define the role of vision in language acquisition, and therefore provides a more precise account of the language development process. This perspective, as McGurk (see Chapter 10) rightly points out, does not, however, help the blind child any further.

Vision may have different roles in development. In the case of blind children following the same developmental path as sighted children, any explanation based on the use of vision must be rejected. If the blind child follows the same developmental path but is slower in his development, vision must be accorded a stimulating factor. If the blind child arrives at the same point but follows a different developmental path from the sighted child, any explanation of acquisition must put vision in relation to the alternative sources of information the blind child uses. As Urwin (see Chapter 13) and Millar (see Chapter 15) discuss, the loss of vision may not necessarily be a handicap.

Obviously, in order to evaluate the language acquisition of the blind child in terms of such aspects as structural differences, functional differences and differences in input, we must be able to put our findings in relation to development in the sighted child. Despite the vast amount of research carried out in the last decade in this area, we often do not have enough information to make a clear comparison. This lack of information makes it very difficult to interpret the findings from blind children, as is evident for example in the chapter by Rowland on interaction. This is especially critical when trying to evaluate whether any differences which may be found between blind and sighted children constitute a risk for the language development and general development of the blind child. It is this information which the therapist needs to have in order to come to a founded decision on intervention. Will differences in input, for example, have a clear effect on the language produced by the child and how important is any resulting difference in the child's language for his continuing development? It may be of no relevance at all; it may be crucial.

The therapist needs to know how to assess any

such deviations in order to determine the necessity of intervention. This is important in all assessments of intervention, as Schaner-Wolles discusses (see Chapter 4), not only with the blind child. The therapist also needs to know what the role of vision is in language acquisition, so that, where deviations attributable to lack of sight occur, alternative compensatory means of presenting the necessary information can be found.

As mentioned above, it is rarely the case that all other things are equal, that is that blindness is the only handicap. According to the evidence presented in the chapters of this volume, it would seem that blindness alone is not sufficient to produce deviant language acquisition. Where blindness comes together with other handicaps of whatever kind, the chances of language disorders are increased. It is therefore necessary to know how to compensate for the lack of vision in order to reduce the effects of other handicaps.

As stated earlier, the contributors to this volume come from a variety of disciplines and represent different standpoints, that of the practitioner concerned with intervention and that of the theorist concerned with explaining language acquisition in general terms. This volume is also intended to be of interest both to those readers working with blind children and to those who have a general interest in language acquisition.

Finally I should like to thank Laura Lane for her help in translating some of the contributions and Gabriele Weiss and Ruth McEwan for their help in preparing the manuscript for publication.

NOTES

1. The symposium was supported by a grant from the Deutsche Forschungsgemeinschaft and the State of Baden-Württemberg.

NOTES ON CONTRIBUTORS

Edna Adelson is Assistant Research Scientist in the Child Language Project at the University of Michigan, Medical Center, Ann Arbor, Michigan, USA.

Richard F. Cromer is a Research Psychologist at the MRC Cognitive Development Unit, London, England.

Barbara Dodd is Lecturer at the School of Education, University of Newcastle-upon-Tyne, England.

Walter Elstner is Speech Therapist at the School for the Blind, Vienna, Austria, and Chairman of the School Committee of the International Association of Logopedics and Phoniatrics.

Michael Garman is Lecturer at the Department of Linguistic Science, University of Reading, England.

Barbara Landau is a Sloan Postdoctoral Fellow in the Department of Psychology, University of Pennsylvania, Philadelphia, USA.

Harry McGurk is Senior Lecturer at the Department of Psychology, University of Surrey, Guildford, England.

Susanna Millar is Research Officer in the Department of Experimental Psychology, University of Oxford, England.

Anne Mills is Lecturer in the Department of English, University of Tübingen, West Germany.

Randa Mulford is Postdoctoral Fellow at the Institute of Child Development at the University of Minnesota, Minneapolis, USA.

Charity Rowland is Director of the Family Focus Research Project, The Morrison Center, Portland, Oregon, USA.

Chris Schaner-Wolles is Lecturer in the Department of Linguistics, University of Vienna, Austria.

Cathy Urwin has a research position in the Child Care and Development Group, University of Cambridge, England.

Ton van der Geest is Professor in the Department of Dutch Language and Literature, Groningen University, The Netherlands.

Paul Werth is Chargé de cours at the Free University of Brussels, Belgium.

Henning Wode is Professor in the Department of English, University of Kiel, West Germany.

Chapter 1.

PRECURSORS OF EARLY LANGUAGE DEVELOPMENT IN CHILDREN BLIND FROM BIRTH

Edna Adelson

THE ROLE OF VISION IN EARLY DEVELOPMENT

A ten-year study of normal delays and detours in the development of infants blind from birth[1] led us to insights about the role of vision in the processes and organization of early development. We also gained an appreciation of the unique adaptive problems faced by the blind infants, their families, and the research clinician.

The central findings of the research are summed up by Selma Fraiberg in Insights From the Blind (1977, pp. 282-3):

> We were able to facilitate the blind infant's development in every sphere of development, but the impediment of blindness could be discerned at every point in development at which representational intelligence would lead the sighted child into the organization of an object world. We could facilitate the affective ties to human partners, but the constitution of those partners as objects was delayed by comparison with sighted child norms. We could facilitate the coordination of hand and ear, but this coordination was still dependent upon the blind child's ability to attribute substantiality to persons and things when only one of their attributes, sound, was given. We facilitated locomotion but we could still discern the impediment to locomotion, the absence of the distant lure usually provided by vision, the reach for 'something out there'. We saw that blindness was not a major impediment to the acquisition of language in the first two years of life when we were able to maximize the experience of the blind child and his language

environment. But the impediment of blindness revealed itself in an impoverished dialogue and in the protracted delay in the constitution of a stable concept of *I*.

In our view, language acquisition has its beginnings in the sensorimotor period, for blind as well as sighted infants. For the young blind child, who must apprehend the world without vision, there is an especially close link between communication and the quality of available experience in prehension and locomotion, and between the extreme difficulties in the establishment of object permanence, and the vicissitudes of human attachment. Our study began with the assumption that strong human attachments would create the essential context for reciprocity and communication between infant and parent. Then, as daily events created a world that was interesting, predictable and enjoyable, infant and parent would have things to talk about, to tell each other. Our task as researchers and clinicians was to decode non-verbal and pre-verbal sets of communications so that the child was not held back from progress toward representational intelligence, language, and abstract and imaginative thought.

THE CASE-STUDY OF KAREN

The problems of Karen and her family present a compelling example of aborted communication, a failed dialogue. The family's difficulties also highlight the problems usually posed by blindness and point to the role of vision in linking partners to one another, in building pathways to a world of objects, words and ideas, in integrating varieties of experience.

Factors Determining Developmental Delay

Karen is blind. When I first saw her at eleven months, her parents described her as being "no trouble at all" - and so she was, since she slept 20 hours a day and did little but suck her pacifier when awake. She seldom laughed or cried or vocalized. She did not like to be held and was unhappy except lying in her baby bed or sitting in her bouncing seat where no toys could be kept within reach. The back of her head was bald. Her hands looked peculiar and useless. Most of the time they were up near her shoulders, bent back at the wrists, half closed. Occasionally when she was upright, she swept at the space behind her head in a strange, apparently purposeless way. She presented a frightening example of a failure to progress after months of unintentional maternal and sensory deprivation.

Mr. and Mrs. Cook are a stable working class couple who were then in their early twenties. They told me the story of her birth and blindness. Karen, their first child, was three months premature, weighing only two pounds three ounces, and it was two months before she could come home from the hospital. Her worried parents tried to hold her then, but she was stiff. She seemed to reject their attention and she did not look at their faces. She was not the way they expected a baby to be, and they could not understand what was wrong. Soon Mrs. Cook became pregnant again. After a while they wondered if Karen could see and they took her to a doctor who insisted that nothing was the matter. Not until Karen was four months old was the blindness officially confirmed and diagnosed as retrolental fibroplasia, a condition which can be caused in premature babies by the supplemental oxygen used in the incubator. She was totally blind.

When Karen was just eight and a half months old, her sister Patty was born, also premature, but not quite as small. Patty spent one month in hospital. Mr. and Mrs. Cook were faced again with fears about a tiny infant and possible blindness, and had nowhere to turn for help.

In spite of their anxiety and fear, they did what they thought was right for both children. They bathed and fed them and kept them quiet. They described infancy as a dull time when babies only eat and sleep, and that was what the girls did. As Karen's first birthday drew near, they waited patiently for her to walk and talk, but were beginning to doubt that she would. A pediatric ophthalmologist who examined Karen then referred the family to the Child Development Project.

On visits to the home to observe and assess Karen and to offer information and support to Mrs. Cook, I also saw Patty. Watching her, I came to understand what Karen's first year may have been like. Patty was not blind, but her days were monotonous and lacking in stimulation. Within the walls of her cot or tilted back in her infant seat, she had nothing to look at, nothing to play with. Her bottle was propped up beside her. She had too much sleep, too little handling. She rarely made any vocal sounds. I made suggestions and brought her toys but they were not used. She began to show similarities to the institutionalized babies described by Provence and Lipton (1962). At seven months an attractive toy was dangled before her. She looked at it silently. She moved towards it eagerly with her eyes, her mouth, her head, but her hands remained out at her sides; she did not even begin to reach for it.

Patty was deprived and delayed in many ways, as we suspected Karen had been. Nevertheless, her future was not in jeopardy to the same extent because she was not blind. She could see her parents and something of the world around her. She was cuddly and comprehensible to her family, and when she grew too big and active to be contained in an infant seat any longer, she began to reach and move toward what she saw, and came alive - a little late, but definitely on her way.

For Karen such an easy change was impossible. For a blind child the world will not suddenly reveal itself after eleven impoverished months. Instead the natural increase in motor energy is more likely to lead to repetitive dead-end behaviours which are not definitely due to blindness, since they also occur in disturbed sighted children. Such behaviours establish themselves as the understimulated blind child attempts to adapt to restricted and fragmented experience (see Smith, Chethik and Adelson, 1969).

We already had a fair grasp of early ego development in the blind. Details of our research and educational programmes are reported elsewhere (Fraiberg, 1977). Briefly, we have found that the milestones of human attachment should be as they are for any child: smiling, preference for the mother, reaction to a stranger, all being shown at the usual times. Sleeping and eating patterns and early speech patterns should also be no different. Crawling and walking are usually delayed in the blind child, but good control of the body in other ways should not be late. Since touch and hearing do not automatically compensate for the missing sense of sight, special care must be taken to ensure from the start that the hands come together at midline, that the fingers become adept and alert, and that sounds come to have meaning. An important finding of our research is that 'reach on sound' (see Fraiberg, 1977, pp. 162-8), which is as important to the blind child as 'reach on sight' is to the sighted child, may not occur until ten or eleven months of age, that is five to six months later than 'reach on sight'. Until it does occur, there will be no attempt to seek something out of reach, no crawling or mobility.

Our central concerns are to establish and support the emotional tie between parent and child, and to build in essential learning experiences of hand and ear during the prolonged period of immobility when the blind infant cannot seek them himself, when his special needs may be misunderstood or underestimated.

We had been able to do this for blind infants whom we saw very early in the first year. Would it be possible to help Karen? In this case report I will touch on each of the developmental areas that prompted our research interest and clinical concern.

Development of Non-Verbal Dialogue

Karen's appearance at eleven months and her parents' reports about her infancy sounded too much like other descriptions and histories in the literature on the disturbed child, for example from Provence and Lipton (1962). Although no developmental scales have been standardized for infants totally blind from birth, we knew from our own research sample and from the study by Norris, Spaulding and Brodie (1957) that Karen was functioning at a seriously retarded level. However, there were several indications that change might still be possible. Firstly, her mother and father cared very much for her and were seeking help. Secondly, there was no evidence from recent medical examinations to indicate other handicaps or brain damage. More important was what we saw in Karen herself. Karen had reacted strongly to her mother's absence at the time of Patty's birth; she had slept even more, eaten less, and her vocalizations had almost stopped. To us this meant she responded to and missed her mother and she was attached in some way. She did smile when spoken to. Her muscle tone was good as she sat in her bouncing seat. Even her awkward hands offered hopeful cues; they did come together to hold her bottle. When I left my hand beside hers, I could feel her fingers move very slightly on mine in tentative exploration. She did not reject the outside world but she had not yet discovered it.

We had to find some way to bring mother and baby together, to let them begin to share small spontaneous moments with pleasure. Nevertheless I always had to respect the family's own style. The home visits, which lasted an hour, were once a week for a while and then twice monthly. The sessions were filmed monthly. The notes taken during the visits and films were summarized and reviewed by the project staff.

Firstly, we noted that Karen would let me hold her for play, but that she was seldom held by her mother. We thought the regular bottle feedings might be a route to bring about change. If Mrs. Cook could hold Karen, then they would have many times together each day. Mrs. Cook listened politely while I described what it meant to a child to be held close, listening to her mother's voice as she enjoyed her bottle, to touch and to be touched, to hear and to be heard. But she continued her routine of propping Karen's bottle beside her and leaving her alone to drink it. When I pressed Mrs. Cook to feed Karen on her lap while I was there, she did so, but mother and child were clumsy, stiff with apprehension. Mrs. Cook looked stoney and cold; Karen looked blank, empty. This was not going to work at all, so I had to rethink my strategy.

Somehow I had to find a bridge between mother and child without usurping Mrs. Cook's central role. On each visit I spent a few minutes sitting on the floor to play with Karen on my lap. I introduced her to the toys I had brought, while making my own unobtrusive assessments. Karen enjoyed these play sessions. Maybe this would be a way Mrs. Cook could more easily hold and enjoy her child, but she was making no moves in this direction. She remained depressed and doubtful. One morning, as Karen played with a bell on my lap, she made some small sound which I firmly said meant that she wanted her mother. Somehow I stood up with Karen and the bell and the toy box and deposited them all on Mrs. Cook's lap. Through it all Karen continued her fascinated exploration of the bell. Mrs. Cook, in her intuitive effort to balance everything, enclosed Karen in her arms and soon was drawn into the play herself. She pulled on the bell gently and held Karen fast; their heads touched and they both smiled. They were comfortable with each other and together they went on to explore the rest of the toys. It was a start. Playing with toys, with its possibilities of active exchange, and demonstrations of intelligence did the trick. A dialogue of play was possible. A dialogue with words was yet to come.

Development of Verbal Dialogue

Mrs. Cook was shy and found conversation a strain. She seldom spoke to Karen to tell her what was happening. It was difficult to convince her that Karen paid attention to her mother's words, that Karen could use language to make sense of an invisible world. The natural course of events provided a clear demonstration. The family dog was scolded all day long. The sudden sharp commands made me flinch every time. One day, just as Karen learned to sit by herself on the floor, the dog wandered by and Mrs. Cook shouted angrily *Get out of here!*. Karen froze, trembled, and began to cry. I comforted her and she resumed playing. Later, a fierce warning was again shouted at the dog, but this time the dog's name had preceded the shout. Karen quieted for a moment, but she did not seem afraid and she did not cry.

There was small hope of getting Mrs. Cook to stop scolding the dog. Perhaps this regular event could prove useful. I commented on the two episodes and asked Mrs. Cook to let me know how Karen reacted at other times. Did she notice a difference when the dog's name was used? Intrigued by Karen's potential cleverness, Mrs. Cook tested it completely before the next visit. She reported with great satisfaction that Karen had never cried when the dog was scolded by name. Her parents were impressed and life became a little more predictable for Karen. Through this occurrence, Karen also became more predictable to her parents. Mrs. Cook said Karen thought about a lot of things and understood more than you might guess.

Conceptual and Motor Development

After four weekly visits, several changes indicated to us that Karen's daily routine was improving and that her parents were more assured of her adequacy. When Mrs. Cook recognized Karen's boredom, she no longer treated it as fatigue and did not hurry her to bed. As a result Karen's sleep decreased dramatically. She took only two naps and her bald spot faded. Her hands had not yet relaxed but she rolled about and could get onto her hands and knees. She sat comfortably on her mother's lap and could also sit unsupported on the floor. This was considerable progress, but her parents could not understand why she did not try to crawl or walk right away.

Like most people, Karen's parents could not understand the unique conceptual problems faced by a blind child. It takes more effort, more time to organize inner and outer experience without vision to aid memory and to confirm and reconfirm what is perceived. For example, how did Karen make sense of the space around her and her place in that space? An interesting clue lay in the odd sweeping gesture Karen made behind her head when she was standing up. For several weeks, it remained a puzzle. Then, one day, after Karen had lost her uneasiness about playing on the floor, she was lying on her back shaking a rattling cube when it fell from one hand landing beside her ear. She moved her arm repeatedly back and forth between her shoulder and head trying to grasp the cube which she could feel with her fingertips. Karen, with many months of experience on her back, was conducting a perfectly good search based on past successes with fallen bottles and pacifiers.

I did not appreciate what all this meant until later during the same visit. After Karen had played with a musical rattle while supine on the floor, I took it from her and sounded it beside her. Lured by the musical note, she rolled over onto her stomach. I shook the rattle in front of her. Karen accurately located the rattle by the sound, stretched her arm straight toward it, touched it with her fingertips but could not quite grasp it. This reaction confirmed that her physiological maturation had advanced, that refined hearing was now available to her which she could use for reality testing, communication, and self/object differentiation. Her subsequent curious behaviour however revealed her mental dilemma. Instead of reaching again to the spot where she had just felt the rattle, Karen bent her arm and brought it back to sweep the space between shoulder and head. It was another attempt at a search and it was quite useless under the circumstances. Yet she repeated the movements, even after the rattle was sounded again and she had reached forward once more to touch it. Her behaviour appeared senseless, irrational to us, yet it made sense to Karen. In Karen's limited world, there was only one place to find things. She knew that in her bed fallen things always landed on the mattress towards her back. Although the floor was now beneath her stomach, she continued to direct her search towards her back. She could unite sound and touch and infer the rattle's existence outside herself, yet she could not appreciate the new relationship between her body, the floor, and the toy. Words alone could not help her with this puzzle.

Karen needed time to learn the new possibilities of her own body. She needed to learn that, if she reached out through the darkness and the silence, there was much to be found at her fingertips. She needed to enjoy play that would give her reliable and accurate mental images of the outer world. We lent the family a playpen and for the next month Karen used this enclosed space to discover what she needed to know about herself and about inanimate objects. With the playpen I left some toys: one from a toy store, one I had made, one an ordinary kitchen item. Mrs. Cook caught on. By the next visit she had bought a better toy, invented a more interesting gadget, and found many kitchen things that Karen liked. Mrs. Cook was also sure Karen preferred those her mother chose for her. Led on by her interest in all these new playthings, Karen thoroughly explored the possibilities within the playpen. She learned that what was out of reach remained near by on the mat or higher up on the rail. It now made sense to search persistently and in different ways for what she wanted and, as she searched, she moved ever more efficiently, first on her stomach, then on hands and knees. While she played, she babbled. She was able to pull herself up to a standing position, and she would always initiate these activities herself.

For the next half year, Karen made progress in many areas. Gross motor changes were rapid and much valued by the family. At 13 months, Karen crawled across the living room. One month later, she knew the entire house. Her mother said, "I never know where she is now." Soon she was climbing into everything. At 17 months, she took her first steps, and by 18 months she preferred walking to crawling. She was upright and active.

Changes in Karen's hands came more slowly. For almost half a year her grasp remained clumsy and immature, a very visible sign of progress still to be made. Mrs. Cook was encouraged to engage Karen's hands at midline with toys or hand play, but these suggestions met with little or no reaction from the mother. They may have called for more physical intimacy than Mrs. Cook could tolerate. She liked to keep things picked up, so that no toys were left lying about. When Karen left the playpen to roam the house, she found few playthings. Nevertheless, I could see that Karen's hands were gradually becoming more adept at seeking and learning.

Another reassuring change occurred. As soon as Karen became active and mobile, the sweeping gesture near her head disappeared. Gradually she brought her hands down from shoulder level, and they became more open. But when there was momentary confusion around her, as, for example, when a stranger approached or when her mother scolded her sharply, her hands went briefly back to the old posture and became a signal to us that she was uncertain or afraid. If Karen's development had not been altered, it is likely these behaviours would have persisted in their inutile forms. Seen several years in the future, they would have been difficult to understand, and even more difficult to change. They would have been tagged as undesirable habits or blindisms.

Development of an Emotional Tie and Language

In this same half year, other very important advances were occurring which alternatively pleased and confused the Cooks or which revealed continuing conflict. Earlier Karen's parents had felt rebuffed and hurt by her stiffness and unresponsiveness. Now Karen could make her feelings quite clear. She made it obvious that she was not about to share attention or playthings with her sister Patty. When Patty was out of reach in the playpen, Karen shouted and fought to get toys away from her. And just as clearly Karen showed she could not do without her mother whom she would follow or seek over any distance and around any obstacles throughout the house.

Karen's move toward her mother was wholehearted and her love and longing were unmistakable to me. Her mother's reaction to this was cautious. Sometimes I spoke for Karen, expressing what I thought she felt when she looked happy or seemed sad, always calling her mother's attention to these reactions. I repeatedly pointed out how Karen smiled at her mother's voice and quieted to mine. I also spoke to Karen, telling her how delighted I was when something I did pleased her, how discouraging it was when I did not know the right thing to do. Karen listened and babbled. Mrs. Cook did not participate in these 'conversations', but gradually she could bring Karen closer to her. When Karen was teething or had a cold, her mother could take her on her lap to comfort her without words and Karen snuggled close. Mrs. Cook began to ask Karen what she wanted or what she meant. Karen picked up the questioning tone and would say *whatsit?* or *whosit?*, when she touched or heard things.

At 14 months Karen tried to stay near her mother, crawling after her, playing beside her, clinging to her. She then began to show normal separation anxiety and could not be left with relatives or friends when her mother shopped. The Cooks felt Karen was becoming spoiled and needed stricter treatment and more separations. I explained that Karen was making up for what she had missed; when she could hold her parents more permanently in her mind, she would move away at her own pace. With this explanation, Mr. and Mrs. Cook were able to give Karen the close contact she needed through this period. By 16 months, she was more tolerant of strangers and had less need to know constantly where her mother was. At 17 months her mother was set free as Karen took off on her own, eager to explore new situations. She was independent and confident. She was at last walking on her own. To her parents this meant she was all right. A month later, for the first time, I heard Mrs. Cook identify herself as *Mama* to her child.

It was in the delayed use of this word *Mama*, and in the reluctant acceptance of Karen's attempts at speech that Mrs. Cook's continuing hurt, doubt, and anger towards Karen showed itself. Karen's language was the last accomplishment to meet with her mother's recognition and approval. From what Mrs. Cook reported, Karen's vocalizations had deteriorated in the months before I first saw her. She had once cried loudly for long spells. Unable to understand or to comfort her, her parents had left her alone in her cot until she quieted. She had once babbled and even shouted the baby sounds she knew, but when I first saw her she neither laughed nor cried. Only a few whispers were the sum of her earlier babbling behaviour.

Slowly, as Karen became more responsive and comprehensible, her mother began to speak to her. She spoke loudly, almost as if she thought a blind child could not hear well, and the loud voice seemed to express a natural anger. It was interesting to note that, when Karen resumed babbling at 13 months, it was with the same angry intensity one heard in her mother's voice. Karen had two words at 1;1.23. She could ask for things at 1;2.7 (tickle game). At 14 months Karen would obey the inhibiting command *no no*. At 15 months she 'talked' all the time in babbled sentences which had little detectable meaning but contained fine conversational inflections. She acquired two new words for family members, *Da-da* and *Sissy*, but no word yet for mother. Karen's father always found some meaning in what she said and judged her as talking quite well. Her mother, not yet hearing her own name from her child, judged her as hardly talking at all.

I could hear Karen's new words and questions clearly. However, most of her attempts to speak were ignored by her mother. Mrs. Cook's response was always *What did you say? I can't understand you.* Suggestions were made of other ways in which one might respond to Karen, but at that point Mrs. Cook was not able to support her child's language development. When Karen was two years old, she began to say *Mama.* From that point on, Mrs. Cook could hear and understand the other things Karen said. Finally, when Karen was two and a half, her mother began to talk comfortably to her, picking up her phrases or questions and giving answers that led Karen into more speech. From then on Karen's speech improved rapidly. She never merely echoed what was said to her. She had two-word sentences at 2;2.13. She quickly mastered the use of *I* and *you* by 2;11.0. In fact, her use of language became quite impressive compared to the other blind children we were following (see Fraiberg, 1977).

SUMMARY

By the age of 18 months Karen's condition was much improved and by 24 months we were even more assured of Karen's adequacy. She was able to enjoy new experiences and integrate the new into a growing repertoire of adaptive behaviours. She and her mother had many dependable ways to communicate. She could walk. She could talk. Concrete experiences could be described in words. Her parents took hope and were proud of her. Dialogue that suited this particular family was possible once we could clarify the distortion and delay in each sphere of nonverbal sensorimotor development. Karen was preparing the foundations for stable memories and for abstract and imaginative thought. Without any vision, all this was difficult but it was possible.

NOTES

1. "The Early Ego Development of Children Blind from Birth" was a study carried out at the Child Development Project at the University of Michigan and was mainly supported by the National Institute of Child Health and Development during 1966-71 (Grant No. HD01-444). Selma Fraiberg was Director and Principal Investigator.

Chapter 2.

PRECURSORS AND THE STUDY OF THE IMPAIRED LANGUAGE LEARNER

Henning Wode

Why should we study the acquisition of language by impaired subjects, for example by blind children? From her case study of Karen, Adelson (Chapter 1.) makes clear the importance of intervention and therapy in promoting the development of the blind child. I wish here, however, to consider some of the theoretical issues which the study of blind children's development raises, particularly in relation to language. Three important issues emerge in my opinion from Adelson's paper. The first issue is a methodological one, that is the suitability of studying a handicapped group, in this case the blind, as a research paradigm to gain insights into the process of acquisition in unimpaired learners. The second issue is the problem of integrating the findings from such a research paradigm in the general development of the field. The third issue revolves around the concept of 'precursor' with respect to language learning. The first and second issue I will discuss together since they are interrelated. The third issue will be discussed separately.

THE IMPAIRED LANGUAGE LEARNER

Most modern studies of language learning have two deficiencies: a. they do not in general refer to the impaired learner, whatever the nature of the impairment, and b. only children learning their first language are studied. As the following brief summary will show, however, these deficiencies reflect the history and development of the field. At the beginning of research on language acquisition around the turn of the century, the focus was on monolingual children, although there were some attempts to include bilingual children, for example by Ronjat (1913), Pavlovitch (1920), or Leopold (1939-1949). Unimpaired children were investigated primarily, although there has been the occasional exception, for example Jakobson's (1941) study of aphasic patients in relation to the development of phonology. However, even after the revival of interest in child language research during the 1960's due to the advent of transformational grammar, the focus remained fixed on first language (L_1) acquisition by unimpaired learners.

During the late 1960's and early 1970's a major breakthrough occurred, in that other acquisitional types besides L_1 were studied. Research on second language (L_2) acquisition in a naturalistic setting was one of the first new types to be established as a field worthy of investigation. Since then, it has become increasingly clear that the fields of investigation could no longer be restricted to either L_1 or L_2 acquisition or even to the study of acquisition in small children. Language acquisition needs to be studied in its entirety, that is in all types of learners, of all ages and in all learning situations, for example, learning a language in a classroom, forgetting a language and relearning it etc. The insights which have already been gained from this reorientation of the field have required drastic revisions of many views popular both among laymen and researchers. It is now questioned, for example, whether adults learn a language in a totally different way from children. Language learning in the classroom is not to be clearly separated from learning outside the classroom. The similarities that exist in all types of language learning situation call for an integrated view (for details and references see Wode, 1981).

Moreover, I think that the most important insight derived from this reorientation is that language learning seems to require specific types of cognitive ability or abilities which cannot be equated with general intelligence, the rise of logical thinking, or the various stages of intellectual development as laid out, for example, in Piagetian psychology. This is where it becomes methodologically almost imperative to broaden the range of investigational options to include language learning by the impaired.

Learning a language means essentially processing speech input in order to extract from it the rules of the target language. Unimpaired learners are likely to make use of the whole range of cognitive and sensory mechanisms at their disposal. It is therefore difficult to identify or observe with precision the exact contribution of each of the individual components of this processing system as long as they are activated together. If, however, some components cannot be activated, as is the case with impaired learners, then the effect(s) of the components can be studied directly by identifying the differences when compared to unimpaired learners. It should be obvious that this provides an excellent opportunity to determine with a greater degree of sophistication what may be due to perceptual processing via the senses as opposed to some more deep-seated cognitive component. Moreover, it is clear that to achieve this the kind of impairment should be identified as precisely as possible, as argued by Schaner-Wolles (Chapter 4). Little will be achieved by broad groupings, such as impaired versus unimpaired learners. For example, there are studies on deviant phonology where various etiologies are lumped together (e.g. Ingram, 1976). It is necessary to conduct studies relative to specific etiologies.

Apart from such general considerations, it seems to me that the study of the blind learner may prove to be a landmark in the development of the field. For example, the preliminary report from the project conducted by Anne Mills at Tübingen on phonological acquisition by blind children (Mills, Chapter 5) convincingly shows that some of these phonological peculiarities relate to specific visual (dis)abilities and not, as one may have been inclined to suspect, to some more deep-seated cognitive abilities that might govern language learning. Similarly, the work by Barbara Landau (Chapter 7), Randa Mulford (Chapter 9) and Catherine Urwin (Chapter 13) makes one wonder why people might have ever entertained the idea that the acquisition of certain discourse skills, of reference, and of the meaning of certain lexical items should not heavily depend on the ability to see.

In short, then, it seems that the study of impaired learners is likely to enrich and refine immensely our understandings of how human beings learn languages. I hope that such studies will, eventually, also be conducted on blind adolescents and adult L_2 learners.

PRECURSORS

The concept of 'precursor', which Edna Adelson discussed, is, in my opinion, an extremely important notion and raises issues which I would like to expand on here. As I see it, there are three possible interpretations of the notion, namely the metamorphic interpretation, the place-holder interpretation and the catalyst interpretation.

According to the metamorphic interpretation, the precursor stands in relation to the subsequent phenomenon as a seed to the adult plant, that is the precursor, as a phenomenon, develops into the subsequent phenomenon through a process of metamorphosis.

According to the place-holder interpretation, a phenomenon A prepares the ground for phenomenon B but there is no metamorphosis of A. To illustrate this in language, a child may use at some stage a non-target-like construction, such as *no* in negation in English in, for example, *I no want envelope* 'I don't want an envelope'. Such a construction is then later replaced by a more target-like structure, in this example when *don't, didn't* start to be used. *Don't* and *didn't* do not however appear to be metamorphized forms of *no* (see Wode, 1977).

According to the catalyst interpretation, the precursor triggers a reaction without being affected itself at all. In language acquisition a phenomenon B will not occur unless phenomenon A has first occurred. For example, learners of German tend not to use the phoneme /ö/, as in *schön* 'beautiful' before /i/, as in *Dieb* 'thief'.

The notion of precursor is extremely important with respect to the cognition issue, that is when thinking about the relationship between cognition and language learning. This issue tends to be discussed primarily in terms of Piagetian theory of cognitive development. Piaget, as is well known, never made language acquisition his object of study. He was interested in how children learn a language as an indication of general intellectual development. It is becoming increasingly clear of late that the kind of cognitive development envisaged in Piagetian theory of child development does not explain those aspects of language acquisition that relate to the structure or properties of the linguistic devices, such as word order, inflectional marking, embedding etc. (see Wode, 1981 for a detailed discussion). Therefore, either the place-holder interpretation or the catalyst interpretation would seem to be most plausible in describing the relationship between general cognition and language. The metamorphic interpretation would seem highly implausible since the formal properties of the linguistic devices would have to be accounted for as growing out of general cognitive operations. The precursors of the linguistic devices, within this interpretation, would have to be formal operations which would be quite different from Piagetian formal operations and which I would want to call linguo-cognitive abilities. The kind of interpretation given to the notion of precursors needs to be carefully considered when studying language learning, particularly when dealing with the impaired learner.

To summarize then, it would seem that the study of impaired learners promises to lead us to a much clearer understanding of the nature of those capacities that underlie the functioning of man's senses and abilities as they relate to the complex phenomena of learning natural languages. Moreover, it seems that research on impaired learners promises to make our understanding much more precise with respect to the contribution of the individual senses. And it may also be the case that our traditional thinking about what may have been a precursor needs to be reversed. It is quite possible, for example, that the ability to see promotes certain developments in language learning, but, on the other hand, that the absence of sight leads to the extension or more speedy development of other language capacities.

Chapter 3.

ABNORMALITIES IN THE VERBAL COMMUNICATION OF VISUALLY-IMPAIRED CHILDREN

Walter Elstner

DEVELOPMENT OF LANGUAGE IN THE VISUALLY-HANDICAPPED: AN OVERVIEW

According to prevailing views, the basic principles of general human development also apply to children with limited sensory perception or children who have lost the use of a particular sense, as in the case of blindness. Of course, such handicaps create particular conditions for development. The important factors here are the point at which the handicap began and the seriousness of the handicap. When serious visual disorders begin at an early age, for example, the entire physical and mental development is altered (Solnzewa, 1975, p. 304). Language development and language abnormalities can only be understood within the framework of development as a whole. Such a description of the development of the blind child has been provided by Solnzewa (1975, 1977, 1980, 1981), among others. The studies of Fraiberg (1974) and Wills (1979), referred to below, are also informative.

The Development of Communication

Children come into contact with their social environment long before they master the sound system of their language. Pre-linguistic means of communication developed at this time, which later become elements of communicative behaviour together with the sound system, function via the various senses and the motor system. At this stage, two aspects of the reciprocal emotional exchange become evident: that of 'being addressed' and that of 'addressing'. It is critical for the blind infant that he lacks the visual triggers for making mutual contact and can only develop compensatory behavioural patterns gradually.

The sighted infant has already developed a large repertoire of visually-determined behavioural patterns by the age of six months. He uses the "smile language" (Fraiberg, 1974, p. 222) and the differentiated "eye language" (Fraiberg, 1974; Argyle, 1980). The blind child, on the other hand, has no way of watching his mother's facial expressions or of observing the joint and simultaneous nature of visual and auditory events. Consequently, he misses valuable stimuli for speaking; he remains poor at expressing himself and loses many communicative opportunities.

Let us also consider the perspective of the sighted people in the blind baby's environment. They unconsciously expect the culturally predetermined reactions and behaviour patterns of sighted babies, which would act as the trigger for their affectionate responses towards the child (Fraiberg, 1974, p. 221). They therefore misinterpret the blind baby's expressionless face as reflecting rejection or lack of interest. As Wills (1979, p. 89) formulates it, the child and the world around him communicate "on different wavelengths". Fraiberg (1974, p. 226) drew attention to the hands of the blind child, however, which do serve as an adequate means of expression and are indicative of an active mind.

One of the early means an infant has of establishing contact is to produce sounds. The blind infant, however, seems to take less advantage of this than the sighted infant, since auditory stimuli cannot be connected with visual stimuli to form perceptual complexes on a higher level. This is the reason, according to Fraiberg (1974, pp. 226-9), that blind children rarely initiate any "vocal dialogues" themselves, even under favourable environmental conditions. The blind infant learns at an early age "to distinguish voices, but they come from the unknown and return to the unknown"[1], (Solnzewa, 1980, p. 36). Thus, blind infants remain dependent on the initiatives of the people around them. Perhaps this is the root of later isolation (Rogow, 1972, p. 36).

The Acquisition of Concepts and Meanings

Semzowa (1961) has demonstrated that, among young blind school children, one cannot expect an increased sensitization of the remaining senses. Rather one finds, if anything, a certain decrease in comparison with the sensory perception of comparable sighted children (Lux, 1933; Elstner, 1955). The auditory threshold for blind children, for example, hardly differs from that of sighted children (Semzowa, 1961, p. 338). Studies of conceptual development in young school children are informative in this connection (Semzowa, 1962, pp. 30-7). These results show that blind children have most difficulty in distinguishing concepts which refer to activities or spatial relationships. The fact that they also have difficulty in the representation of concrete objects was established by Solnzewa (1975, p. 306). In this study, young pre-school-age blind children could only identify 27.7 per cent of the objects presented to them, whereas a comparable group of sighted children achieved 100 per cent with the same objects. Without sight, the "great organizer of perception" (Wills, 1979, p. 91), the remaining senses are much less capable of making sense of the environment. The child who cannot see finds it difficult to abstract the information which is essential, for example, for the recognition of people, animals and objects, for understanding the course of events and their relationship to one another, and for orienting himself. He can rely only on the use of the senses of hearing, touch, and smell. These difficulties lead to a deficit in concrete representations, and as a consequence to a lack of interest in an external world whose signals cannot be united into meaningful entities. For this reason, help on the part of caretakers, teachers, etc. at an early stage, especially in the motor development of the blind child, is of extreme importance (see Solnzewa, 1977, p. 107, among others).

With the beginning of language, the blind child gains a tool for the expansion of his conceptual world. The time of greatest development for the blind child who is not multiply-handicapped is between 1;6 and 5;0 (Solnzewa, 1977, p. 107). His first verbal utterances are above all a means of communication with the people in his environment (Solnzewa, 1981, p. 233). Many blind children show an increased ability in imitating speech sounds, and later words and word combinations, especially if they are of the "auditory type" as defined by

Mansfeld (1952, p. 48). This ability is also positively reinforced by an affectionate response from the child's caretaker. The use of language for purely communicative purposes, however, is an obstacle to the acquisition of concrete reference in language. Since the blind child is severely limited in terms of the physical area in which he lives, the danger exists of perception in the auditory mode remaining distinct from perception in the other modes. This may be the explanation for the finding that blind children remain at the stage of echolalia for a prolonged period (Wills, 1979, p. 116; Rogow, 1972, p. 37), and tend to so-called 'verbalism'. At a later stage, if the conceptual content of utterances is incomplete, tasks are solved on a purely verbal basis (Solnzewa, 1977, p. 108).

The Development of Morphology and Syntax

In the previous section, it was argued that the main difficulty for blind children of normal intelligence lies in comprehending the concrete nature of verbal expressions and differentiating between concepts; they appear, however, to acquire formal structures with relative ease. Solnzewa (1980, p. 38) reports that blind children imitate sounds from their surroundings, such as animal voices and the noise of engines etc., later than sighted children, but speech sounds earlier. This willingness to imitate also lasts longer and, as mentioned above, can lead to echolalia at a later stage. As discussed earlier, the blind child's early language is primarily communicative in nature. It is also characterized by the playful manipulation of sounds, phrases and compounds. Wills (1979, p. 112 ff) illustrates this playfulness with many examples from her observations of the linguistic development of two blind children. For these children, speech sounds acquire a life of their own (Wills, p. 112). The speech of blind children is much more freewheeling and independent, and not so restricted by the constraints of meaning as the speech of sighted children (Wills, 1979, p. 86).

The sound of some patterns and combinations in language greatly fascinates certain blind children. Their production of such patterns then triggers off the production of new similar-sounding combinations through a process of association. Wills (1979) describes many examples of this behaviour. I, myself, taped a ten-year-old girl many years ago, who played with such sound patterns and put them into song form. This playing with sounds also occurs in the context of speech therapy. The therapy consists of practicing particular combinations of consonants in nonsense syllables with different vowels. This phonetic training, which usually inspires great merriment among the children, gradually earns the title of 'fun exercises'; it picks up on the children's own enjoyment of sound games. Often the children vary the basic material with similar-sounding examples from the sound patterns they are familiar with from the spoken language. It is conceivable that children with an auditory orientation first acquire grammatical structures and syntactic sequences as sound patterns and only gradually assign content to them.

The level of concrete, direct language that the blind child needs in order to cope with life around him, lags somewhat behind his control of formal structures acquired through sound patterns. Wills (1979, p. 113) describes one of the children she observed who, in spite of a high syntactic level in his "freewheeling" language, could not express his real needs verbally, and was largely dependent on his mother's help. The other child observed by Wills could produce longer sentences. However, he was not able to construct these himself, but produced exact repetitions of what he had heard. He had learned these utterances as whole sentences from their sound structure.

Phonological Development

It has been reported that a sighted infant can already imitate mouth and tongue movements at the age of two months (Trevarthen, 1974). That the sighted child babbles over an extended period is common knowledge. The blind child, on the other hand, babbles much less (Fraiberg, 1974, p. 229). The absence of visual stimuli in the pre-verbal stage seems to be responsible not only for the lack of babbling, but also for particular phonological characteristics and the large number of articulatory mistakes among young blind children.

Typical examples of these mistakes, observed by many authors, are the tentativeness or lack of precision in the articulation of particular phonemes, although this inaccuracy rarely impairs communication. Instances from German are the bilabial formation of /v/ and the interchanging of /m/ and /n/ (eg. *Mikolaus* instead of *Nikolaus* 'Father Christmas') or of /st/ and /sp/, in either initial or final position (Lux, 1933; Elstner, 1955 and 1966; Häusler, 1968). Mistakes in English include the substitution of /l/ or /r/ for /w/, /ʃ/ for /s/, /ð/ and /θ/ for /f/, and /n/ for /m/ (Fladeland, 1930; Wills, 1979). Kostjutschek (quoted in Solnzewa, 1975, p. 307) made similar observations about Russian. Göllesz (1971) reports deviant lip articulation among Hungarian blind children. In a study of 14 blind pupils in the Budapest School for the Blind, he established that blind children show more lateralization and less movement of the lower lip than sighted pupils.

Mills and Thiem (1980) recently investigated the interaction of visual and auditory information in the perception of speech sounds. They define four visual categories of German consonants which play an important part in determining perception under experimental conditions and which can function as aids in discrimination under normal conditions. The fact that these discriminatory aids are not available is a possible explanation for the high number of phonological abnormalities among visually-impaired children. This is discussed in more detail in Mills' paper (Chapter 5).

Rogow (1973, p. 107 ff) points out that blind children often have less sensorimotor experience in the area of the mouth. They generally 'explore' various objects with their lips and tongues much less than sighted children. This is significant not only for lexical and semantic but also for phonological development. One must also consider the finding, which is confirmed by our own observations, that blind children are often fed solid food at a much later point than sighted children. The consumption of solid food requires differentiated chewing and swallowing movements which function also as the precursors of articulatory movements.

In the preceding remarks, I have shown that even a blind child who is not multiply-handicapped is exposed to certain dangers in his development. A healthy environment can avert these dangers to a large extent and can effectively help compensate for the adverse effects of blindness. These effects are critical, however, for multiply-handicapped blind children or for children who grow up in an unfavourable milieu. This explains the fact that in many of the studies which deal with the verbal abilities of blind children, such a large percentage of speech abnormalities is observed.

LANGUAGE ABNORMALITIES AMONG BLIND AND PARTIALLY-SIGHTED CHILDREN IN SCHOOLS FOR THE BLIND

Incidence of Language Abnormalities

Before starting the discussion proper, I wish to mention briefly the problem of defining any abnormality in language. Baumgarten (1979, p. 73)[2] gives the following definition:

> Linguistic behaviour is labelled abnormal by the individual himself or by the people around him, when it deviates from the various language norms defined by social groups or authorities. Language may be abnormal on phonological-articulatory, morpho-syntactic, or lexical-semantic levels. Depending on the nature of the abnormality, the individual will suffer a handicap not only in his ability to act on the world but also in the areas of cognition, emotion, psycho-motor ability and social learning.

This is, in my opinion, the most complete definition as yet produced and covers the kind of abnormalities found in blind children very well. By using the term 'language abnormality' one avoids classifying the behaviour prematurely as a specific disorder. The term 'disorder' is moreover used in widely differing ways by different authors, so that a comparison of different findings is problematic.

Some of the authors who study the mental development of blind children also report the presence of, what they call, speech disorders. According to most studies, more than 40 per cent of the children have speech abnormalities, when different age groups are studied.

The following table shows the percentage of children with speech disorders reported in various studies. These statistics, however, are not strictly comparable. Stinchfield (quoted in Maxfield, 1928, p. 71) investigated the entire population of blind children including pre-school children and the educationally-subnormal in Philadelphia and Watertown, the largest institutions for the blind in the United States. Miner (1963) studied seven- to sixteen-year-old blind and partially-sighted[3] pupils at schools in Michigan and Illinois. Häusler (1968) examined school-age pupils at eight German schools for the blind, including both blind and partially-sighted children. He excluded, however, children in vocational schools, the educationally-subnormal and pre-school children. Elstner (1971), like Stinchfield, studied the whole population of pupils at the Vienna school for the blind. This institution is only for the totally blind, since there is a special school in Vienna for the partially-sighted.

Table 3.1: Percentage of Visually-handicapped Children with Language Disorders

Author	Period of Data Collection	Language Disordered (%)	Population (n)
Stinchfield	1923, 1925	49	404
Miner	1961-2	33.8	293
Häusler	1967	45.25	411
Elstner	1969-70	44.27	131

Source: Stinchfield (1928), Miner (1963), Häusler (1968), Elstner (1970)

In 1971, the author also carried out a more limited study of the blind children just starting school, and compared his results with those of German and Soviet investigations. The results are presented in Table 3.2. As would be predicted, the figures relating to language-disordered children were somewhat higher than they were for the population as a whole.

Table 3.2: Percentage of Visually-handicapped School Beginners with Language Disorders

Author	Period of Data Collection	School Beginners - Language Disordered (%)	Population (n)
Elstner	1969-70	57	102
Semzowa & Solnzewa	1962-3	40	62
Häusler	1967	62	53

Source: Elstner (1970), Semzowa and Solnzewa (1966), Häusler (1968).

The highest incidence of language disorders was found among pre-school children, especially pre-school multiply-handicapped children. I will discuss these groups in the following sections.

In contrast to the studies which report a higher occurrence of language abnormalities among visually-handicapped children than among sighted children, the investigations of Fraiberg (1968, 1974) and Wills (1979) show almost no speech disorders among congenitally blind children, but just a somewhat retarded speech development. According to Brieland (1950), the difference between the speech of blind and sighted children is also small.

These apparent contradictions can be explained when one considers the fact that the results here are taken from observations of completely different groups. Reports of non-deviant language development come from congenitally blind children or children blind from an early age with no further disorders, and who have developed in an optimal milieu. Experience at the school for the blind has taught us, however, that such children are the exception. The majority of children in schools for the blind have not had such favourable social conditions, and a large number of them have further primary or "consecutive disabilities" (see Bracken, 1969[4]). Not one of the 93 children in the author's study had had the advantages of the same favourable conditions as the children observed by Fraiberg or Wills.

The diversity of individual circumstances makes it impossible to draw statistically valid conclusions. No two children are exactly the same with regard to those variables which are significant for mental and physical development, and therefore also for linguistic development. The following list summarizes the variables already mentioned earlier:

- degree of visual faculty (total or partial blindness)
- time of onset of visual impairment (congenital blindness, blind since early childhood etc.)
- cause of the visual impairment
- age of child (infant, pre-school child, school-age child)
- additional disorders (deafness, mental or physical handicap, learning disorder, minimal cerebral palsy, emotional and/or behavioural disorders)
- social factors (social class, neglect/overprotection, hospitalism, suitable training - especially at an early age).

The incidence of a multiple-handicap is far higher than blindness alone and is strongly associated with a language disorder. In the past few years, questions about the education and development of multiply-handicapped children have been debated with increasing frequency. In particular, the pronounced increase of minimal cerebral palsy and the ensuing handicaps is a topic of current discussion (Benesch, 1974).

Classification and Relative Frequency of Language Abnormalities

My own work at the Vienna Institute for the Blind will be described here in more detail in relation to the kinds of abnormality that occur, their relative frequency and the factors associated with an abnormality in language development. Only those abnormalities are counted here which required speech therapy. The study is limited to children at pre-school age attending the two kindergartens[5] (KG I, KG II) of the Institute between 1970 and 1981. The populations are described in Figures 3.1 and 3.2. Diagnosis was made on school entry.

Figure 3.1: Frequency of Language Disorders among Children in Pre-school Institutions for the Blind and Partially-sighted Compared with Sighted Children

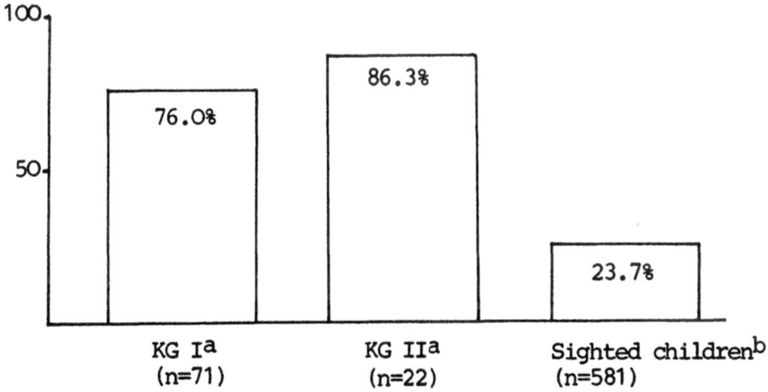

Source: a. Elstner
Source: b. Hess (1955)

Figure 3.2: Frequency of Language Disorders among Visually-handicapped Pre-School Children According to Sex and Kindergarten.

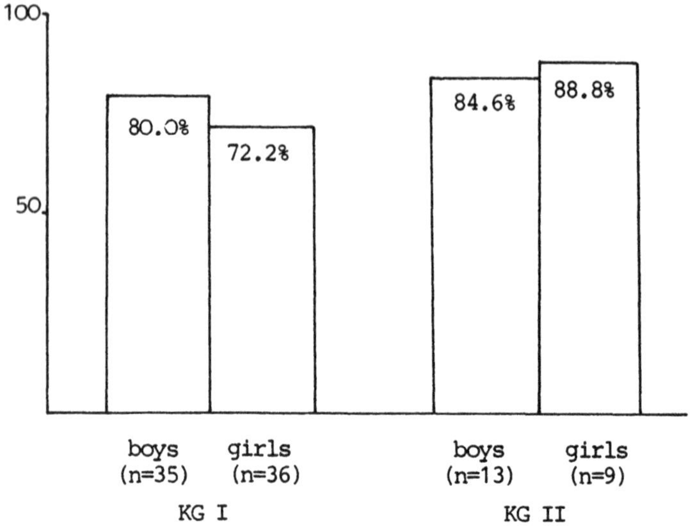

Comparison in the number of disorders (Figure 3.1) is made with a group of sighted children from kindergartens in Lucerne, Switzerland, investigated by Hess (1959, p. 201). Table 3.3 gives the age structure of the children studied.

It is striking that pre-school children in the Vienna Institute for the Blind (KG I and KG II) have a higher frequency of language disorders than the comparable group of sighted children, and that the children in Kindergarten II (KG II) have more language disorders than the children in Kindergarten I (KG I). These two findings were to be expected, since, firstly, earlier studies have found that blind and visually-handicapped children have had more language disorders than sighted children. Secondly, language disorders are more frequent in younger children and children with additional handicaps (Elstner, 1955, 1966, 1971; Häusler, 1968).

Table 3.3: Distribution across Age Groups of Language Disordered Visually-handicapped Children at the Time of Diagnosis from KG I and KG II

Age[a] (years)	Totally Blind		Partially Sighted		Total
	Boys	Girls	Boys	Girls	
3	1	2	1	1	5
4	4 (1)[b]	7 (1)	0	2	13 (2)
5	8 (2)	9 (3)	3 (1)	2 (1)	22 (7)
6	8 (3)	4 (2)	3 (1)	4	19 (6)
7	3	1 (3)	3	1 (1)	8 (4)
8	0	0	2 (1)	1	3 (1)
9 and older	2	0	1	0	3
Total	26 (6)	23	13 (3)	11 (2)	73 (20)
Mean Age	5.7 (5.3)	4.8 (7.3)	6.4 (6.3)	5.4 (6.0)	5.6 (6.2)

Note: a. It will be noticed that some of the children are older than school age (6 years in Austria). In certain circumstances it is possible for a child to remain in a kindergarten, for example when there is difficulty in making a clear diagnosis of the child relevant to determining his future education.

Note: b. The figures given in brackets refer to the visually-handicapped children with no language disorder, for the purpose of comparison.

Classification according to sex (see Figure 3.2) reveals an almost equal frequency of speech disorders among boys and girls. According to the data from sighted children, one would have expected a higher incidence (almost double) in boys than in girls.

Surprisingly, a further classification of the results according to degree of visual faculty showed a higher occurrence of language abnormalities among the children with partial vision than among those who were completely blind (see Figure 3.3). Earlier studies (Häusler, 1968; Elstner, 1971) have found the reverse relationship, that is that totally blind children show a greater incidence of language disorders than the partially-sighted. Among the partially-sighted children in this study, there are a large number of multiply-handicapped and educationally-subnormal, so it can be argued that this sample is not representative of the whole population of partially-sighted pupils at schools for the blind.

Figure 3.3: Comparative Frequency of Language Disorders in Totally Blind and Partially-sighted Pre-school Children.

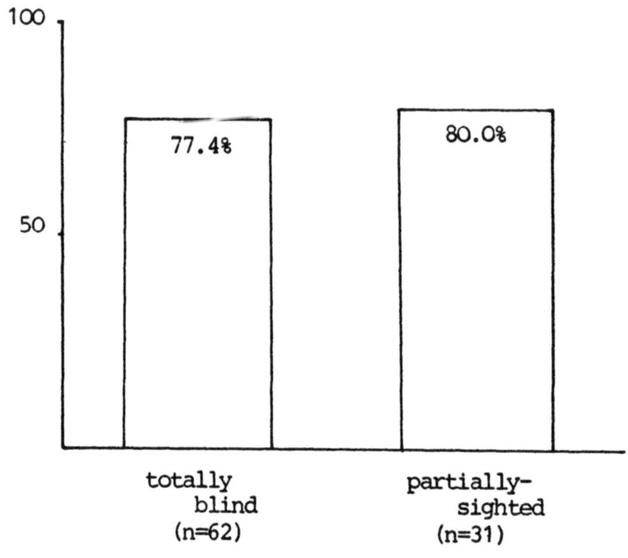

Following is a survey of the proportions of different types of language disorders within the total number of language abnormalities (= 100%) which were found among completely blind and partially-sighted pre-school children (see Figure 3.4). Again, the statistics from Hess about sighted kindergarten pupils are given for comparison. Disturbances in the flow of speech (stuttering and cluttering), which have not previously been mentioned, are also included. Neither these nor the abnormalities listed under 'other disorders' (nasality and vocal impairments, among others) are considered to be important in view of disorders in language development in general, so they may be disregarded here.

It appears that the morpho-syntactic and lexical-semantic abnormalities, when compared to the phonological-phonetic abnormalities, account for a greater proportion of disorders among blind and partially-sighted children of pre-school age than among sighted kindergarten pupils. Phonological-phonetic abnormalities constitute approximately half of all disorders among blind and partially-sighted children, whereas they make up three quarters of sighted children's disorders. The difference between the visually-handicapped and sighted children in terms of disorders in morpho-syntactic development is even more pronounced; approximately one third of all disorders are of this type among visually-handicapped children, compared with only four per cent among sighted children. This leads one to the conclusion that visually-handicapped children have particular problems with the structural and semantic aspects of language in comparison with sighted children.

As is to be expected, many of the visually-handicapped children had multiple language disorders. Almost all children with disorders in morpho-syntactic development also had problems with articulation. It is of course not possible to determine if phonological abnormalities occur among the children with 'almost no speech'. They are 'potential' stammerers, however, since their poor ability to differentiate phonemes only improves gradually, even when favourable results are obtained in therapy.

Figure 3.4: Proportional Distribution of Language Disorders in Blind and Partially-sighted Children Compared with Sighted Pre-school Children

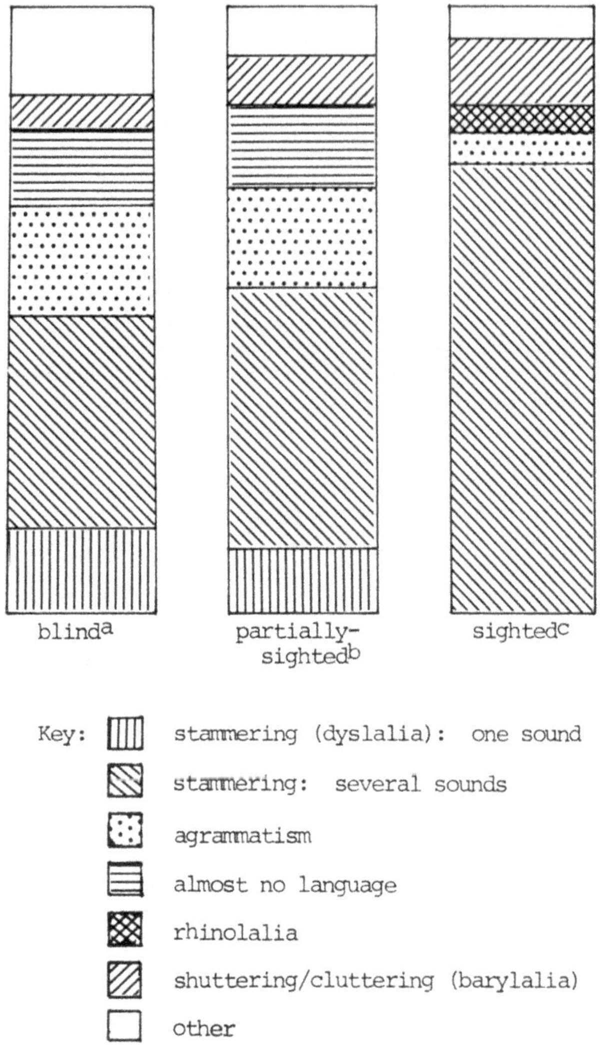

Source: a,b. Elstner; c. Hess (1955)

Note: a. blind children (n= 48); disorders (n= 71)
Note: b. partially-sighted (n= 25); disorders (n= 37)
Note: c. sighted (n=138); disorders (n=141)

In Figure 3.5, the two language abnormalities, 'stammering: single sound' and 'stammering: several sounds', are combined under the heading phonological-phonetic disorders, and are compared with the two disorders in morpho-syntactic development, 'agrammatism' and 'almost no speech'. The figures from the two kindergartens (I and II) were combined; the children were grouped according to sex and visual faculty (totally blind - partially-sighted). As was mentioned above, it was to be expected that children with the greatest loss of vision would have the most disorders in every aspect of language tested. The only result of this comparison which agreed with predictions was the relationship between completely blind and partially-sighted children in terms of morpho-syntactic abnormalities: completely blind children had proportionally more morpho-syntactic abnormalities than children with partial vision. All other comparisons did not match predictions.

Figure 3.5: Comparison of Phonological/Phonetic and Morphological/Syntactic Disorders in Totally Blind and Partially-sighted Boys and Girls

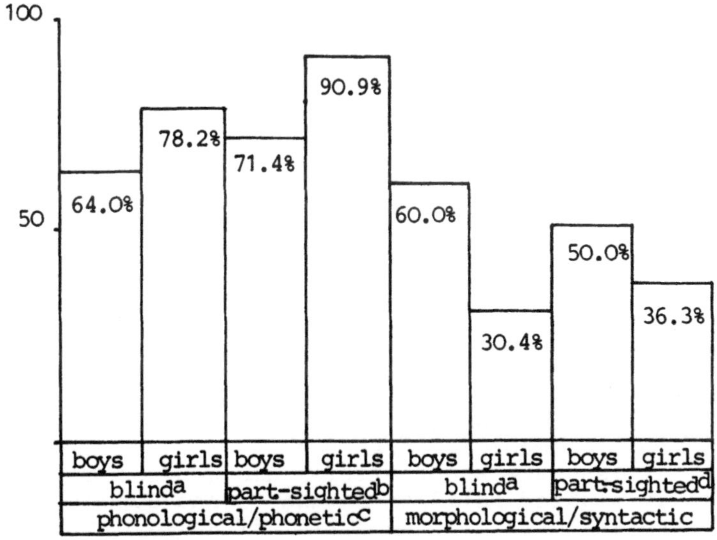

Note: a. blind children (n=48)
Note: b. partially-sighted children (n=25)
Note: c. includes stammering of one or several sounds
Note: d. includes agrammatism and 'almost no speech'

When the phonological-phonetic and morpho-syntactic language abnormalities of children in KG I are compared with those of children in KG II, it appears that children in KG I make more articulatory mistakes but fewer structural (grammatical, syntactic, lexical and semantic) errors (see Figure 3.6). No mistakes in articulation were included from children listed under 'almost no speech'. This can easily be explained by the fact that the children of KG II had additional handicaps, particular mental handicaps, and therefore had greater problems with the formal properties of language.

Figure 3.6: Comparison of Phonological/Phonetic and Morphological/Syntactic Disorders amongst Boys and Girls of Kindergartens I and II.

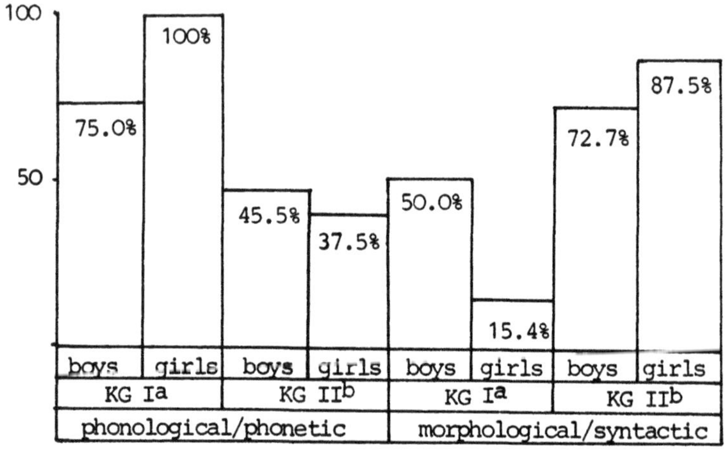

Note: a. KG I - boys (n=28), girls (n=26)
Note: b. KG II - boys (n=11), girls (n= 8)

Discussion of the Results

There are presumably several reasons for the large number of language abnormalities among blind and partially-sighted children at the Vienna School for the Blind (Figures 3.1 and 3.2). Firstly, one must recall all the dangers and problems which threaten the visually-handicapped child's mental and physical development, and therefore language development as well. These were discussed fully in the first section of this paper and were found in all areas of language and communication.

The age of the children investigated (see Table 3.3) certainly contributes to the high incidence of language abnormalities. Many children of pre-school age have evidently not yet completed their language development. It is well known that sighted children also have far more language abnormalities at this age than later as school children, what Scholz (1970) calls "temporally influenced development".

The factor of social class seems also here to be relevant (see Table 3.4). It has been shown by some research, for example by Thimm (1977, pp. 79-80), that social class affects the rate of language development and skill in verbal expression. The children studied here belong predominantly to lower social groups. With the exception of one child, one could not expect pronounced verbal stimulation from the social environment. The two lower social groups show approximately the same incidence of language disorders.

Table 3.4: Categorization of Children in KG I and II according to Social Class

	Academic	Agricultural and Clerical Workers, Craftsmen	Unskilled
KG I (n = 71)	1 (1)[a]	56 (42)	14 (11)
KG II (n = 22)	0 (0)	13 (11)	9 (8)

Note: a. The figure in brackets refers to the number of language-disordered children.

An additional handicap to blindness seems to be the most important factor in explaining the high incidence of language abnormalities. As discussed above, children from KG II had relatively more abnormalities overall, especially in the dimensions of morphology, syntax, lexicon, semantics, and pragmatics (Figures 3.1, 3.2, 3.6), but fewer phonological problems. This can be attributed to the greater number of multiply-handicapped children in KG II. The most important of these handicaps were mental handicap and learning deficiencies, usually due to brain damage in early childhood, and pathological brain mutations with their corollary handicaps, such as physical handicap, hearing disorders and motor disabilities. There was also one case each of diabetes and muscular dystrophy. Of the pre-school children from KG I 56.4 per cent (40 out of 71) were multiply-handicapped and from KG II 90.9 per cent (20 out of 22). Corroborating evidence can also be found in the literature. According to Graham (1968), almost half of all blind children who are multiply-handicapped are without language. It can be assumed with considerable certainty, that a large percentage of the remaining half have speech disorders.

Mental handicap correlates particularly strongly with language disorders. According to Young and Hawk (1955) approximately a quarter of the 53 children in their study had normal speech upon entering nursery school; on the other hand roughly the same number were without language, and over half had retarded or impaired speech. In 1968, Knolke reported that 19 out of 28 educationally-subnormal, blind children also had speech disorders. Among the subjects of our study, approximately 25 per cent of KG I and 86 per cent of KG II can be classified as educationally-subnormal or mentally-handicapped.

Educators of the blind point out that there is a constant increase of cerebral disabilities among blind pupils, which has critical consequences for the development of language. In this connection, Benesch (1974, p. 143) refers to the organic psychosyndrome (defined by Bleuler) with its striking behavioural and motor disorders. According to the criteria set up by Benesch, signs of minimal cerebral dysfunction are already in evidence among nearly 50 per cent of the pupils at the Vienna Institute for the Blind and one can expect a further increase in the incidence of this brain disorder in the future. This necessarily implies a reconsideration of the educational consequences.

When there is a pronounced retardation in the development of pre-school children, one must always consider the possibility of the concurrence of cerebral disorders and social deficit. We were able to observe five-year-old children who were not yet toilet trained, had still not learned to walk properly, and refused solid food, because up to that point they had only received food of purée consistency or liquids (compare Rogow, 1972). Language development had not yet begun for these children, or had come to a standstill. The question should be raised here as to what extent one can make up for missed phases in development or compensate for developmental disorders (Elstner, 1966, p. 35). Few of these children get the opportunity to enter educational institutions for normal children, and many turn out to be ineducable. The results cited earlier by Rogow (1973), Graham (1968), as well as Young and Hawk (1955) pertain to this issue.

The high proportion of disorders in language development leads one to ask whether the lack or limitation in spoken language is due to mental deficiency, or should be called a language disorder or language retardation[6] (from Leischner, 1967). Linck and Haberkamp (1976) and Kruse (1980) have contributed to the differential diagnosis of central disorders in language development. According to their work, a language disorder is now defined as organic damage of different brain functions or centres, whereas language retardation is defined as a "purely maturational problem in the language mechanism"[7] (Kruse, 1980, p. 208). Deafness and mental deficiency are not considered in the formulation of these definitions. A differentiated and specialized diagnosis at the Vienna Institute is not yet possible for several reasons. From the development we have observed over the past decades, however, we can conclude, that in approximately half the cases disorders in verbal communication are due to mental deficiency; approximately a third of the cases are to be classified as language disorders as defined above, and the remaining cases as language retardation problems.

When analysing the incidence of phonological-phonetic disorders and morpho-syntactic and lexical-semantic disorders between totally blind and partially-sighted children, it was found that, contrary to expectations, the totally blind did not show a generally higher incidence of disorders compared with the partially-sighted. This surprising result leads one to the conclusion that loss of vision is less of a crucial factor in causing a language disorder than the presence of an additional handicap or an unfavourable social background. Both of these factor have already been shown to be present in both the totally blind and partially-sighted. This conclusion is also supported by the data presented in Figure 3.6. This shows, in a comparison of the multiply-handicapped children (KG II) with the only visually-handicapped (KG I), that the multiply-handicapped have a higher number and more severe disorders especially in the areas of morphology, syntax, lexicon and semantics.

We see no contradiction in the fact that there

were fewer occurrences of articulatory mistakes among the severely handicapped children of KG II. This was because no phonological abnormalities were observed among the children without language from KG II, since no phonemic differentiation had begun yet. The children listed under 'almost no speech' could not rely on the spoken language alone for the purposes of communication. In the course of further linguistic development, however, more stammering is to be expected.

The prevalence of language abnormalities among children with partial vision (Figures 3.3, 3.4, 3.5) does not correspond to predictions made on the basis of previous studies (Häusler, 1968; Elstner, 1977). One can assume, however, as was indicated earlier, that this finding is not representative of the total population of blind and partially-sighted pupils, due to the small numbers and the negative selection with respect to additional handicaps. The partially-sighted pupils who entered the school at a later time had far fewer additional handicaps and therefore far fewer language disorders than the pre-school children.

We cannot explain the prevalence of language abnormalities among girls in KG II (Figure 3.2), the phonological-phonemic abnormalities of the children in KG I (Figures 3.5 and 3.6) or the morpho-syntactic abnormalities of the children in KG II (Figure 3.6), other than to attribute them to chance.

Figure 3.7: Causes of Difficulties in Verbal Communication in Visually-handicapped Pre-school Children

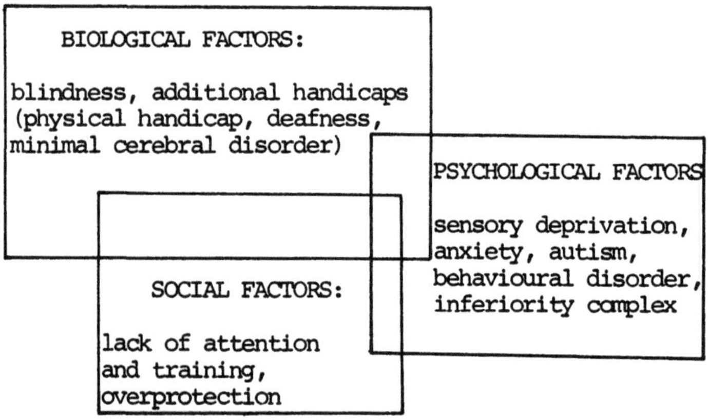

Although the different comparisons have produced no definite results, and it was not possible to conduct a statistical analysis, certain facts seem clear. Generalizing from these results, it can be said that children, as they enter pre-school institutions for the blind today, have comparatively more phonological-phonetic, morpho-syntactic, and lexical-semantic language abnormalities, as well as more difficulties with speech flow than sighted kindergarten children. The reasons are biological, mental and social in nature. These three factors overlap, as the preceding figure shows (see Figure 3.7).

Speech Therapy for the Visually-handicapped

To conclude this paper I would like to give a brief description of speech therapy work with the visually-handicapped child. On the whole it can be said that the general principles of speech therapy apply equally to the treatment of the visually-handicapped as to the treatment of the sighted (Elstner, 1971, p. 238). It is always an advantage to conduct therapy sessions in the environment where the child lives and plays, that is in his familiar physical and social environment.[8] The speech therapy then has the advantage of being "communicatively open" (Homburg, 1981, p. 273), that is, able to meet the wishes and needs of the child in the most natural way.

Training exercises for the various senses should accompany specifically language exercises, as has already been discussed in more detail (Elstner, 1971, p. 241 ff; Kiphard, 1972; Affolder et al., 1980). I have also published a collection of such exercises suitable for the visually-handicapped elsewhere (Elstner, 1972). It is important that everyone who has regular contact with the child be involved in such a programme to maximize the possibilities of improvement.

The exercises for the treatment of phonological and phonetic problems are also basically those used with sighted children. A clear diagnosis of the phoneme inventory has to be made, taking account of the age of the child, before therapy can begin (Scholz, 1970, p. 98). In order to introduce new sounds into the child's repertoire it is useful to proceed from characteristics of the sounds already known, what we have called the "deductive method" (Führing, Lettmayer, Elstner and Lang, 1981). Since there appears to be a need to improve auditory perception (Lux, 1933; Elstner, 1955; Häusler, 1968), exercises to increase auditory attention and discrimination are used. Using the sense of touch, children follow movements of the lips and tongue, as well as perceive with the finger tip the size of mouth-opening appropriate for a particular articulation. These are possible compensatory exercises for the missing visual information (see Mills, Chapter 5).

In dealing with problems in the morpho-syntactic, semantic and pragmatic areas, it is important to refer to the stages of development in non-handicapped children, as has often been stated by other authors (eg. Miller and Yoder, 1971 quoted in Schiefelbusch and Lloyd, 1974, p. 543; Kubiak, 1979, p. 363). Emphasis has shifted within linguistics in the last decade from syntax to semantics and pragmatics. It is important that therapy also reflects the results in these areas (Ihssen, 1977, p. 171).

It must be stressed that no coherent description of acquisition in non-handicapped children is available for the speech therapist. With special reference to the visually-handicapped, a more complete analysis of the role of vision in language development is needed. Until such a description is available, the explanations offered for the high incidence of language disorders can only remain imprecise. Speech therapy must then also suffer from not having a clearly formulated basis for compensatory teaching.

NOTES

1. [Stimmen zu unterscheiden, aber sie kommen aus dem Unbekannten und kehren ins Unbekannte zurück.]

2. [Sprachverhalten wird von der Umgebung und/oder dem Individium selbst als auffällig beurteilt, wenn es auf der phonologisch-artikulatorischen, morphologisch-syntaktischen oder lexikalisch-semantischen Ebene gegenüber den von sozialen Gruppen und Instanzen unterschiedlich formulierten Sprechnormen abweicht, wobei je nach Auffälligkeit des Sprachverhaltens neben der kompetenten Handlungsfähigkeit des betroffenen Individiums auch Beeinträchtigung seines Lernverhaltens in den Bereichen Kognition, Emotion, Psychomotorik und Soziabilität wahrscheinlich sind.]

3. Partially-sighted pupils can be instructed in the same way as sighted pupils, with the help of special teaching aids. They do not learn Braille.

4. [Konsekutive Verbildungen] These disabilities are the consequence of a primary handicap and are frequently psychological in nature.

5. KG I: For visually-handicapped children who would probably have otherwise received a normal education. KG II: For visually-handicapped children with additional, particularly mental, handicaps who would probably have nevertheless required a special education in the absence of blindness.

6. [SpEB - Sprachentwicklungsbehinderung], [SpEV - Sprachentwicklungsverzögerung]

7. [reine Reifungsstörung der Sprachanlage]

8. Since most (ca. 90%) visually-handicapped children live in residential schools, this would be in the living quarters of the family group.

Chapter 4.

SPEECH THERAPY FOR THE BLIND

Chris Schaner-Wolles

In the previous chapter Elstner provides an excellent opportunity for a person inexperienced in the field of blind-research, like myself, to gain insight into the problems involved in the physical, psychological and linguistic development of blind children, and their relation to the task of speech therapy.

The study which he presents covers all types of language problems which were present in pre-school children at a Viennese institute of education for blind children. In view of the extensive data sample and the large variety of problems dealt with, I will confine myself here to the discussion of a few of the more important points.

Mainly, I should like to emphasize the urgent need for linguistically and psycholinguistically based tools for diagnosis and analysis of pathological language development in children generally and that of blind children in particular. In the German speaking world at least, linguistics has not dealt with these problems in any satisfactory way. This affects not only Elstner's work, but is also a major stumbling block to the whole current practice of language therapy (see Dressler and Schaner-Wolles, 1981).

A well-founded diagnosis on a linguistic basis should draw up as complete a profile of all linguistic abilities of the child as possible. Such a general diagnosis requires a distinction to be made between the various linguistic levels, namely phonetics, phonology, morphology, syntax, semantics, lexicon and text, and for these to be correlated with different modalities, such as perception, imitation and production. Only after a complex analysis of all these levels will the nature and genesis of disorders become sufficiently clear to base an adequate treatment on the insights gained into the specific features of the linguistic development of the handicapped child.

In practice however, disabilities at the phonetic level (disorders of articulation, fluency and voice production) are over-emphasized, whereas those disabilities at the other linguistic levels are still neglected, because of the lack of knowledge about structure, function and development of language (see Ihssen, 1978, p. 63). Elstner's work reflects the confusion between linguistic levels which is common in research into language disorders. For example, the distinction between speech and language disorders is not kept clear; a large number of so-called "language" or "phonological" disorders turn out on closer scrutiny to be at the phonetic level. Morpho-syntactic disorders are lumped together without any subdivisions; semantics and lexicon are touched upon unsystematically at best, while the textual level is neglected completely.

Since the population of Elstner's study is very heterogeneous - a feature to which I will return below, it seems worthwhile to check for deviant, delayed or "mixed" (Crystal, 1980, p. 127) language development. Does the development of a blind child differ in quality from normal language development with respect to the various linguistic abilities (Menyuk, 1964, 1969)? Hence, are the inferences drawn from comparison with the development of normal children necessarily fallacious? Or will the visually-handicapped child pass through - with a certain time-lag - the same stages of mental and linguistic development as the normal child (Lenneberg, 1967)? It seems that the search for the answers to these questions has been hampered by the lack of linguistically-based diagnostic tools and, for German at least, the lack of comparative data from language development of non-handicapped children (see Mills, forthcoming, for a review).

Unfortunately, the consequences for therapy are serious. In my opinion, it is impossible to work out a systematic and effective therapy programme without a clearly defined, detailed diagnosis. A therapy programme which is linguistically tailored to the individual child must be based on a diagnosis which establishes which aspects of the language abilities are delayed and which are deviant, and furthermore, the extent of deviance and delay. While, in the case of deviance, the programme has to focus on the specific characteristics of the language inventory of the individual child, in the case of a delayed development, it is the acquisition pattern of the normal child which has to be taken as the basis for therapy.

Elstner seems to be intuitively aware of these faults in speech therapy work. He mentions, for example, the frequent confusion of /m/ and /n/ in the language of blind children, in contrast with sighted children, and suggests an explanation. On the basis of this explanation, he then tries to draw conclusions for speech therapy, which in this case could not be inferred from experience with visually normal children. He emphasizes the serious problems of speech therapists in the area of morphology and syntax, as well as with respect to the lexical and semantic fields. He stresses the urgent need to work out concrete principles in therapy work based on the already existing vast body of theoretical literature, but for the individual therapist this is out of the question (see Rieder, 1980, p. 4).

My contribution therefore is not so much intended to be a straight critical evaluation of Elstner's work, but rather to be a plea for an interdisciplinary collaboration in research on pathological language development in children. The conference on which this volume is based, indicated that the first steps in this direction are being taken.

The point I should like to discuss finally is not only crucial for the work under consideration, but rather is a good illustration of how long the road to cooperation still is, at least from an Austrian point of view.

How reliable are the results of a study which is based on a heterogeneous sample? The only property common to all subjects is, at worst, the fact that they are all blind or partially-sighted. Brain damage, mental retardation, or hearing impairment, to mention just a few factors which certainly have an impact on language development, could not be checked in detail by Elstner before gathering his data. This is the case simply by virtue of the fact that, for whatever reason, a differentiated and specialized medical and psychological diagnosis has not yet been introduced at the Viennese Institute.

From my own experience with mentally-retarded children, I am well aware that this situation is no exception in Austria, nor, I presume, in many other European countries. I wonder how a speech therapist can do reasonable work under these circumstances: a question therapists are increasingly asking themselves.

It is the task, and duty, of research workers in the medical, psychological and linguistic fields to make their findings accessible to those who wish to apply them, particularly in therapy work. The cooperation envisaged here has recently proved its value in research on aphasia (see Peuser, 1978). Interdisciplinary work such as this volume represents will hopefully bring us a good deal nearer to that goal!

Chapter 5.

ACQUISITION OF SPEECH SOUNDS IN THE VISUALLY-HANDICAPPED CHILD

Anne E. Mills

THE ROLE OF VISUAL INFORMATION

The role of visual information, that is of the seen articulatory movements, has not been the subject of much research, although it has been known for a long time that the seen articulation can improve comprehension when the acoustic conditions are bad. This has been shown by O'Neill (1954) and by Sumby and Pollack (1954) in perception experiments. Models of speech perception therefore have not included visual information but have been based on the processing of auditory information related in some ways to articulatory movements.

The many studies which have investigated lipreading (for example Alich, 1960; Woodward and Barber, 1960; Fisher, 1968; Walden et al., 1977) have shown that the number of visually distinctive sounds are smaller than the number of phonemes in a particular language (called a "viseme" by Erber, 1974). This number is determined by several factors, for example the distinction between a voiced and a voiceless sound does not appear to be visually distinctive. The precision of the articulation and the conditions under which the articulation is observed can also effect the number of distinctions that are possible. The groups of consonants, based primarily on the German phoneme repertoire, which are visually distinctive under the most favourable conditions are presented in Table 5.1.

It is not possible to describe the processing of auditory information in detail here. What is most important are the relationships between the various acoustic parameters in the perception of sounds. Miller and Nicely investigated the perception of sounds under different levels of white noise. They found that the information necessary to distinguish voiced from voiceless sounds and the information determining manner of articulation was lost less quickly than the information determining place of articulation.

Table 5.1: The Visual Groups of Consonants tested by Mills and Thiem (1980)

Visual Group	Consonants[a]
1	b,m
2	v
3	ð
4	ʃ
5	l
6	r
7	z
8	d,g,n,ŋ,x,h

Note: a. Voicing is not relevant here.

Miller and Nicely wrote (1955, p. 352): "The place of articulation, which was hardest to hear correctly in our tests, is the easiest of the features to see on a talker's lips. The other features are hard to see but easy to hear."

Visual and auditory information seem to complement one another. The exact interaction between the two has not been the subject of much detailed investigation, although this topic has attracted interest in recent years (Ewertsen and Nielsen, 1971; Dodd, 1977; McGurk and MacDonald, 1976, 1977; Summerfield, 1979; Mills and Thiem, 1980; McGurk and Buchanan, 1981). The results obtained by Dodd (1977) suggest that visual information does not just support auditory information but plays an independent part in perception. The results obtained by McGurk and MacDonald (1977) also suggest this conclusion. They presented adult subjects with a dubbed film in which a speaker articulated syllables with the structure consonant + vowel /ɑ/. The film was dubbed in such a way that the articulatory movements of one syllable were presented with the sound of a different syllable. The subjects frequently perceived illusions which did not agree in many instances with either the seen or the heard syllable. For example if /gɑ/ was presented visually and /bɑ/ auditorily, the subjects generally perceived /dɑ/ which is called a fusion. On the other hand, if they were presented with /bɑ/ visually and /gɑ/ auditorily, they most frequently perceived /bgɑ/, called a combination. On the basis of their results, McGurk and MacDonald formulated a manner-place hypothesis, since rejected, according to which the information as to the place of articulation is visual and the information as to the manner of articulation is auditory. This explanation however does not explain the two different types of illusion. According to this hypothesis the last case should lead to the perception of /b/ since this consonant is also a stop.

In a larger experiment including consonants which occur in German (Mills and Thiem, 1980) a greater range of consonants was tested in this way to see if a more exact explanation of the illusions could be found. According to the results of this experiment, four groups of consonants appeared to be visually distinctive in German (see Table 5.1), namely visual groups 1,2,3 and 4-8. In general the auditory information determined the voicing of the percept and the manner of articulation. The visual information determined the visual group of the percept. This still does not offer an explanation for the two different types of illusion, fusions and combinations. The perceived sound seems to depend on the articulatory possibilities which the visual picture allows as a whole. For example if a bilabial closure is presented visually (vis.gp.1) the lips are first closed then opened for the articulation of the vowel. As the lips open, they move through positions which match the articulation positions necessary for visual groups 2,3, and 4-8. When a sound from these groups is presented auditorily, it is possible to interpret the visual information as matching two different sounds, that is a combination. If the visual stimulus shows a greater lip opening than that necessary for the auditory stimulus then the perception of a combination is practically impossible. In the cases where the visual group contains a sound which has the same manner of articulation as the auditory stimulus, then a fusion is perceived.

These results suggest that the visual information determined to a very large extent what is perceived, in that an adjustment of the auditory information is more readily made than an adjustment of the visual information. This dominance implies that the information from the auditory and visual modalities are compared with one another. A sound must be stored with its acoustic properties but also with the visual information about the articulatory movements. Models of speech perception must take visual information into account.

VISUAL INFORMATION IN THE ACQUISITION OF SPEECH SOUNDS

Under normal conditions of conversation visual information does not play such a critical part, firstly, because such discrepancies as were manipulated under experimental conditions are not possible and secondly because semantic and pragmatic information plays an important part in perception when words are involved. In the period of language acquisition in children, however, it is quite possible that visual information is more important than in adults. There is some evidence already to support this. In many diaries of child language development it is reported that the child around the age of six months watches mouth movements. Children often copy such movements without sounds (Scupin and Scupin, 1907). Wundt (1911) claimed this observation of mouth movements was critical in language development in that it formed the impulse to speak. An earlier study (Mills, 1978) with a sighted child (0;9) showed that the child used visual information in his imitations. The child tried to copy the different lip positions of the adult models.

From the hypothesis that sighted children use visual information in the acquisition of phonology follow certain predictions:

1. that sighted children will learn the articulatory movements that they can see more quickly and with less error than those that they cannot see.

2. that sighted children will make phonological substitutions within a visual group rather than across visual groups. The substitutions within a visual group will be made on the basis of other factors such as acoustic similarity. If a visual group has only a few members and these are not acoustically similar to one another, the sounds will not be substituted for one another.

3. that blind children will not be influenced in their phonological substitutions by visual groups but by other factors such as acoustic similarity. Substitutions will therefore be made across visual groups and a pattern will emerge which is different

from that of the sighted child.

Subjects and Method

To examine the accuracy of these predictions, a group of blind children are being studied in their early language development[1]. Here the analysed data from one blind child, Hanna, will be compared with the data from two sighted children. Hanna is a girl born of German parents. She is congenitally blind (Leber's tapetoretinal degeneration) with no apparent additional handicap. She has normal hearing and is well developed in motor and cognitive skills (well within the normal range). At the time of the recording of the data to be discussed here (1;9 to 2;1), she was just beginning to produce the first two-word utterances. The one sighted child, Joanna, is a girl of English parents. She is within the normal range in development, has normal hearing and was just beginning to produce two-word utterances at the time of recording, that is at the age of 1;6. The second sighted child, Amahl, is a boy of English father and Indian mother whose phonological development in English was described by Smith (1973). The data presented by Smith start around 2;2 since the boy began to speak late, at approximately 1;10.

The data collected from Hanna and Joanna consist of spontaneous utterances and elicited imitations of syllables with the structure consonant + vowel /ɑ/. Among the spontaneous utterances a distinction can be made between imitations of words occurring in the adult's previous utterance and productions which do not appear to have an immediate model. This distinction did not appear to have any effect on the data collected so that this distinction is not pursued. The data collected by Smith are predominantly spontaneous utterances and those considered here were collected between 2;2 and 3;0.

Elicited Imitations

The first comparison will be made between the elicited imitations of syllables from the blind child Hanna and the sighted child Joanna (see Table 5.2). The syllables are grouped according to the visual groups discussed earlier. Where it was not possible to elicit an imitation, a dash appears in the table. The data here are few since the imitation game was not always successful but in one instance they are of particular interest.

Table 5.2: Elicited Imitations of Syllables from One Blind Child (Hanna) and One Sighted Child (Joanna)

Visual Group	Model	Hanna	Joanna
1	b	b	b
	m	m/n/v	m
2	v	v	w
4-8	d	d/g	d/g
	g	g/d	-
	n	n	n
	s	-	j/g
	ʃ	ʃ/s/ç/θ	-
	l	l	l

Hanna and Joanna both make errors in their imitations, mainly in substituting sounds within visual group 4-8. Hanna uses a sound from a different visual group in two instances: she produces, in imitation of /m/ (vis.gp.1) [n] (vis.gp.4-8) and [v] (vis.gp.2); in imitation of /ʃ/ she produces in one instance [θ] (vis.gp.3). Joanna makes substitutions within group 4-8 except for the substitution of [w] in imitation of /v/. This sound was not used in the illusion experiment which forms the basis of categorisation, since /w/ is not a phoneme of German. On the basis of Walden et al.'s results (1977) with English, it can be confused in a lip-reading task both with sounds of group 4-8 and group 2. It cannot therefore be clearly assigned to a visual group.

Spontaneous Utterances

More information is available from the spontaneous utterances. For the purposes of this analysis the initial consonants of the words produced were compared rather than the consonants occurring later in the word. Smith's data are used in this comparison. For the sake of brevity I will discuss the errors that occurred with visual groups 1 and 2 (see Tables 5.3 and 5.4). Firstly, the total number of target words beginning with a consonant from the visual group is listed for each child. Secondly, the number of words always produced with that consonant are listed. In the next two columns the substitutions in these words are classified: where the consonant was omitted and where the consonant was substituted by a consonant from a different visual group. Errors in voicing were not classified as errors, so that in visual groups 1 and 2 no substitutions occurred within the visual groups. In the last column all the other words produced by the child were considered; the number of times a consonant from visual groups 1 and 2 was substituted in these words is listed. Errors where the first consonant of a consonant cluster was omitted, such as /s/ in /sm/, were not considered.

Looking at Table 5.3 first, which reports the errors involving consonants from visual group 1, it can be seen that the blind child makes more errors across the visual groups. The figures from Smith's data are presented for two periods since the errors were concentrated in the first two months of observation. Even in this more restricted period the number of errors involving substitutions across visual groups is still far smaller as a proportion of the number of words involved than in the blind child. If the actual errors are considered, the difference between the sighted child and the blind child becomes more marked. In every instance except one, the sighted children's errors can be explained by the influence of a consonant occurring later in the word. For example, Amahl and Joanna produced [beɪbu] for *table*, Amahl produced [bʌbə] for *rubber*, [mɪbu] for *nipple*. The one exception is [maɪp] for *knife*. Hanna's errors can only be explained in this way in two instances. The other errors are different. She produced [deɪdi] for *Baby*, for example, that is a vis.gp. 4-8 consonant is substituted for a vis.gp.1 consonant; *tief* 'deep' was produced as [pi:f] (a vis.gp.1 consonant is substituted for a consonant from gp.4-8), *weg* 'away' as [mɪp] and *fahren* 'drive' as [pɑ:l] (a vis.gp.1 consonant is substituted for a vis.gp.2 consonant).

It could be argued that fewer errors are made by the sighted children because these particular individuals are more accurate phonetically. Smith's data, since they are more extensive, were examined to make a comparison of the productions of target words beginning with /d/ and /t/ (vis.gp.4-8). Of the 171 target words beginning with /d/ and /t/, 32 (19%) are produced with a different consonant (voicing errors are not considered). The main substitution was with [k] or [g] which are also from visual group 4-8.

Table 5.3: Substitutions in Spontaneous Utterances from One Blind Child (Hanna) and Two Sighted Children (Joanna and Amahl) which involved Consonants from Visual Group 1 (/b/, /p/, /m/).

Child	Number of target words with initial vis.gp.1	Correct	Consonant omitted	vis.gp.1 substituted by different vis.gp.	vis.gp.1 substituted for different vis.gp.	
Hanna	20	17	0	3	5 out of	95
Joanna	12	12	0	0	1	24
Amahl						
2;2-2;3	68	68	0	0	7	355
2;2-3;0	328	324	2	2	8	1400+

Table 5.4: Substitutions in Spontaneous Utterances from One Blind Child (Hanna) and Two Sighted Children (Joanna and Amahl) which involved Consonants from Visual Group 2 (/f/, /v/)

Child	Number of target words with initial vis.gp.2	Correct	Consonant omitted	vis.gp.2 substituted by different vis.gp.	vis.gp.2 substituted for different vis.gp.
Hanna	16	7	0	9	6 out of 99
Joanna	3	0	0	3 (all by /w/)	0 33
Amahl 2;2-3;0	96	64	0	32 (26 by /w/)	9 1600+

This number of errors is proportionally higher than the number of errors with /b/, /p/ and /m/, which suggests that Amahl is not generally accurate phonetically. This also supports prediction one, namely that sighted children will make fewer errors with the sounds which involve articulatory movements which can be seen than with those whose articulatory movements cannot be seen. Of the 13 words beginning with /d/ or /t/ which Hanna produced, three (23%) were produced with a different consonant, which indicates that she is not generally retarded in her phonological development.

Table 5.4 shows the substitutions involving consonants from visual group 2. A similar picture emerges. Again the blind child made a far greater number of errors across visual groups. The two sighted children, both English speakers it will be remembered, substituted /w/ in the majority of the cases. The status of /w/ is unclear in terms of its visual distinctiveness but, even if it is assumed to be distinct from visual group 2, the sighted children still make fewer substitutions across visual groups. In the nine errors produced by Amahl four words began with the morpheme *some* which was produced around the age 2;6 as [fʌm]. The other five substitutions were in words beginning with the cluster /sw/ which was produced as [f], for example *swing* as [fɪŋ]. The nine words can therefore be reduced to two rules, only one of which clearly involves a substitution across visual groups. Hanna's errors are again distinct, and are not clearly the results of any rules. In words beginning with /f/ or /v/, she produced for example [las] for *Wasser* 'water', [haɪkə] for *weiter* 'further', [søːlə] for *fühlen* 'feel'. /f/ was substituted in *Schuh* 'shoe' to produce [fuə], *Sack* 'sack' is [fak].

Discussion

Although the sample from the blind child is comparatively small, the evidence here is in support of the predictions made earlier. In support of prediction one, that is that sighted children will learn the articulatory movements that they can see with less error than those that they cannot see, Amahl made fewer errors in words beginning with /b/, /p/, and /m/ (vis.gp.1) than in words beginning with /d/ or /t/ (vis.gp.4-8) whose distinctive articulatory movements cannot be seen. The blind child made more substitutions across visual groups than the two sighted children and these substitutions did not appear to be the result of any rule, such as assimilation, which was the case for the sighted children. From the evidence presented here the three predictions appear therefore to be upheld.

The question now remains to be asked what relevance this different pattern of substitutions has for the development of phonology and language in general for the blind child. In the case of Hanna, her general language development was within the normal range as far as structure and function were concerned, so that no overall effect could be observed. Her phonological development is retarded in comparison with that of the sighted child only in respect of those sounds which have an observable articulation, that is the sounds in visual groups 1 and 2. Her production of consonants which do not have clearly visible articulation however appears to be at the same level as the sighted children, so that she cannot be said to be generally phonetically retarded. From the evidence presented here, Hanna's different pattern of substitutions is not therefore to be classed either as retarded or deviant in the sense of a language disorder, but it is a different, marginally slower, developmental pattern. It is predicted that she will finally make use of acoustic information sufficiently to correct her substitutions and to conform to adult norms.

Considering Elstner's data (Chapter 3), it remains an interesting question, whether the different pattern of substitutions observed in Hanna could in itself lead to the development of different phonological rules and finally a language disorder. It would seem unlikely that this would result but, compounded with some other factors such as an additional handicap, it could well lead to a disordered phonology requiring therapy. Further research should throw light on this question.

NOTES

1. This research project 'Die Rolle der visuellen Information beim Spracherwerb' is being conducted at the University of Tübingen and is funded by the Deutsche Forschungsgemeinschaft.

Chapter 6.

THE VISUAL AND AUDITORY MODALITIES IN PHONOLOGICAL ACQUISITION

Barbara Dodd

The results presented by Anne Mills in Chapter 5 demonstrate that speech perception involves not only the processing of auditory cues, but also, if it is available, visually perceived lip-read information. This conclusion has now been reached by several researchers using different paradigms, and is true for English and German (McGurk and MacDonald, 1976; Dodd, 1977; Mills and Thiem, 1980). Mills' paper raises two important issues. One is the role of lip-read information in the acquisition of phonology; and the other is concerned with how lip-read information is coded for speech perception.

THE ROLE OF LIP-READ INFORMATION IN PHONOLOGICAL ACQUISITION

Teachers of profoundly deaf infants claim that instruction in lip-reading can usefully begin as early as six weeks of age. If they are right, then very small infants should be aware of lip movements i.e. be able to extract some information by observing the changing pattern of lip shapes. I attempted to test this hypothesis (Dodd, 1979) by observing 10 to 16 week old infants' reaction to nursery rhymes presented with speech sounds and lip movements in-synchrony and out-of-synchrony.

Twelve healthy, full-term infants, acted as subjects. The babies were seated in an infant chair, and their attention drawn to a mirror in which they could see reflected the face of an experimenter who was inside a sound-proof box. The experimenter attracted the baby's attention by calling the child's name and making noise. Once the baby was attending to the in-synchrony speech in this brief familiarization period, the experiment began.

Each experimental session lasted a minimum of four minutes. During this time the experimenter recited nursery rhymes, brightly, maintaining eye-contact with the infant wherever possible. Every 60 seconds the stimuli changed from being in-synchrony to being out-of-synchrony or vice versa. The out-of-synchrony presentation was achieved by using a tape recorder delay, so that the auditory information arrived at the loudspeaker behind the mirror 400 ms. after it was actually spoken. Alternate infants began with an out-of-synchrony presentation. Each infant had two trials of each type of speech; each trial was one minute long. Two observers, who had a good view of the infant, pressed 'inattention buttons', that were connected to a polygraph recorder, whenever the infants were not looking at the face, that is, for example, when they were fretting, pulling clothing over their heads, had their eyes closed. The polygraph measured the time course of the experiment in seconds, the type of stimuli presented, and the two observers' perception of the infants inattention. Agreement between observers was 95 per cent.

Table 6.1: Percentage Inattention to in- and out-of-Synchrony Presentation

Subject	In-synchrony	Out-of-synchrony
DC	20.3	50.4
MK	17.0	87.0
VH	6.5	25.1
JM	25.0	28.5
SB	5.4	26.9
MM	29.2	36.6
RH	2.9	1.0
DJ	6.6	43.8
JD	15.8	44.2
ZC	8.3	10.4
CW	34.0	29.9
AF	8.0	27.7
Mean	14.9	34.3

Source: Dodd (1979).

The results showed that infants attended significantly less to the out-of-synchrony presentation than to the in-synchrony presentation (Wilcoxon $T=5$, $N=12$, $p<0.01$). This finding was confirmed by the fact that several infants became distressed during the out-of-synchrony presentation. Thus it would seem that infants as young as ten weeks of age are aware when speech sounds and lip movements do not match, even though they do not understand what is being said. If it is not an innate ability, then it is acquired very soon after birth.

One implication of the finding that lip-read information can be processed in infancy, is that vision may play an important part in the acquisition of speech perception and production abilities. The obvious way of measuring the role of vision is to study the development of blind infants.

The literature shows an increased incidence of phonological disorders in the blind school-age population (see Elstner, Chapter 3). However, blindness per se is not a sufficient condition for disordered phonology, since most congenitally blind children acquire a normal phonological system, though their development may be slightly delayed. Therefore the role of vision must be assessed in terms of differences in the developmental pattern of phonology between blind and sighted children.

Anne Mills' case study of a blind child has provided some fascinating data which point to the conclusion that normally sighted children often make substitution errors from the same visually distinct class of sounds, whereas blind children may maintain the correct manner of articulation but tend to substitute a sound from a different place of articulation.

Some years ago, I collected language data on a 21-23 month-old little girl, Nicola, who had been born without eyes, but who was otherwise normal. I have therefore reanalysed the phonological data, according to Mills, to see if it lends support to her findings. Note that the subject's general language development was well within normal limits.

The phonological data analysed consisted of 100 words that could be unambiguously discerned from tape recordings of Nicola's spontaneous speech. These were compared, on a word for word basis, with the phonological realizations of a normally sighted little girl over the age range 17 to 27 months. However, 61 words out of 100 were produced by the sighted subject between 21 and 23 months of age, the same age as Nicola at the time of data collection.

A summary of the data is shown in Table 6.2.

Table 6.2: Comparison of Blind and Sighted Children's Phonology

Response Frequency	Blind[a]	Sighted[a]
Pronounced correctly	42	19
Both children pronounced correctly	14	14
Both children made same error	32	32
Pronounced differently	54	54
Error Types (per cent)	**Blind**	**Sighted**
Substitution from same visual category e.g. [mɔl] *ball*	15.4	36.1
Substitution from different visual category e.g. [sɪp] *ship*	23.1	12.8
Cluster Reduction e.g. [bɒk] *block*	39.9	21.3
Deletion e.g. [ɪŋ] *sing*	24.6	29.8

Note: a. Number of words = 100.

The data show that the sighted child was more likely to substitute a sound from the same visual category, whereas the blind child was more likely to substitute a sound from a different visual category. The finding supports Mills' data, and indicates that sighted children do use lip-read cues as a source of information in planning their phonological output.

This is not surprising since lip-reading provides information about how to make a sound whereas an auditory stimulus merely provides an abstract target to aim at. Blind children should therefore be at a disadvantage in acquiring phonology, and this is reflected by reports of delayed phonological acquisition, and a high incidence of phonological disorders.

PROCESSING OF LIP-READ INFORMATION

The results presented by Mills show that lip-read information is important for normal development of phonology, and for speech perception. Thus heard and seen speech perceptions must be integrated at some point in processing. The nature of the code in which they are combined has yet to be determined.

Three possible codes have been suggested. Lip-read information may be immediately recoded into a code derived from audition, and then processed as if heard rather than seen. MacDonald and McGurk (1978) suggest, on the other hand, that it is possible to modify the Motor Theory of speech perception (Liberman et al., 1967) to include visual information, that is lip-read perceptions could be processed in a code derived from articulatory feedback. However, evidence from studies of the lip-reading and phonological abilities of the pre-lingually profoundly deaf indicates that neither of these candidate codes is adequate.

The deaf can identify rhymes (O'Connor and Hermelin, 1978), match homophones (Dodd and Hermelin, 1977), develop a spoken phonological system (Oller and Kelly, 1974), convert lip-read nonsense words to graphemes (Dodd, 1980), primarily on the basis of lip-read inputs. In other words, the deaf can abstract a phonological code from lip-read information. An alternative candidate code, a non-modality specific phonological code, seems worth considering. Such a code would be capable of processing and combining speech information derived from audition, vision and proprioception (Dodd, 1980).

A sensory handicap, like deafness or blindness, would reduce the efficiency of the coding leading to disordered phonology, or abnormal developmental patterns. However, because of the non-modality specific nature of the code, neither handicap would preclude the acquisition of phonological skills.

Chapter 7.

BLIND CHILDREN'S LANGUAGE IS NOT "MEANINGLESS"[1]

Barbara Landau

THE NATURE OF THE HANDICAP

A central issue in the study of blind children's language has been the extent and nature of their handicap. It is usually assumed that the blind child's experience lacks some essential component or components that promote normal language learning, and that this experiential deficit is reflected in distortions of the language system. On first thought, one might indeed assume that blindness must have a wide range of devastating effects; for example, it is clearly more difficult to navigate smoothly through space without vision, it is often more difficult to determine the addressee in a conversation, etc. For the blind infant, the situation could be worse yet, since he must learn about the world without the benefit of rich visual information specifying the shapes, sizes, and textures of objects, spatial layouts and their transformations over movement, and socio-emotional communicative signals from caretakers. Sensitive observers of blind infants, notably Selma Fraiberg (1977) have proposed that these deficits in information have drastic consequences for the blind infant, resulting in delayed object permanence, distorted emotional relationships, and deviations in language. Yet it is not so obvious to all that these proposed delays and deficits are necessary consequences to blindness.

Consider the case of language learning by blind children. The crucial theoretical question there must be whether or not vision is in some principled sense necessary for language learning. Three possible hypotheses come to mind. Firstly, based on Bruner's (1974/5) analysis of the importance of gaze in establishing mutual reference, one might wonder whether or not blindness would impede this first step in language learning. Secondly, Wexler and Culicover's (1980) work on learnability theory suggests that situational-interpretive input may be necessary to guarantee language learning under real time constraints. On this view, one might wonder whether or not blindness would reduce the availability of situational interpretations, and thereby reduce the availability of meaning-surface string pairings necessary for syntactic learning. Thirdly, one might wonder whether or not blindness could impair the development of concepts standing behind word meanings, thereby rendering blind children's language 'meaningless', even if well-formed.

This latter hypothesis seems particularly well-favoured in the literature, based on the following general rationale: where relevant experience is lacking, concepts cannot develop; and where concepts are lacking, word meanings cannot be learned. On one level, it has been claimed that a wide variety of concepts, hence word meanings, must be different for the blind than for the sighted child; it is often supposed that lack of vision means lack of many concepts. Specifically, various educators and psychologists have claimed that use of "visual terms" by the blind are 'verbalisms' - empty and meaningless for lack of supporting visual experience (Cutsforth, 1951; see Warren, 1977, for review). Yet, the evidence adduced for these claims has been limited, because of both flaws in methodology and lack of theoretical articulation. Most investigators have not attempted a serious discussion of what, exactly, could be lacking in the blind child's experience, nor how this lack could significantly interact with the learning process.

THE INVESTIGATION OF BLIND CHILDREN

For the past several years, we have been studying language learning in blind children, to assess the role of 'context' - carried by the sight of objects, properties, events, and scenes - in developing meanings (Landau, 1982; Landau and Gleitman, forthcoming). We have wondered whether, indeed, the function from sensory experience to language is so tight that variation in or absence of modality-specific input will lead to deviation and/or distortion in expressed meanings. Our specific questions have been: 1. How do blind children express early vocabulary of objects and events, and later predicate-argument structure (object-event relationships)?

2. In particular, what consequences does blindness have for the development of visual terminology? 3. Are usages of these words indeed empty?

Our three subjects have all been blind since birth, or shortly thereafter. Angie was a full-term baby, a victim of congenital deformation of the optic nerve, with some possible light perception in one eye. At her first interview (29 months old), she was already functioning at a sophisticated linguistic level, with mean length of utterance (MLU) 3.60. Angie's language was comparable to sighted subjects of the same linguistic level, to the extent it could be analyzed by the standard measures of expressed meanings.[2] The other two children were three and two-and-a-half months premature respectively, and were victims of Retrolental Fibroplasia. Kelli is totally blind; Carlo has some light perception. Both of these children were studied from onset of language through 42 months.

Language Onset

Onset of single words was at about 23 months for Kelli, and about 26 months for Carlo. These ages are uncorrected for prematurity, but even if corrected by three months, they still indicate a delay, relative to the sighted mean (14.2 months, Bayley Scales of Infant Development). A general initial delay for the blind subjects is corroborated by normative data on blind children from Norris, Spaulding, and Brodie (1957), although most of their subjects as well as Kelli and Carlo still fit within the normal range (10-23 months, Bayley Scales).

Expressed Meanings: Vocabulary and Predicate-argument Structure

Given the general onset delay, one might wonder whether blind subjects are deviant or different in what concepts they express, and what words are used to express them. Kelli's and Carlo's early vocabularies shown in Figure 7.3, are compared to sighted children studied by Nelson (1973). Kelli's sample was recorded between 23 and 28 months, and Carlo's between 26 and 29 months. Nelson's subjects were between 15 and 24 months when they achieved the 50-word level (mean: 19.75 months).

Figure 7.1: Early Vocabulary of Two Blind Subjects Compared to Sighted Children[a]

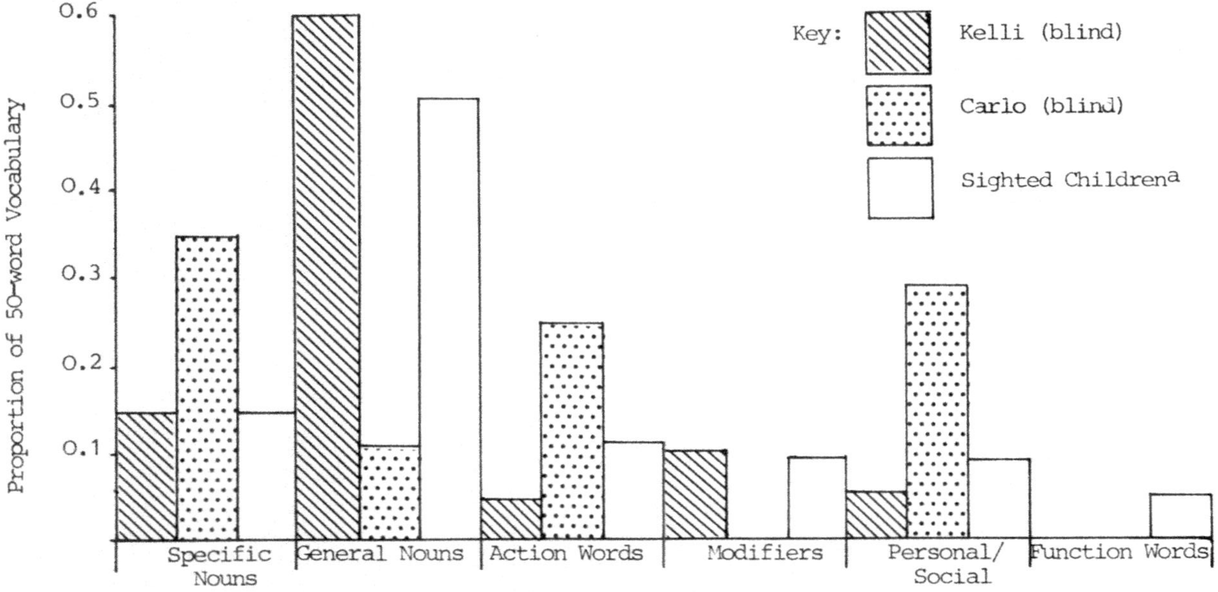

Note: a. Data for sighted children and categories from Nelson (1973)

Note that the early words expressed by both blind and sighted children are primarily objects and people (subsumed under specific and general nouns), and also include some action words (e.g. *go, up*) and personal-social words (*please, no,* etc.). Thus, despite the onset delay, there is no evidence from these data that blind children cannot express words for the concepts normally expressed by young children.

Next, consider the children's expressed meanings at a later language level, that is in early syntactic utterances. In Figures 7.2 and 7.3, the children's early multiple-word utterances are shown, compared to those of sighted children studied by Bloom and her colleagues, and using their coding system (Bloom, Lightbown and Hood, 1975).[3] In the earlier sample (Figure 7.2), both blind children express many action utterances (e.g. *Carlo open, Kelli eat*) and many locative actions (where the goal of movement was a change in location, e.g. *put in tape*). There are somewhat fewer locative states (where there is no movement effected, e.g. *Mommy sit*, when the mother is in her chair), states (expressions of wants or needs, e.g. *Carlo want cookie, Kelli sick*), attributes (e.g. *big truck*), and comments on the existence, negation, and recurrence of objects and events (e.g. *a dolly, no dolly, more dolly*). Note that Carlo shows fewer types of expressed relations than Kelli or Bloom et al.'s subjects. But in the later sample (Figure 7.3), both blind children express semantic relations covering all the categories.

These data suggest that knowledge of language is not diminished by blindness. Blind children do talk about objects and their locations in space, actions, and events, and do so in just the same way as sighted children at the same linguistic level.

However, some might still believe that the blind child is handicapped in language, choosing stronger examples to demonstrate this deficiency. The argument could be made that blind children can talk about objects and events since, after all, they can touch objects, and they can hear some events occurring. Yet their handicap exists since they do not have as much first-hand sensory experience with visual aspects of the world. This lack of experience must have some consequence: blind children can never know the meanings of words like *red* and *look* and *picture*, that refer to the visual world.

Figure 7.2: Early Sample of Semantic-syntactic Relations Expressed by Two Blind Subjects Compared to Sighted Children[a]

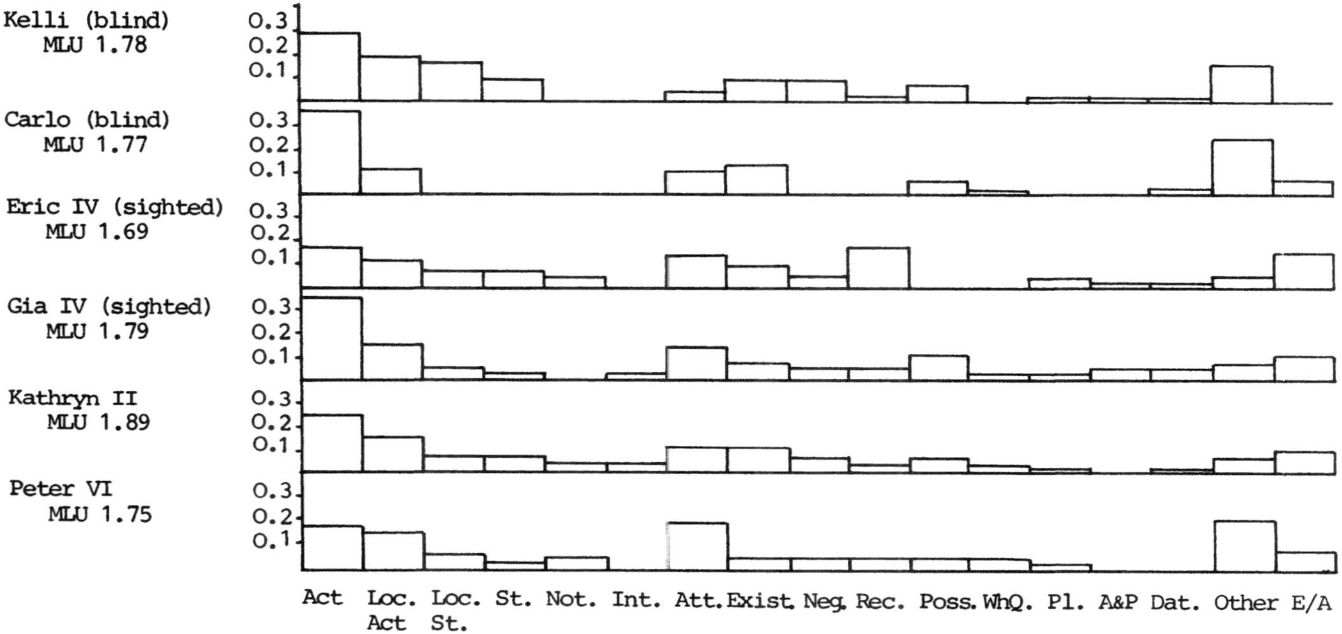

Note: a. Data for sighted children and categories taken from Bloom, Lightbown and Hood (1975)

Figure 7.3: Later Sample of Semantic-syntactic Relations Expressed by Two Blind Subjects Compared to Sighted Children[a]

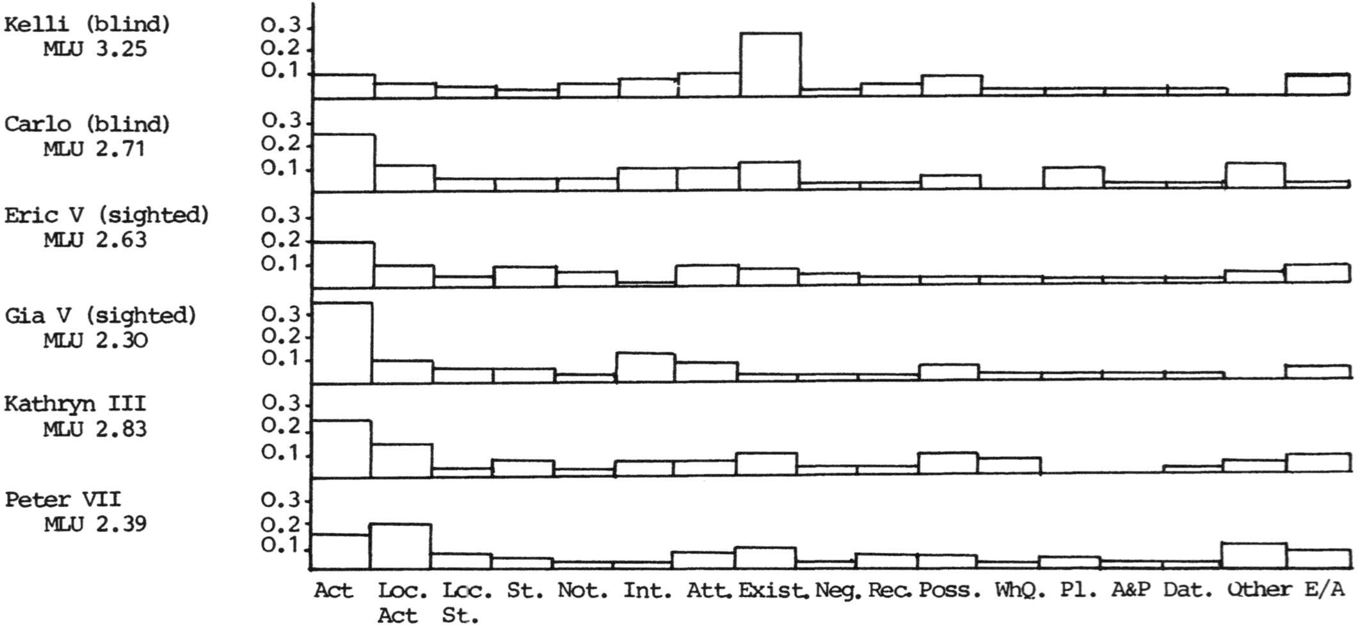

Note: a. Data for sighted children and categories from Bloom, Lightbown and Hood (1975)

Such a claim is certainly worth testing, although informally, we know that blind adults do use language to refer to visual aspects of the world - for example, they do say *look* and *see*. Defenders of the deficiency notion emphasize that the use of such visual words by the blind is 'verbalism', or empty and meaningless usage. Yet the evidence for such a claim is merely a handful of studies, using methods such as word association, elicitation of imagery, and the semantic differential (see Warren, 1977, for review). These methods are at best highly indirect and at worst irrelevant in assessing the blind person's meanings (or lack thereof) for visual terms.

What would be convincing evidence that verbalisms are a function of deficient concepts? One possibility would be data demonstrating that use of the terms reflects an impoverished, inconsistent, or bizarre concept. For example, it might be that the blind person uses the work *look* to mean simultaneously "scratch the left elbow" and "buy milk at the corner store". This would certainly be bizarre, and would provide some preliminary evidence that sighted concepts are not constructable without relevant sensory input.

Is there any such evidence? We do not believe that there is, but much more importantly we have evidence that is altogether counter to the belief that use of visual terms by the blind is semantically empty. Our evidence is in the form of intensive observation and experimentation on one of our totally blind subjects.

Use of Sighted Terminology for Haptic Activity

Kelli began using the visual term *see* when she was 28 months old, approximately the same age at which sighted children begin to use verbs of perception. From the beginning, Kelli's use of the word *see* was far from meaningless. To people around her, she seemed to use the word when she wished to touch some object; and she was satisfied when her request to "see" something was followed by letting her touch it. This behaviour suggested that visual verbs like *see* and *look* meant "touch" to Kelli.

Indeed, it did seem to mean "touch", for in a first series of experiments, we asked Kelli to *Look up*, and she responded by straining her hands upwards above her head, as if to reach some object. This is hardly the response of a sighted child to the same command, and it is not even the response of a sighted child deprived of vision by blindfolding. When four sighted control subjects were blindfolded and asked to *Look up*, they responded by tilting their heads upwards, as if genuinely trying to look at some object. So Kelli's use of *look* was surely different from the sighted child's use. Yet it was not bizarre, since her method of contact is manual; nor was it inconsistent, for when she was asked to *Look down, Look in front of you, Look behind you, Look over here,* or *Look over there*, she responded with the spatially appropriate movement of her hands, "looking down" by touching the floor, "looking behind" by touching the floor in back of her, etc. Note, too, that Kelli did not understand the word *look* in its broader sense, that is, either to mean "perceive in general", or to mean "understand", as we sometimes use the term (e.g. *I see,* or *Look at what you're saying*). Rather, *look* was differentiated from other verbs of perception; for when Kelli was asked to taste something, she put it to her mouth, and when asked to listen to something, she put it to her ear, or simply quieted, attending to some expected sound. But when asked to look at or touch some object, Kelli reached out, contacting the target object with her hands.

If Kelli's meaning for *look* was synonymous with *touch,* this would have been an interesting finding. But as it turned out, her meaning was not simply identical to *touch;* rather, *look* seemed to mean "perceptually explore with the hands", while *touch* meant "simply contact with the hands". We discovered this during a long series of queries to Kelli, starting with the command *Touch (some object) but don't look.* To this potentially contradictory command, Kelli merely laid her hands on the object, without exploring it. When she was told to *Look, but don't touch (some object),* she either explored manually (the normal response to *Look*), or responded with confusion. This initial set of behaviours suggested the distinction between *look* (perceptually explore) and *touch* (merely contact), which we then documented in a series of 30 commands, modifying the verbs *look* and *touch* along four dimensions: spatial, intensity, temporal, and instrument of perception. For example, we asked Kelli to *Look* or *Touch under/here/behind; Look* or *Touch real hard/gently/ real good; Look* or *Touch once/not yet; Look* or *Touch with your finger/foot/nose/mouth/ear.*

On many of these commands, Kelli differentiated *look* from *touch*, always "looking" by exploring and manipulating, and "touching" by coming into manual contact in a non-exploratory way. For example, if asked to *Look behind you*, she searched for an object behind her; but if asked to *Touch behind you*, she touched her back. When asked to *Look real hard* at some object, she rubbed it up and down, but when asked to *Touch it real hard*, she would bang the object with her hand, or scratch it with her fingers. When asked to *Look with your nose* or *Look with your mouth*, she performed the appropriate modality-specific behaviour, for example, bringing the object to her mouth as if to taste, or to her nose as if to smell. But when asked to *Touch with your nose* or *Touch with your mouth*, she bent down, and pressed that part of her body to the object.

So it seems that Kelli did use *look* in an internally consistent and meaningful fashion, to mean "explore with the hands", and contrastively with *touch* which meant "simply contact the object". At least from this evidence, it again seems that the blind child does use words like *look* and *see* in a meaningful fashion.

Learning that *Look/See* Means "Explore with the Hands"

How could Kelli have learned these words? First, of course, the words have been used by people around her. In fact, the simplest explanation of Kelli's usage would be that she has directly imitated usage by some model, say her mother. If Kelli's mother used the words *look* and *see* in just those contexts when Kelli was manually exploring an object, then perhaps the fact that Kelli developed a meaning for these words is not at all mysterious.

But it is indeed mysterious, since Kelli's mother did not use *see* and *look* exclusively to refer to Kelli's tactial-haptic perception of objects. Rather, her mother used the words in many other ways as well: to mean "visually perceive" to her sighted child, Kelli's younger sibling; as a simile (e.g. *Kelli, you look like a kangaroo*); and in contexts where Kelli could not possibly look at an object with her hands (e.g. when Kelli was in another room). And it is important to note that Kelli's mother herself was quite unaware of her child's meaning, for she was astonished when Kelli's arms flew upwards to the command *Look up*. She was astonished, for she and her husband had taught Kelli to tilt her head upwards to the command *Look up*, and downwards to the command *Look down*.[4] Kelli's novel response to these commands in the experimental situation is a powerful demonstration that some abstract representation of the word *look* was guiding her response (rather than some memorized routine).

How, then, did Kelli learn these meanings for *look, see,* and *touch*? First, note that many natural languages carry the same distinction for verbs of perception as the one that Kelli made: the distinction between the exploratory mode of perceiving, and the non-exploratory mode. For example, in English, we have such a distinction for verbs of vision, with *look* versus *see*; and for verbs of audition, with *listen* versus *hear*.[5] Further, we have the expression *to set eyes on*, meaning "merely direct one's eyes towards", as in *I never even set eyes on him, much less knew him well*. Wasco (an American Indian language) also encodes this distinction for visual verbs, but more succinctly than does English: there are two monomorphemic items, one corresponding to the English phrase "set eyes on" ("put two eyes on"), and one to the phrase "visually explore". For tactual verbs, French encodes the distinction, with the verbs *tâter* meaning "palpate", and *toucher*, meaning "merely come into contact with the hand". These similarities across languages in encoding the exploratory/non-exploratory distinction for perception verbs provide insight into how Kelli came to make the distinction between *look* and *touch*. In particular, it seems to be a fact about humans that it is important to distinguish between these two modes of perception. Language, reflecting this distinction, often (though not always) separates the two modes by allotting a different basic word to each. Kelli, of course, is human, so it is presumably important to her to differentiate between active and non-active perception with her dominant modality - the tactile-haptic system. Kelli was not provided with a direct linguistic reflex of this distinction in English; so she must have commandeered the work *look*, an otherwise stranded word, and used it to mean "haptically explore".

Learning that *Look/See* Means "Perceive with the Eyes"

Let us now return to the notion of handicap in blind children's language. Earlier, we mentioned that a favoured hypothesis about the source of this handicap is the notion that sensory experience furnishes the building blocks of concepts, which, in turn, stand behind word meanings. In the extreme, it has seemed self-evident to some that the blind child could never know what was meant by visual terms.

Yet Kelli has furnished us with evidence forcing rejection of this claim for a handicap induced by blindness: as we have just seen, the use of words *look* and *see* by this blind child is far from meaningless. Rather, the child has created her own meaning, one which is internally consistent, and far from bizarre, as it is a distinction normally carried by natural languages. One might say, at this point, that it is the strictly visual use of visual words that is the handicap; for example, Kelli could never come to know what it means for a sighted person to "see".

But we also have evidence that she has this knowledge, too. We have documented Kelli's comprehension and production of visual verbs referring to the activity of sighted persons; and we have found that Kelli knows well that vision conforms to the laws of Euclidean geometry. She knows that sighted poeple need to have objects correctly oriented in space to be able to see them, that sighted people cannot see through barriers (although they can hear through barriers), that large objects must be displayed differently from small objects for sighted people to see them at a distance, that certain spatial operations on an object can make it invisible and that these are different from the operations that can make an object inaudible (see Landau, 1982; Landau and Gleitman, forthcoming, for details).

Is Kelli then aware that sighted people are different from blind people? We believe she does have a growing awareness of what her own blindness means, since we have observed her commenting on occasion *Mommy, because I can't see?* or *Because I'm blind?*. These comments occur in contexts that are deeply related to her experience as a blind person, for example, when she is puzzled that others can "see" photographs, or airplanes, or birds in the sky. It seems that Kelli's knowledge of blindness grows with her knowledge of the meanings of sighted words.

Kelli's knowledge of the sighted meanings for visual terms, although surprising, can be understood. Clearly, the environment provides a basis for learning from experience. Kelli has learned about vision through her knowledge of space (see Landau, Gleitman and Spelke, 1981), and through language, since there was never any parental restriction on the use of sighted words to her. So, for example, several occurrences of her mother saying *I can't see you* when occupying various locations relative to Kelli might suffice for the inference that sighted people can see only if there are no barriers (and, if the object is correctly oriented). Or, the similarities in linguistic structures over different verbs of perception might suffice to indicate there is an active-stative distinction for the visual mode of perceiving. For example, the distinction between active-stative modes is carried by syntactic context. That is, to the question *What are you doing?*, one might reply *I am looking/listening*, but less plausibly, **I am seeing/hearing*. In short, various kinds of knowledge have entered into Kelli's learning, by inference, that sighted *look* and *see* mean something quite different from her own, haptic *look* and *see*.

CONCLUSIONS

Kelli has demonstrated that blindness need not lead to deficits in language learning; and indeed, that rich representational capacity underlies even use and understanding of visual terminology. Why, then, did anyone ever think of visual language by the blind as a deficit? Most likely, because of underlying theories about human learning, in particular, about how we come to have the concepts we do, and how we proceed to learn the language that expresses those concepts. The notion that the blind child cannot learn to use visual terms meaningfully comes close to the heart of the classical Empiricist programme on issues of concept acquisition. The radical Empiricist view of these issues is, roughly, that the primitive base of concepts is occasioned as a direct reflex of the sensory apparatus; complex concepts are built out of these primitives. Where there is no sensory reflex for a primitive - e.g. colours for the blind man - there should be no concept (see Fodor, 1981, for discussion of the pitfalls of this programme). John Locke, representing this view, wrote:

> I think it will be granted easily, that if a child were kept in a place where he never saw other but black and white till he were a man, he would have no more ideas of scarlet or green, than he that from his childhood never tasted an oyster, or a pineapple, has of those particular relishes. (Locke, 1690)

According to this view, then, the blind child has no appropriate sensory reflex for terms referring to visual experience, and further, does not have the materials necessary for learning the terms (see Fodor's discussion of the differences here between the empiricist and rationalist programmes). The layman's or educator's version of this theory finds the blind child deficient when he uses visual terms, and discourages such use.

Without the case of the blind child, we might speculate that this view is too simple; for we do learn words like *truth, liberty,* and *humanitarian,* whose meanings (or meaning features, if one could decompose them) seem far removed from any specific sensory experience. But the case of the blind child forces us to modify the radical empiricist view of concept and word-learning, by providing one simple and direct example: the blind child learns concepts for *look* and *see,* even though she cannot look or see. Her knowledge is gained through experience, but the relevant experience is far more complex than a direct reflex of the sensorium. Rather, the experience is the subtle product of a complex interaction between internal biases about the assignment of words to concepts, and knowledge from other conceptual domains - such as space and language.

Finally, if we adhered to a direct and simple view of the relationship between the sensorium and language, we would overlook important theoretical and practical issues. First, we would obscure theoretically important facts about the nature of human language learning, for example, the internal biases that bring a learner like Kelli to create a lexical distinction between exploratory and non-exploratory tactile-haptic perception. And second, practically, we would be misdirected in our suggestions for parental treatment of blind children. We might suggest, as Cutsforth did decades ago, that the blind child be discouraged from using visual terminology, lest it lead to "loose thinking". Could use of visual words lead to "loose thinking"? I believe Kelli has shown us that the opposite is true: for free use of visual terms has allowed Kelli both to make crucial linguistic distinction for her own means of perceiving, and to understand what is meant by the other, visual, means of perceiving. Ultimately, this knowledge can lead Kelli to profound insights into the nature of her own blindness.

NOTES

1. All of the work reported in this paper was done jointly with Lila R. Gleitman. I wish to thank

her for her extensive theoretical insights and involvement in every aspect of the project. In addition, I thank her for copious comments on previous drafts of this paper. Thanks also go to Dr. Gilberto Pereira and Ms. Anne Farren of Children's Hospital of Philadelphia for locating subjects, and to Lenora Knapp and Marcia Glicksman for analyzing data. This work was supported by a Social and Behavioral Sciences Research Grant from the National Foundation - March of Dimes to Lila R. Gleitman, and a National Research Service Award from the National Institute of Mental Health to Barbara Landau.

2. The measures we used were developed by Nelson (1973) to characterize early vocabulary, and by Bloom, Lightbown and Hood (1975) to characterize semantic-syntactic relations in early syntactic utterances. Therefore, the measures were more appropriate for analyzing language at an earlier growth point than Angie's level at her first interview.

3. Note that these comparisons are again between the sighted and blind children at the same linguistic level (MLU). As with previous analyses, the blind children are older than (delayed relative to) their sighted controls.

4. Her parents had taught Kelli to *Look up and look down* with appropriate (sighted) head movements in the context of a nursery song, simply as part of the action accompanying the song.

5. The contrast between *touch* and *feel* is ambiguous, since *feel* can be used either in an exploratory or a non-exploratory way, for example, *Feel this fabric,* versus *Can you feel* (i.e. sense) *that?*.

Chapter 8.

MEANING IN LANGUAGE ACQUISITION

Paul Werth

MEANING IN PSYCHOLINGUISTICS

In recent years, psycholinguistic studies of meaning have tended to make certain simplifying assumptions about their object of study: (1) that meaning resides in, is the property of, words; (2) that the analysis of word-meaning should be componential, i.e. composed of minimal elements, arranged in some order; (3) that the acquisition of word-meanings is gradual, i.e. component by component, rather than holistic; (4) that the relationships between components are actually acquired by way of a procedure (which may be based on logical or ontological knowledge).

Consider the following quotation from Clark and Clark (1977, p. 509):

> When children acquire the meaning of a word, they construct an entry for it in their mental lexicon. They start off with a very simple entry containing only a few of the components relevant to its use by an adult. And as they learn more about its meaning and how it contrasts with other words, they may add further components and, if necessary, discard irrelevant ones. Eventually, their entry comes to coincide with the adult entry.

This by now orthodox view embraces points (1-3) above; for point (4), see Clark and Clark (1977, p. 439 ff) and Miller and Johnson-Laird (1976, p. 122 ff, and *passim*). From the more purely linguistic point of view, we should clearly want to know more about (a) the "adult entry", i.e. what components it contains, and how they are arranged, and (b), more generally, what is the nature of these components, whether they come from a set of universal semantic primes, or a language-specific set, and what are the restrictions on their possible combination and structural-hierarchical arrangement.

In the previous chapter Barbara Landau was concerned with the sensory language of sensorially-deprived children. She provides us with a method and some data which bear upon two areas of great importance in the study of human cognitive development: (1) the relationship between the linguistic-conceptual systems of the blind and those of the sighted; (2) the nature of the meanings acquired by children, and where and how they originate.

Underlying the first area is a tradition of received beliefs and fallacies about the language of the blind, while beneath the second area are the various competing theories of meaning. The re-examination of the first area requires us to apply what we know about language and cognition in general in the explanation of new facts emerging from the study of the language of the blind, enabling us to preserve or modify one or another theory in the second area.

THE MEANING OF PERCEPTION VERBS

Let us begin by quoting Miller and Johnson-Laird (1976, p. 585) on verbs of perception, (including those studied by Landau): "*Perceive*... is a predicate that denotes the process involved when an internal representation of the external world is constructed out of information from the receptors."

Assuming this definition to be substantially correct, the implementation of the process poses some interesting empirical questions, two of which Landau concentrates upon: (1) What do blind children mean (do) when they employ visual terms? (2) How do they construct such meanings, and particularly, from what input?

Visual Meanings in the Blind

Landau argues that the *see/look* modality has been translated - for at least one child - into the *touch* modality. It seems clear that in very broad terms, this is correct, for Kelli substitutes manual exploration for visual examination. But there are some disturbing weaknesses both in her experimental design (casting some doubts on the reliability of her findings), and in her linguistic assumptions (revealing a crucial gap in her experiments). First, (a perhaps unavoidable problem for most small-scale psycholinguistic research), there is a risk with small numbers of subjects that any findings are, at best, merely anecdotal, and at worst, actually misleading because they may accidentally be unrepresentative. Notice that the philosophy of science meta-argument appealing to existential generalization (i.e. that the existence of a single case is sufficient to require the modification of a general theory), does not serve to generalize the behaviour of Kelli to all blind children or, for example, Washoe-behaviour to all chimpanzees. Rather, it applies when the single case is a case of some phenomenon which the theory is directly or indirectly setting out to explain, for instance, in a theory of grammatical sentence-types, a sentence-token of the language under scrutiny. But we have to ask: what counts as a 'sentence token' here? In fact, a 'single' sentence-token represents not a single case of linguistic behaviour, for example one utterance of one speaker on a single occasion, but a set of recurrent behaviour patterns across a group of speakers. What makes it 'acceptable', both to speakers and as a datum for such a theory, is (a) that it is recurrent, and (b) that it is generalized across a 'dialect'-group. In other words, the 'single' sentence represents a large number of utterances or judgments, and not merely one. Kelli's behaviour with *see* and *look* certainly seems to be recurrent, but we have no evidence yet that it is generalized. Without amassing a lot of corroborative evidence from a statistically-significant number of other cases, we have no real indication that this is anything more than Kelli-behaviour (which could be originally random, and reinforced by some chance contingency; cf., for example, the 'private languages' of twins).

Fortunately, such a defect is easily remedied. More worryingly, however, there are occasional weaknesses in Landau's experimental design, particularly when it comes to controlling for variables. A small example: to test whether Kelli understood the difference between *touch* and *look*, Landau gave the child such instructions as *Touch but don't look at* some object; Kelli then duly distinguished between the two verbs. The problem is that the very instruction itself invites a contrast, and thus obscures the difference between a natural distinction and a forced opposition; any child at all asked to *Touch but don't feel* or *Look but don't see*, or

Talk but don't speak would be likely to force some differentiation, just to be compliant.

Another methodological problem arises out of the inevitable play element in this kind of research with small children. Given that comprehension or intended meaning are typically investigated via non-linguistic response (usually involving the manipulation of toys), what counts as a successful (or meaningful or useful) answer might vary from a thoroughgoing performance of an appropriate activity right through to a more or less reduced iconic representation of it (e.g. *Taste the dolly* - Kelli puts the doll to her lips). Just as a young subject might be anxious to please this nice adult who brings interesting toys, and spends time playing with her, so might the researcher run the risk of 'over-interpreting' the responses. Especially if her data consist of the iconic type of response, the researcher is in danger of misrepresenting her results by making possibly untenable assumptions based on inadequately-specified responses.

CONSTRUCTION OF MEANINGS, AND THEIR INPUT

The input of a semantic system such as Kelli's for *see/look*, argues Landau, must come from (a) spatial knowledge and (b) syntactic contexts. She makes some interesting observations in support of these, but does not adduce any really strong evidence or theoretical argument to back them up. We must consider, therefore, what would constitute such evidence or argumentation.

Spatial Knowledge

For the sighted speaker, the verb *touch* in its primary sense requires the object to be within reach of the bodily extremities; *feel* as a haptic verb implies substantial bodily contact; *look* and *see*, on the other hand, suggest non-contact. All - unlike *hear* and *smell* - imply the absence of some kind of intervening material. For Kelli, though, *touch, feel, look* and *see* are all contact-verbs when transitive (*Look at the doll*), but not necessarily so when intransitive (*Look behind you*). Given this distinction, it would be interesting to find out something more about the precise meaning for Kelli of the intransitive cases: what exactly does *Look behind you* mean when translated into the touch modality? I suspect that for a sighted speaker it is a more precise instruction than it is for Kelli (viz. *Turn through a semicircle until your eyes are ± 180° from their present position,* as against *Scan the hemispherical space to your rear*). I suggest this for no better reason than the sheer physical difference between the optic and the haptic modalities. Spatial knowledge presumably derives from all sensory inputs together: relatively close space from all senses; further space from vision primarily, less from hearing. But the most important faculty for the acquisition of any knowledge is of course the symbolic-conceptual - what we may call 'central processing', (or perhaps, specifically, "the ability to reason" (Miller, 1967, p. 15) or "deductive information processing" (George, 1970, p. 140) or even "logical competence" (Wason and Johnson-Laird, 1972, p. 41)). Central processing, we may hypothesize, is not only responsible for the interpretation and classification of sense-percepts, it is also responsible for building up a conceptualization from the various sources at its disposal: the senses, memory, the (developing) language system, and particularly its semantic component, together with problem-solving and decision-making skills. In the absence of any visual input, presumably the most important source of spatial information for the blind child must be language (Landau certainly seems to assume this). Let us therefore consider the role of linguistic context for these perception verbs.

Syntactic Context

Landau suggests that the active/stative distinction in English, between *look* and *see*, or *listen* and *hear*, for example, would have become obvious to Kelli from the usage of those around her, illustrated in Example 1.

Example 1. (What are you doing?) I am {looking / listening}

*I am {seeing / hearing}

There are several syntactic points to make here. First, note that Example 1 as presented is rather rare and highly context-dependent, as in Examples 2a and 2b.

Example 2. (a) (Can I help you sir?) No, it's alright, I'm just looking.
(b) Will you please be quiet. I'm listening.

In such contexts, where the object of attention is either non-specific or obvious, the normally transitive verbs *look* and *listen* may occur without an overt object. From Example 1 alone, a blind child would be able to infer no more than the information that looking and listening are activities, while seeing and hearing are not. In their normal contexts, however, *look* and *listen* take objects (with prepositions). Second, it is a well-known teaching point about English that the verbs of "inert perception" (Leech, 1971) do not accept the continuous aspect, so that *see* and *hear* in Example 1 would be discounted on those grounds anyway. However, and thirdly, even without the continuous aspect, *see* and *hear*, being verbs of "inert" perception, are not usually possible responses to questions with *do*:

Example 3. (What did he do?) *He $\left\{\begin{array}{l}\text{saw}\\ \text{heard}\end{array}\right\}$ the accident.

Moreover, there are several other possible contexts which Kelli could have been exposed to:

Example 4. V + Adj.

$$\text{John}\left\{\begin{array}{l}\text{looked}\\ \text{felt}\\ {}^{*}\text{saw}\\ {}^{*}\text{touched}\end{array}\right\}\text{amazed, silly, tired...}$$

Example 5. V + Prep. phr.

$$\text{Myrtle}\left\{\begin{array}{l}\text{looked}\\ \text{felt}\\ \text{saw}\\ {}^{*}\text{touched}\end{array}\right\}\text{over, through, around... the room.}$$

Example 6. V + THAT-comp. S

$$\text{Oedipus}\left\{\begin{array}{l}{}^{*}\text{looked}\\ \text{felt}\\ \text{saw}\\ {}^{*}\text{touched}\end{array}\right\}\text{that his mother was ready.}$$

Example 7. V + Obj. + Manner adv.

James { looked at / felt / *saw / touched } the newspaper carefully.

Example 8. V + IF/WHETHER-comp. S

Go and { look / feel / see / *touch } if the bed is dry.

We can see from these examples that there is not a great deal of apparent consistency here: on the face of it, *look* variously behaves like each of the others, and enters into almost all the possible combinations. However, this apparent confusion is at least partially resolved when we look at the regular semantic distinctions which operate within the category of perception verbs as set out in Table 8.1.

Table 8.1: The Semantic Distinctions between Verbs of Perception

Sense (Perceive)	Sense Receptor Activity	Sensory Exploration	Appear To Senses
See	Set eyes on	Look at[a]	Look
Feel$_S$	Touch	Feel over[a]	Feel$_A$
Hear$_S$	Attend to	Listen to[a]	Sound
Smell$_S$	Sniff at	Smell$_E$	Smell$_A$
Taste$_S$	Savour	Taste$_E$	Taste$_A$

Note: a. or another preposition

We can see from Table 8.1 that the four forms in the *see* and *hear* modalities are distinct from each other (taking the prepositions to be part of the form). *Feel, smell* and *taste*, however, are more ambiguous - nevertheless, if they are differentiated by indices, as has been done in the table, we can go a long way towards sorting out the contextual chaos.

Thus, Example 1 has the sensory exploration meaning, Example 4 has the appear-to-the-senses meaning, and Example 6 has the perceive meaning. Examples 5, 7 and 8, though, are still mixed. We can explain Example 7 in this way: the manner adverb is sensitive not to this particular categorial set, but to the active/stative distinction (cf. Ross, 1972), which brings the sense-receptor meaning and the sensory-exploration meaning together as activities. Example 8 is somewhat harder: it seems to me that the basic meaning here is 'perceive' and the non-perception verbs (*look*, and perhaps *feel* too) are portmanteau-forms:

Example 9. Go and [look at / feel over] the bed and [see / feel] if it is dry.

In Example 9 the first parenthesis encloses exploration-verbs, and the second, perceive-verbs. This leaves as our only remaining mystery, Example 5: basically, this seems to be the sensory exploration meaning (the preposition performing an important role here), though it evidently allows of a more receptive sense with *see*. Of the other perceive-verbs, *hear* also has an occasional prepositional use as in Example 10.

Example 10. Evan heard through my explanations in silence.

The question remains, however: are there sufficient surface clues to enable these meanings to be distinguished from each other? Given the evidence that we have examined so far, it seems doubtful that there are. But this is as true for sighted learners as for blind ones: in fact, how does anybody learn to distinguish these meanings? Presumably, given that all speakers can correctly differentiate them, the cues must be more diverse and subtle than we have so far accounted for, and there is no particular reason to suppose that lack of visual cues provides any special difficulty.

However, Table 8.1 does reveal a glaring deficiency in Landau's argument. She strongly implies that, for Kelli, *look (at)* has ousted some of the area of meaning which for sighted people is occupied by the word *touch*: such that *look* has come to mean "explore", while *touch* now means "degraded contact But this is not in fact the case: *touch* never normally bears an exploratory or even a perceive sense.

As Table 8.1 shows, it is exclusively used for sense-receptor activity, i.e. it normally means something like "contact with the hand". The appropriate exploratory verb in the *touch*-modality is thus not *touch*, but *feel(over)*. But not one of Landau's experiments has apparently sought to investigate the meaning of *feel* for Kelli, and its relationship for her with *look*. What would Kelli have made of the instruction - perfectly coherent to a sighted person - *Feel over but don't look at the doll*? In fact, in the light of a systematic table such as Table 8.1, it would seem advisable for Landau to carry out a more extensive programme of testing all the oppositions involved.

To these suggestions, I think it would be helpful to add another. Perhaps with somewhat older children, it would be interesting to study how a blind learner deals with the meaning of more specific vision verbs such as *watch, stare, peep, peek, glimpse, glance, notice* and *glare*. These add further distinctions, not all of which would be directly perceivable by the blind child (e.g. both *watch* and *stare* suggest intentionality and prolonged duration, and the latter adds social impropriety; *glimpse* suggests the object is partly hidden, while *peep* suggests the perceiver is partly hidden, and so on). Would such distinctions be evident to, or difficult for, the blind child?

IMPLICATIONS

I now come to a more general discussion of the implications of Landau's paper. One of the notions which she quite rightly castigates is that of "meaningless language" or "empty verbalisms". She demonstrates that one blind child's visual language is not "empty". But is the notion of "empty verbalism" even coherent, even notwithstanding Kelli's example? Clearly, there are possible interpretations of the expression which make sense: the mere 'parroting' of unknown languages might be one such. But it would perhaps be more precise to call that a 'vocalism' rather than a 'verbalism', since the latter implies linguistic status for the utterance, and I find it dubious that something devoid of meaning for the speaker can be accorded linguistic status. Natural language certainly contains morphs which are "empty" in the sense that they have only syntactic function while lacking semantic content (e.g. *do* in questions and negatives, expletive *it* and *there*).

It is also of course possible for speakers to employ words of whose meaning they have not the foggiest notion (though they will characteristically know a great deal about their syntactic and even collocational behaviour). But morphs and words do not exclusively make up language; in fact, they are largely artefacts of analysis. In the terms we are examining, "language" and "verbalisms" refer to spoken utterances, necessarily. Utterances, unlike sentences or propositions, are real-world phenomena whose meanings are governed not by truth-conditions, but by relevance-conditions (cf. Grice, 1975; Werth, 1981; Wilson and Sperber, 1981). Thus, even in the case of a speaker deliberately violating the relevance-condition by including fictitious words in his utterance (like the comedian Stanley Unwin, for example), the utterance as a whole will still bear pragmatic, or contextual, meaning, even if this is only the implicature that the speaker is being deliberately unhelpful, or facetious. But this is unconventional behaviour, of course, even if it is interpretable. In the case of sensorially-deprived children such as Kelli, however, that sort of choice can still be made. The question of linguistic deficit, though, has arisen for areas of linguistic behaviour where it is assumed no such choice is possible; specifically, it seems to be assumed that a sightless person lacks experience for that area of conceptualization, and therefore cannot employ visual language other than "emptily". But this seems to be based on a fallacious premise, namely, that the input to the conceptualization of a given sense-experience is necessarily and exclusively the evidence afforded by that particular sense-modality: thus, goes this theory, a blind child has no input at all to visual conceptualization, and hence his visual language will be "empty". But consider again Miller and Johnson-Laird's definition of perception, given above. Let us assume, with them, that although there are five sensory input systems (sight, sound, taste, smell and touch), they all feed into a single perceptual system (our "central processor"). If this is so, we can then hypothesize that a child deficient in any of the input systems will nevertheless still be able to construct some sort of model of the world in his conceptual system, using evidence from his non-defective inputs (in which there may even be compensatory development). It seems that Kelli has been able to do something of this kind; but to test the hypothesis properly, we obviously need much more information from deaf and other sensorially-handicapped children.

Moreover, if the hypothesis is true, a further interesting question arises: can we predict which sensory system will substitute for a given defective one? In Kelli's case, we can see that sight and touch have been related through a common concern with external form. Furthermore, Kelli's substitutions can only be possible where it is external form which is under consideration. Asked to look at colours or images or non-discrete phenomena, such as sunsets, Kelli would clearly be unable to comply, using touch or any other non-defective sense. But touch is not in fact the only conceivable modality which could be substituted for vision. With modern technology, such as the adapted sonar for the blind, one can imagine a sight-vocabulary using terms derived from an auditory one. For the deaf, loudness might be interpretable in terms of size or proximity (spatial systems), or via intensity of light or colour (visual systems).

To conclude, I will try to answer the question: is Kelli's language "deficient"? In the sense of "containing a meaningless set of visual terms", the answer is clearly that it is not deficient. But I must nevertheless say that we should not allow ourselves to get carried away by the discovery that *look* for Kelli has a regular and coherent meaning. The sad fact is, that the language of Kelli and children like her is inevitably deficient in at least these ways: (a) spatially: while it seems clear that Kelli has been able to construct some model of the world from her other senses plus deductive powers, nevertheless it is reasonably obvious that any such model will be incomplete and distorted (in ways systematically different from the individual distortions made by sighted children); and (b) lexically: for instance, though Kelli has at least partially substituted *see/look* for *touch/feel* etc., we must still ask what has become of the existing distinction between *see/look* and *touch/feel*. My guess would be that for Kelli it is there, but in a dormant way. She has a set of haptic meanings for both modalities so that for most purposes she will treat them as synonyms. However, if pressed, she has been able to construct some sort of second-hand conceptualization of vision which she can refer to. Obviously, though, it cannot be as full or detailed as that of a sighted child, and she will usually ignore a sighted distinction which, for her, is unproductive. Nevertheless, at this point, we may begin to wonder exactly how far-reaching the effect of such a handicap is on concept-formation, anyway, given that only a certain proportion of our conceptual store is formed through direct perception, and even that has to go through central processing, including memory, reasoning etc. The remainder comes from secondary experiences, mainly linguistic, and for blind and sighted people alike, the resulting concepts will most probably be incomplete, distorted and false. The difference is that for blind people there is an area of experience which can never be detailed at first hand - but given that so much of human language is non-visual (abstract, mental, emotional, "displaced" - cf. Hockett, 1960), we may perhaps take comfort in the realization that blindness may not be an overwhelming handicap at the conceptual level, at least.

Chapter 9.

REFERENTIAL DEVELOPMENT IN BLIND CHILDREN[1]

Randa Mulford

INTRODUCTION

Of the several functions of language that a child must master on his way to becoming a fluent adult speaker, the referential function is one of the most basic and one of the earliest to emerge during development. By the "referential function" is intended a speaker's ability uniquely and unambiguously to identify for a listener the entity or entities being talked about. The development of reference has been a topic of considerable interest among language acquisition researchers in recent years. It has been approached from a variety of perspectives, for example, by developmental semanticists (e.g. Nelson, 1973; Bowerman, 1978; Clark, 1979), pragmatists (e.g. Bates, 1976; Atkinson, 1979; Ochs, Schieffelin and Platt, 1979), psychologists (e.g. Piaget, 1951; Bruner, 1975), and theoretical linguists (e.g. Halliday, 1975a; Lyons, 1975). These researchers and others have traced aspects of the development of linguistic reference from its prelinguistic roots through the mastery of complicated and subtly differentiated referring expressions. Of course, there is still much to be learned about many details of referential development, but its general outlines have become clear.

For a number of reasons, the development of reference is a particularly appropriate topic on which to focus an investigation of blind children's language. First of all, knowledge of the 'normal' course of development in this area is relatively detailed. This puts researchers in a favourable position when trying to formulate specific bases for comparing language acquisition in blind and sighted populations. While gross measure of language development in the two groups (e.g. Norris, Spaulding and

Brodie, 1957; Fraiberg, 1977) have generally shown few differences, more detailed comparisons of particular aspects of development (e.g. Rowland, 1980; Mulford, 1981) suggest that there are indeed differences, some more striking than others, in the course and rate of language acquisition for blind and sighted children. If comparative studies are based on well-documented aspects of normal development, then it is more likely that comparisons can be made that are sufficiently fine-grained to reveal the subtle differences, or perhaps the similarities, between the two populations.

A second motivation for considering referential development is that there is good reason to expect blind children to face particular challenges in this area. Accounts of sighted children's development suggest that vision contributes in several significant ways to the growth of the referential capacity. It might, therefore, be expected that visually-impaired children will encounter difficulties at various points in development where the role of vision appears to be crucial. The second part of this paper will be devoted to trying to anticipate the kinds of problems blind children may encounter in learning to refer successfully and to illustrating both some of the problems and some of their solutions with evidence from the existing literature on language development in the blind.

Finally, the topic of referential development is one in which two major lines of current research on blind children's language, mother-child communication and semantic development, converge nicely. As will become clear below, learning to refer successfully involves both taking into account and manipulating aspects of the communication situation and using linguistically appropriate referring expressions. These are precisely areas where much previous and ongoing work on blind children's language has focussed. It therefore seems useful to make explicit some of the links that exist between lines of research which, at first glance, might seem to be only vaguely related.

A FORMULA FOR ESTABLISHING REFERENCE

Before taking up the referential function from a developmental perspective, it is necessary to consider what is involved for any given "act of reference" to be successful. Imagine the following situation: a speaker (A) wants to convey to an addressee (B) that a particular object, say, a pencil, is broken. To convey this message, it is not enough for A to sit alone in his room and say *B, the pencil is broken.* Nor is it enough for A to enter a room where B is engaged in conversation with someone else and to say *It's broken.* Even if A takes B aside, looks him straight in the eye and says *It's broken* or *The pencil is broken*, it is still quite likely that B will not be able to figure out what A is talking about. The referent is unclear and the referring act is unsuccessful. More conversation will be necessary before A can get his message across to B.

Here is a 'formula' for how to refer successfully to some entity X, like the pencil in the example above. It is based on similar schemas proposed by Martin Atkinson, Eleanor Ochs and Bambi Schieffelin (see especially Keenan and Schieffelin, 1976; Atkinson, 1979; Ochs et al., 1979). It involves the following five steps or (self-)instructions to the speaker:

1. Assess whether the listener is paying attention to you.
2. If the listener is not attending to you, do something to get his attention.
3. Assess whether the listener is attending to the referent X.
4. If the listener is not attending to X, do something to direct his attention to it. (Repeat steps 3 to 4 until the listener is attending to X)
5. Refer to X with a sufficiently definite, unambiguous referring expression.

In the hypothetical situations sketched above, the speaker A violated this formula in various ways. In speaking to someone who was not there, he failed to assess adequately the listener's attention. Even when he was in the same room with the speaker, he at first failed to gain B's attention before beginning to talk. When he succeeded in securing B's attention to himself, he failed to make sure that the referent object (the pencil) was also in B's attention. He further failed to use explicit enough referring expressions. Thus B was unable to interpret what particular object A had in mind when he used the word *it* or the phrase *the pencil*. A speaker must comply with all five steps of the referring formula before a given act of reference can be succesful.

There are many things a speaker can do to assure that the listener is paying attention to him and to the potential referent. In practice these two goals of attracting and directing the listener's attention are very often accomplished simultaneously. Ochs et al. suggest a number of strategies, both verbal and non-verbal strategies, that speakers typically use to accomplish these goals. (L refers to the listener and X to the referent entity.)

Non-verbal	Verbal
- initiate eye contact with L	- name L (vocative)
- move toward L	- name X (use some referring expression)
- touch L	- use greeting term (e.g. *Hi!*)
- point at X	- use deictic pronoun or adverb (e.g. *there, that*)
- look at X	- use expressive particle (e.g. *Uh-oh, Ow!*)
- touch X	- use locating device (e.g. *Look at X*)
- reach for X	- ask a question (e.g. *What's that?*)
- show X to L	- use a prosodic device (e.g. whine, change speech volume or register)
- give X to L	

The strategies that a speaker uses to attract attention to himself are probably primarily determined by the social and/or physical situation. For example, touching the listener may only be appropriate in an informal context, or when making noise (e.g. by saying the addressee's name) would be undesirable. Strategies used for directing attention to the referent, however, are highly dependent on its physical location relative to the speaker-listener dyad. To return to the hypothetical situation discussed above, the means that speaker A can use to assure listener B's attention to the pencil in question will depend largely on whether the pencil is in fact on the scene. If it is physically present, then A has several options. For instance, he can point at, look at, or hold up the pencil and then say *It's broken*, assuming that B will be able to relate the gesture and the pronoun. Or he can use, instead of a gesture, some verbal device, for example a definite referring expression, to pick out the pencil. So A might say *Do you see the yellow pencil lying on my desk?* and then add *It's broken*, thus creating a linguistic link between the pronoun and the object it refers to. Or the speaker can combine both verbal and non-verbal devices to bring the pencil to B's attention. For example, he can hold up the pencil, saying *See this pencil?*. Then he can go on to complete his message *It's broken*. Certainly this combining of strategies is very common in normal conversation when the referent object is physically present.

If, however, the pencil is not physically present at the time A wants to convey his message to B, then the only means he has of identifying the referent are verbal. Non-verbal strategies like pointing, touching or showing can only be used to draw attention to aspects of the physical environment, not to referents which exist only in memory or in shared knowledge. A is limited to saying something like *Do you remember the pencil I bought when we were shopping yesterday? Well, it's broken*. He must bring the referent to B's attention by introducing it into the conversation, in other words, by using language only. This kind of reference to an entity not present in the 'here-and-now' of the speech context has been called "displaced reference". The capacity for displaced reference is one of the defining properties of human language.

Whether a speaker intends reference to the 'here-and-now' or to a more remote context, he is obliged to use a linguistically appropriate referring expression or the referential act will be unsuccessful. The speaker who, for example, points at a pencil and says *The crayon is broken* will certainly confuse his listener. Even saying *It is broken* in the same circumstances may not be precise enough, as the speaker could be intending the pencil as a whole or only some smaller part of it (e.g. the eraser). Successful reference requires the use of a referring expression which is sufficiently explicit to allow the listener to uniquely and unambiguously identify what the speaker is talking about. The linguistic and extra-linguistic conditions determining what is "sufficiently explicit" in any given speech context may be very complex; they will not be taken up further here. Every language user has, however, undoubtedly had many experiences where, as a listener, he has had to ask for clarification of a referent or, as a speaker, he has had to make his reference clearer. Thus this kind of referential failure is certainly very familiar.

The formula for establishing reference outlined here represents steps that any speaker must take whenever he intends to refer. As was pointed out above, in the course of actual conversation, many of the "steps" can be and often are accomplished simultaneously, with speakers and listeners continually assessing and directing each other's foci of attention within the physical and verbal contexts. (For a more complete discussion of reference in discourse, see Keenan and Schieffelin, 1976; Ochs et al., 1979.) The particular referring expressions the conversational participants use are also highly determined by the entire discourse context.

NORMAL DEVELOPMENT OF THE REFERENTIAL FUNCTION

The sequence of steps within a referential act also reflects in interesting ways the typical developmental sequence as a child masters the referential function of language. Research with sighted children shows that the development of reference proceeds along the general path to be outlined below.

Attracting Attention to Self

Infants become adept at attracting attention to themselves considerably before they begin to talk. At first their success at drawing attention to themselves is quite unintentional. They cry, smile, gurgle and vocalize in reaction to internal or external stimuli, but their actions frequently have the effect of attracting the attention of those around them. Later, beginning around nine months, infants start to make deliberate efforts to attract the attention of others (Bates, Camaioni and Volterra, 1975). They use basically the same repertoire of behaviours which has been successful in eliciting notice unintentionally, but now they may initiate the crying, vocalizing, smiling, etc. and persist in the behaviour until they are satisfied that someone is attending to them. Attracting attention to self, then, is developmentally one of the earliest steps in learning to refer.

Assessing the Listener's Focus of Attention

How infants learn to assess other people's foci of attention has perhaps been examined in less detail than other aspects of pre-referential and referential development. It is clear, however, that from an early age babies are sensitive to others' direction of gaze. They will look in the same direction as someone else from about four months of age

(Bruner, 1975). Even before this, they seem to recognize making eye contact as a sign of mutual attention. Although vision seems to play a primary role in assessing attention, infants also learn to recognize and accept auditory proof of attention, for example, adult imitations or other reinforcements of the baby's vocalizations. Infants also undoubtedly recognize very early that touching, holding and other tactile exchanges may be signs of attention. Typically adults will show their attention to the infant with a combination of signals, e.g. vocalizing, gazing and touching simultaneously.

Directing Attention to External Referents

Shortly after infants have become successful at attracting attention to themselves, they begin to try to direct others' attention to objects and people outside themselves. Again, deliberate attention-directing seems to have its roots in the baby's unintentional activities. For example, infants may mouth, bang, vocalize at or look at objects in their own explorations of them; adults may then treat the infants' actions as deliberate attempts to bring the object to adult attention. Intentional attention-directing begins to appear when the infant is about ten months old. Initially it draws upon the earlier repertoire of object behaviour. Then some specifically attention-directing behaviours begin to emerge, for example, showing an object and communicative pointing. These gestures come to be combined with vocalizations during the pre-linguistic period. Children may be motivated to combine vocalization, and later language, with gestures as they become aware that in some situations gestures alone are not enough. If, for instance, the other person is not looking at you, it is impossible to attract or direct his attention by pointing alone.

As the first words begin to appear, they are very often superimposed on attention-getting and -directing gestures. One of the earliest items in the vocabulary of most infants is some kind of deictic or "attention-directing" word (e.g. *that, there, look,* or some baby variant of these). It is invariably accompanied by pointing or some other gesture (see further Nelson, 1973; Carter, 1978; Atkinson, 1979). Infants also come to use other words, for example, the names of people and objects, with these gestures; ultimately they are able to use the verbal devices alone to draw attention. Typically, however, gestures continue to be used along with language in many situations (Pechmann and Deutsch, 1980).

Early Development of Referential Language

A baby's first uses of language with referential intent may not be very accurate. A one- or two-year old has, after all, only a limited vocabulary and typically uses the words he has with meanings that do not exactly correspond to the conventional meanings of the adult language. When, for example, a child says *dog* to indicate a cat, horse or other animal, he is not using the referring expression very accurately. Semantic development is a gradual process and such errors of meaning are very common in early child language (Bowerman, 1978; Clark, 1979). Other more subtle problems in learning to use the full range of referring expressions of the adult language continue to plague the language-learning child well into his school years (see, for example, Karmiloff-Smith, 1979). Complete mastery of the accurate use of referring expressions continues for many years, probably as long as a speaker is learning new vocabulary.

Development of Displaced Reference

The child's first uses of verbal devices for reference are very strongly tied to the immediate speech context, to the 'here-and-now'. Referring expressions are first used to indicate aspects of the perceptible physical surroundings, to name people, objects, actions and properties that are on the spot. First attempts at displaced reference generally appear from about age 18 months and are initially limited to the immediate past (i.e. comments about what has just happened) or to the child's intentions for the immediate future. Generally early displaced references are triggered by some aspect of the current situation (Sachs, 1977). The capacity to talk about more distant places and times depends crucially on the child's ability to use language alone, without the support of non-verbal attentional strategies, to make clear for the listener what he is talking about. Children under about three years of age are not very adept at displaced reference, especially when the listener is not a familiar person. They are still very dependent on the non-verbal context to support their referential acts and are still mastering those verbal devices which specifically signal intention to refer to another time or place, such as tense markers or phrases like *Do you remember...?* (Ochs et al., 1979). They are also not very good at assessing the listeners' knowledge of non-immediate situations and thus make many assumptions about other people's abilities to figure out what they mean.

POTENTIAL PROBLEMS FOR THE DEVELOPMENT OF REFERENCE IN BLIND CHILDREN

Clearly, the development of reference, as we understand it so far, is a very complex and drawn-out process. Let us turn now to the particular challenges blind children may face in mastering the referential function. At each step of the referring act, problems are likely to confront a blind speaker. Some of these problems, and some of the solutions that blind speakers might exploit, can be illustrated with examples from naturalistic speech samples collected during a longitudinal study of the language of three blind children. The subjects of this research were three totally congenitally blind boys between the ages of five and six. All were considered to be 'successful' blind children by the adults who worked with them. Two, Robert and Joshua, were identical twins whose blindness was due to retrolental fibroplasia (RLF). The third one, Alex, had Leber's amaurosis, a genetic retinal disorder. None had any other diagnosed sensory or central nervous system impairments. The children were recorded in various settings, but primarily in their pre-school or kindergarten classrooms or at home. The children and the data collection methods have been described in more detail elsewhere (Mulford, 1981). In the following dialogues, SC indicates a sighted child. Where more than one adult is involved, identity is indicated by a numerical subscript.

Assessing the Listener's Attention to the Speaker

Unless the blind child is already participating in a conversation with someone, he may have trouble determining whether his intended addressee is listening to him (Examples 1-2) or whether the person he wants to talk to is even present at all (Example 3).

Example 1. Joshua is walking across the classroom to a table where $Adult_1$ is sitting. In his path is another table where $Adult_2$

Example 1. (cont'd)

is seated. Joshua doesn't know $Adult_2$ and hasn't been aware of her presence.

$Adult_1$: *Over here, Joshua. Careful. You're gonna run into the table with Mrs. Edwards.* [=$Adult_2$]

Joshua: [to $Adult_2$] *Where's (your) car?* [$Adult_2$ doesn't answer]

$Adult_1$: *Say "Hi, Mrs. Edwards".*

Example 2.

While walking to the kindergarten classroom, Robert and $Adult_1$ have been talking about asking $Adult_2$'s permission to go to the parking lot to see $Adult_1$'s car. They enter the kindergarten classroom, where $Adult_2$ is seated at a table at the opposite end of the room, out of earshot.

Robert: *Becky* [=$Adult_2$], *could I see Randa's* [=$Adult_1$] *car, please?*

$Adult_1$: *Becky's at the - way at the other side of the room. (You) have to go down there (to where she is).*

Example 3.

Robert, Joshua, $Adult_1$, and $Adult_2$ are seated at a small table. The boys have been playing 'the object game' together; Robert is now playing alone while the others observe. Mike, a high school student who often comes as a teacher's aid, is absent.

Joshua: *(Mike), are you doing the objects with Robert?*

$Adult_1$: [not understanding who Joshua intends to address] *Yep, we're watching him. O.K.?*

Joshua: *Mike?*

$Adult_1$: *Mike's not here today.*

Knowing that the intended addressee is physically present (e.g. touching the child or making noise) is no guarantee that he is paying attention. Even if the blind child has been conversing with another person, he may have a hard time assessing whether the listener's attention has shifted to someone or something else, since he cannot rely on visual cues to the listener's continuing attention. For example, the listener may be looking elsewhere (Example 4) or may have moved out of earshot.

Example 4. Adult$_1$ and Adult$_2$ have been talking with Alex about changing cars. Then they switch to consulting a map together.
Alex: [to ?] *(Er-)um-am I going in your car?* [being ignored] *Am I? Am I?*
Alex is apparently unaware that the adults' attention has shifted to the map.

It seems likely that blind speakers rely heavily on auditory or verbal confirmation of listener attention and actively try to elicit such confirmation.

<u>Attracting the Listener's Attention to the Speaker</u>

As discussed above, many of the sighted child's earliest attention-getting strategies are non-verbal. Some of the most effective of these, such as initiating eye contact, are unavailable to the blind child. If the listener is close by, then initiating physical contact, for instance, by touching (Example 5) or pinching (Example 6) may be effective, if not always socially acceptable.

Example 5. Adult$_1$, Adult$_2$, SC, and Robert are in the classroom. Adult$_1$ has been talking to Adult$_2$ and SC, not to Robert.
Robert: [feeling Adult$_1$'s clothes] *Do you have a dress?*
Adult$_1$: *Do I?*
Robert: *Or pants?*
Adult$_1$: *I have on pants.*

Example 6. Robert is sitting next to Denise (SC) during group time in kindergarten. He pinches her.
Denise: *Ah!*
Robert: *What's your name?*
Denise: *You pincheded* [sic] *me.*
Robert: *What's your name?*
Denise: *Denise*

Making some kind of non-linguistic noise may also be successful (Example 7).

Example 7. Adult$_1$ has been talking to Joshua, then leaves. Adult$_2$ is nearby.
Joshua: [making some grunting noises]

Example 7. (cont'd)
Adult$_2$: *What a silly noise that was.*
Joshua: [makes more noises]
Adult$_2$: *Hey, what kind of noise is that?*

Consider also the attention-attracting 'fake' cough that Rowland noted in one of her pre-verbal subjects (1980, p. 95).

Although using non-verbal devices is one available option, these five-year old blind children relied most heavily on verbal means to elicit listener attention, sometimes in conjunction with physical contact, as in Examples 5 and 6, but often alone. These verbal devices included vocatives (Example 8), expressive particles (Example 9), greeting terms (Example 10) and questions (Example 11).

Example 8. Alex, Adult$_1$ and Adult$_2$ are sitting together at a picnic table.
Alex : *Mom? I mean...I mean-um...I mean-um...um...Laura?* [=Adult$_1$]
Adult$_1$: *Yeah?*
Alex : *I mean, Randa?* [=Adult$_2$]
Adult$_2$: *Yeah? What?* [pause] *Yes, what do you want?*

Example 9. Alex is playing with the power controls on the car seat. Adult$_1$ and Adult$_2$ are seated nearby.
Alex : *Whoops.* [seat is stuck]
Adult$_1$: *Whoops, what?* [goes to investigate]

Example 10. Robert and Adult$_1$ are in the kindergarten classroom. Adult$_2$ enters.
Adult$_1$: *Who came in the classroom right now?*
Robert: *Donny. Hi, Donny.* [=Adult$_2$]
Adult$_2$: *Hello.*

Example 11. Alex, Adult$_1$ and Adult$_2$ are talking about piñatas. Then Adult$_1$ directs some commands to Adult$_2$.
Alex : [interrupting] *Are piñatas heavy to carry?*
Adult$_2$: *I guess it depends on how big they are.*

Vocatives and questions are especially effective in eliciting a verbal response from the listener, a clear sign that he is paying attention. They were very frequently used by the children in my study, such that up to one third of all their utterances in some samples were questions. Urwin also reports the early and persistent use of such devices for eliciting listener response in at least one of her subjects, Suzanne, who began using the expression *Ay?* by the age of twelve months (1978, pp. 341-9).

Assessing the Listener's Attention to Referent X

The blind children's difficulties here will be similar to those of assessing the listener's attention to the speaker, at least in situations where the referent is found in the physical surroundings. Again, they miss all visual cues as to the focus of listener attention, such as direction of gaze, so they may misjudge it (Examples 12-13).

Example 12. Robert and Adult$_1$ are walking through the parking lot. Robert hears a motor running. There is also a car driving away nearby.

Robert: *I wanna see that car...I wanna say hi.*
Adult$_1$: [attending to car driving off] *Well, that car already left.*
Robert: *No, that car when it's running.*
Adult$_1$: *That's a truck.*

Example 13. Adult$_1$ is helping Robert with an art project. Adult$_1$ is gluing tooth-picks on the paper; Robert is feeling the tip of the metal core of a pipe-cleaner.

Adult$_1$: *We're gonna make our ladder nice an' wide.*
Robert: *Is it pi- is it got a pin in it?*
Adult$_1$: *What?*
Robert: *Put a pin in.*
Adult$_1$: *A pin?*

The blind child's problem is compounded, of course, because he may not perceive all aspects of the situation which could attract, or distract, the attention of a sighted listener. Thus in Example 12, Robert seems initially unaware that there is a second vehicle that the adult could be paying attention to.

In contexts where the referent is not physically available, blind children are in basically the same position as the sighted. They must determine whether the intended referent 'exists' in the ongoing discourse, that is, whether it is already on the listener's mind. Or the referent entity may potentially 'exist' in the shared knowledge of the speaker and listener; again the child must judge whether a particular listener is likely to have access to the same past experiences or the same knowledge of the broader context as he does. Being able to see bestows no particular advantages when it comes to assessing whether the listener is attending to the same piece of the invisible world as the speaker. The kinds of misassessments that blind children make are very like those of sighted children (Example 14).

Example 14. Alex, $Adult_1$, and $Adult_2$ are talking together. Neither $Adult_1$ nor $Adult_2$ was present when Alex had his 'Big Bounce' (a kind of toy).

Alex : *You remember when I had a Big Bounce?*
$Adult_1$: *A Big Bounce?*
Alex : *Yeah.*
$Adult_2$: *(Where) was that?*
$Adult_1$: *I don't remember that. Was I there?*
Alex : *What?*
$Adult_1$: *I don't think I was there when you had a Big Bounce.*
Alex : *Oh.*

Directing Listener Attention to Referent X

Again the blind child's range of options for directing a listener's attention to a physical referent is more limited than the sighted child's. He cannot just look at X, indicating his focus of attention by his direction of gaze. Nor do blind children point to objects that attract their attention or spontaneously show objects to others. For the most part, they are limited in their non-verbal attention-directing strategies to physical contact with the referent, like touching (Example 15) or holding (Example 16). Sometimes they may try to bring the listener into contact with the focal object as well (Example 17).

Example 15. Alex and $Adult_1$ are sitting in the car.
Alex: [touching the button on the car door that controls the window]

Example 15. (cont'd) Alex: *Is that the window shade opener?*

Example 16. Alex, $Adult_1$ and $Adult_2$ are sitting in the car. Alex is holding a bag of candies.
Alex: *This is a candy bag that - that - an' it has candy.*

Example 17. Robert and Joshua are sitting at a small table. Joshua is practising on the Braille writer, which Robert would like to use. Robert pushes a spiral notebook at Joshua, getting it in his way.
Robert: *Here's your notebook, Josh.*
Joshua: *No.*
Robert: *Here's you- here's your notebook, Joshua.*
Joshua: *No!*
Robert: *You-(right) here's your notebook.*

Blind children are much less constrained by their impairment, however, once they begin to use verbal attention-directing strategies. They can name or describe what they are attending to, either alone, as in Examples 18 and 19, or in conjunction with a non-verbal strategy, as in Example 17 above.

Example 18. Alex, $Adult_1$, and $Adult_2$ are walking through the park and pass close to the corral by the pony ride.
Alex : *I smell the ponies!* [adults laugh]
$Adult_1$: *So do I. They stink.*

Example 19. In the car. Alex had been playing with the motorized control to raise and lower the driver's seat. Now he is sitting on the passenger side. $Adult_1$ runs the motor to adjust the seat.
Alex : [teasing voice] *Who's making that seat go up an' down?*
$Adult_1$: *I'm makin' it go forward so I can reach the pedals.*

Referring to X with a Definite, Unambiguous Referring Expression

Several recent studies of blind children's semantic development (Herron, 1974; Bernstein, 1980; Mulford, 1981; Landau, Chapter 7), as well as the earlier discussions of "verbalism" (e.g. Cutsforth, 1932; Nolan, 1960; Harley, 1963; Dokecki, 1966), have focussed on the issue of blind children learning to use referring expressions accurately. Blind children, like sighted ones, have to learn how to use language to pick out precisely and uniquely the entity or entities they are focussing on. Both must learn the definiteness conditions on referring expressions. Although all children typically have problems in learning to use some kinds of words correctly, the blind child may face additional difficulties with words whose referents are primarily or partially distinguished by visually-perceived attributes. The most obvious examples of problem domains are totally visual words like colour terms or *light-dark* (see Millar, Chapter 15). Other classes of words may also pose problems because the information necessary to correctly identify and label the categories they refer to is most readily perceived visually. For example, two of the children reported on here had difficulty for a time with the pronouns *he* and *she*, so that they sometimes used *he* for girls and *she* for boys. The interesting point was that these confusions only occurred when they were talking about other children, not about adults. It is not hard to imagine that the clues sighted speakers generally use to distinguish five-year old boys from five-year old girls are relatively unavailable to a blind child and that the clues he must rely on, such as voice, relative size or even clothing, are not always sufficient for identification. Example 12 above is also a case where the child makes a perceptual misidentification, calling a truck a car based on its sound, and thus confusing the listener temporarily. Further problems arise, too, because blind children may not always be aware of potential referential ambiguities in the speech context, as in Example 20.

Example 20. Joshua is feeling a ring on Adult's hand; there are two rings there.

Joshua: *I want the ring on.*
Adult : *Which-which ring?*
Joshua: *I (wanna) put the ring on.*
Adult : *Which ring?*
Joshua: *I put the ring on.*

Example 20. (cont'd)	Adult :	*Which ring? My little ring?*
	Joshua:	*Yeah.*
	Adult :	*Or my big ring?*
	Joshua:	*My* [sic] *little ring. Big ring.*
	Adult :	*My big ring. O.K.*

Joshua does not seem to have noticed that there are two rings and that therefore the phrase *the ring* is not definite enough. Particular kinds of expressions (e.g. spatial deictics) may take a very long time for blind children to learn to use with complete referential accuracy. Some words may never be used with just the same meanings by blind and sighted speakers.[2]

DISCUSSION

Although a number of examples have been presented here to illustrate various kinds of referential problems faced by blind speakers, it should be pointed out that, generally speaking, these three five-year olds were quite successful referrers, at least judging by the responses of their listeners. Two main factors seem to account for their relative referential success.

First, by the age of five, these blind children have already mastered a number of effective verbal and non-verbal devices for establishing reference. They have become relatively proficient at assessing listener attention and, if anything, may err in the direction of 'over-attracting' attention by an excessive use of vocatives and questions. Although they are still learning the conventional uses of some kinds of referring expressions, they make few blatant meaning errors. We need more detailed information on the use of referential devices by sighted children of the same age in similar settings for comparison, of course, but one suspects that the performance of the two groups will be similar.

The second factor which contributes to these children's apparent referential success is the very active role of their adult listeners as interpreters of intended reference. In all these speech samples, the children were interacting with familiar and attentive adults, for the most part in surroundings also very familiar to the child. The adults were able to exploit their knowledge of the particular children and, in almost all cases, arrived at interpretations of potentially ambiguous utterances which seemed to correspond to the children's intentions. Of course, all conversations involve listener interpretation as well as speaker intention, and the parents of sighted children as well as blind ones typically need to read a lot into their youngster's early communicative attempts. It seems clear, however, that successful interaction with blind children requires some special skills in assessing their foci of attention and in interpreting their utterances from the perspective of a speaker without vision. As Fraiberg (1977) and Rowland (1980) have suggested, some of these skills may have to be taught to people who have not had experience with blind children. It is also a common practice to teach blind children some of the gestural conventions for indicating attention, for example, turning to face the person one is addressing. This type of training may facilitate their communication with unfamiliar listeners to some extent. It is necessary to gather more data on how referentially successful blind speakers are, both children and adults, in situations where their listeners are relatively unfamiliar and unskilled interpreters.

Much more information is also needed on the development of referential skills among younger blind children. Although Rowland (1980) and Urwin (1978a) have made valuable contributions with their studies of children under the age of three, there are still many unanswered questions. We can anticipate that problems of referring will be especially severe for the younger language-learning blind child for two reasons. First, the young sighted child talks primarily about his immediate surroundings and relies heavily on non-verbal means for assessing, attracting and directing attention. Many, if not most, of these strategies involve vision. Not only is the blind child's perception of his physical surroundings more limited than the sighted child's, but he also lacks access to those non-verbal attentional strategies that depend on vision. Secondly, although blind children may eventually learn to use verbal devices very successfully to accomplish reference, the development of a repertoire of such strategies is undoubtedly gradual. What is more, among sighted children, the use of certain verbal devices is normally preceded by the use of conventional non-verbal devices. For instance, sighted children only begin to use pointing words like *that* or *there* after they have come to use pointing gestures; the words first appear only in combination with the gestures (Bates, 1976; E. Clark, 1978).

Since young blind children do not use these conventional gestures, language acquisition data from blind children should help to resolve the issue of whether such gestures are in fact prerequisites for specific, verbal developments or only typical precursors. The answer which seems to be emerging from Rowland and Urwin's work is that blind children can master the verbal devices without first having recourse to the non-verbal ones, but that their development proceeds along a somewhat different course, possibly through the use of unconventional gestures and/or language rituals, and perhaps at a different pace than that of sighted children.

CONCLUSION

This discussion of referential development in blind children has been intended to outline in some detail the range of problems which need to be investigated. Only very sketchy solutions to these problems exist so far. This paper has concentrated only on the development of the blind child as a speaker, but certainly his complementary role as listener and interpreter of reference needs to be explored, too, to arrive at a broader understanding of how he learns to communicate. As more is learned about how and to what extent individual blind children overcome the potential obstacles their impairment poses, child language researchers will be in a better position to suggest ways of enhancing the development of referential communication among young blind speakers. Ultimately, we should have a better understanding of the necessary, as opposed to the characteristic, role of vision in the development of the referential function of language.

NOTES

1. This chapter is based on portions of my unpublished doctoral dissertation "Talking without Seeing: Some Problems of Semantic Development in Blind Children", Stanford University, 1981.
2. I will skirt entirely the issue of whether or not any two speakers, sighted or blind, ever use the same word with precisely the same meaning.

Chapter 10.

EFFECTANCE MOTIVATION AND THE DEVELOPMENT OF COMMUNICATIVE COMPETENCE IN BLIND AND SIGHTED CHILDREN

Harry McGurk

A number of issues recur in the chapters of this volume, three of which I wish to select for particular discussion. These are issues, it seems to me, which must be resolved if we are ever to make progress in this area. Firstly, I wish to consider the nature of the samples involved in research on the development of communication in blind children, secondly, to consider the extent to which there are specific factors in the development of communicative competence which are attributable to the absence of visual input, and thirdly, the extent to which there may be differences between totally blind and partially-sighted children in their acquisition of communicative competence. Throughout this discussion my perspective will be that of a developmental psychologist rather than that of a linguist, and I will illustrate my comments with reference to psychological research.

SAMPLE HETEROGENEITY IN RESEARCH ON COMMUNICATIVE COMPETENCE IN BLIND CHILDREN

It has been repeatedly pointed out, for example by Elstner (Chapter 3) and Schaner-Wolles (Chapter 4), that visually-impaired children are frequently handicapped in other ways in addition to their deficient visual experience. These additional handicaps tend to confound the interpretation of data when it comes to assessing the extent to which any communicative delay or deviance shown by such children may be attributed directly to their visual deficit. One solution to this problem is to conduct research with subjects whose sole handicap is visual, as reported, for example, by Barbara Landau (Chapter 7). Moreover, if it is possible to select subjects whose handicap varies in degree from total blindness, through a moderate degree of visual impairment to normal vision, then we can assess the extent to which dependent variables are also transitively ordered between subjects from the different categories. If such transitive ordering is observed, then we can be confident that the phenomena under scrutiny are related to blindness.

However, such a strategy raises other, equally important methodological and ethical questions. The population to which the results of a study designed along the above lines could be generalized is clearly a minority one among visually-handicapped children; as we have noted above, the vast majority of such children are also handicapped in other ways. We also noted above, however, that only by working with otherwise normal children who happen to be visually-handicapped can we learn what, if anything, is specifically visual about the development of communicative competence. In this sense, we are using the occurrence of the congenital visual defect as a natural experiment, a context in which to evaluate hypotheses about the role of vision in the development of communication. Perhaps in so doing we need to acknowledge explicitly that it is the blind who are serving us and our theories, rather than we who are serving the blind. Of course, data from research designed to address theoretical issues can serve as a basis for the development of strategies to enhance the acquisition of communicative skills among children from handicapped populations. However, the development of such strategies needs also to be addressed directly and it is a moot point whether the interests of the modal visually-handicapped child are served by research investigations on samples from highly restricted populations.

DOES VISUAL HANDICAP HAVE SPECIFIC EFFECTS ON THE DEVELOPMENT OF COMMUNICATIVE COMPETENCE?

In Chapter 2, Wode raised the question of whether the visually-impaired, but otherwise normal, child showed deviant patterns of communication, or whether such children were merely delayed in arriving at communicative competence. The question can also be asked whether, should deviance indeed be manifested, it can be causally attributed to lack of, or reduced, visual input *per se*, or whether there are other factors which covary with visual handicap but which contributed more directly to the development of communication. The bulk of the evidence presented in the other chapters of this volume suggests that blindness is associated with delayed rather than deviant communicative development. Only the data presented by Anne Mills (Chapter 5) and by Barbara Dodd (Chapter 6) have revealed highly specific effects attributable to blindness and these were confined to a fairly circumscribed, though theoretically significant, aspect of phonological development. In the main, the evidence reported here indicates that, although he takes longer to traverse the route, the visually-impaired child follows the same path to communicative competence as his sighted peers, and the level of competence he eventually achieves is well within the range of reaction we accept as normality. Visual impairment, rather than having specific, determinate effects, thus seems to have general moderating or modulating influences upon the development of communicative competence.

R.W. White (1959) has argued that there is an endogenous, overarching human psychological motive to be effective, to have reliable effects, to be competent in exchanges with the physical and social environment. This effectance motivation is enhanced by experiences of agency, of events in the world being contingent upon one's behaviour. On such experience is the motivation to acquire competence based. With respect to the development of communicative competence work by Kaye (1977) and Collis and Schaffer (1975) suggest how normal patterns of caretaker-child interaction serve to provide the infant and young child with the experience of such contingency within the context of communicative exchanges. Kaye's analysis of feeding episodes shows how mothers of newborn babies monitor the infant's sucking rhythms and interpolate such behaviour as talking to the baby or adjusting body posture into the pauses between sucking bursts. These interpolations have the effect of lengthening such filled pauses relative to unfilled pauses. Thus, the on-off pattern of infant sucking influences the phasing of maternal caretaking behaviour and this, in turn, influences the temporal relationship between pausing and sucking. Kaye argues that the origins of dialogue are to be found in these reciprocally contingent, turn-taking exchanges between infant and mother.

Collis and Schaffer (1975), working with twelve-month old infants and their mothers, illustrate how the mother, by monitoring the direction of infant regard, identifies the focus of infant attention and may comment appropriately. Thus, the infant's visual behaviour specifies a topic upon which the mother provides commentary. Murphy and Messer (1977) also show how direction of regard, pointing and other deictic behaviour on the part of the normal infant provide opportunities for contingent exchange between infant and caretaker.

The absence of such visually mediated deictic behaviours from the repertoire of the blind or visually-impaired child severely constrains the opportunities for contingent interaction over shared referents both before and during language acquisition. Very young sighted infants produce their own visual and other referential gestures and can follow the gestural referents of others. The visually-impaired child thus misses out on a whole range of opportunities for self and other initiated contingent exchanges and, to that extent his competence-enhancing experiences are restricted. Such restrictions can be expected to have a generalized delay effect upon language acquisition.

Some of the filmed material presented during this conference, together with comments made by Edna Adelson in her paper (Chapter 1), confirm that visually-impaired children do display components of the orienting reaction other than direction of visual regard. For example, on introduction of new or novel objects or events they show interruption of ongoing behaviour and general stilling. A sensitive adult can use such behaviours as a guide for specifying topics on which to comment and thereby enhance the contingency experience of the child. In so doing, the adult enhances his or her own contingency in interaction with the child; from the film material and from observations by Adelson it is evident that contingencies are deficient for <u>both</u> adult and child in interaction sequences involving blind children. Thus, the blind child may not only have a reduced sense of agency, but is also deficient in providing contingent feedback in interaction with others. Unless steps are taken to overcome this deficiency, it can only serve further to reduce the child's contingency related experience and to delay further the development of communicative competence.

Because the blind child's non-verbal behaviour so often fails to provide topics for comment, parents frequently adopt an interrogative mode in interaction with blind children. Moreover, data attest to the fact that parents of blind children employ direct questions to the child with much greater frequency than do parents of sighted children.

Although questioning may facilitate a rudimentary form of turn-taking between parent and child, because the initiative is always with the interrogator, the practice does not enhance the child's experience of agency. This is particularly so with closed as opposed to open-ended questions. Interestingly, in this regard, some recent work by Blank (1981) has shown that parents of sighted but linguistically retarded children employ many more questions during parent-child interaction sequences compared with parents whose children display normal language development. Of course, there is something of a chicken and egg problem here, but Blank's work also suggests that the adoption of a freer interactive style with language-delayed children does enhance the quality of their linguistic output. It might be valuable to determine whether the same holds true with respect to the development of communicative competence in blind children, for here also we have a factor which may be implicated in the general deficiency in these children's linguistic development.

COMMUNICATIVE COMPETENCE IN BLIND COMPARED WITH PARTIALLY-SIGHTED CHILDREN

In this area there is a considerable amount of potentially conflicting evidence. For example, in Walter Elstner's study (Chapter 3) he observed that the partially-sighted subjects showed the same degree of speech and language impairment as the totally blind. As we noted previously, however, Elstner's sample was a very heterogeneous one and the probability exists that additional handicaps contributed to linguistic impairment of the blind and partially-sighted alike. On the other hand, Barbara Landau (Chapter 7) stressed that in her work with otherwise normal children little difference was revealed between the language performance of blind, partially-sighted and normal children with respect to such general measures as mean length of utterance (MLU). During discussion at this conference, cases were reported which were at variance with these observations, cases involving substantial differences in communicative competence between blind and partially-sighted subjects, the latter being much closer to the normally sighted than the former.

It seems important, for theoretical and for practical reasons, that this issue should be addressed and resolved. Resolution, of course, will require careful description of the degree of visual impairment manifested by partially-sighted subjects and its relationship to communicative competence across a range of linguistic and paralinguistic variables. The pay-off for such detailed analysis is potentially considerable. At a theoretical level, the outcome would enhance our understanding of those specifically visual processes which may contribute to the development of communicative competence. Practically, such work would be of importance for the development of intervention procedures directed towards maximizing the potential utilization of residual vision in the developing child. Irene Neilson (1981) has illustrated how spatial cognition and spatial mobility can be facilitated by intervention programmes initiated early in the partially-sighted child's infancy; if intervention is delayed, then little benefit accrues thereby. With this in mind we would do well to inform ourselves whether partial vision is of significance to the acquisition of communicative competence, and, if so, to determine whether its effectiveness can be enhanced by specifically developed, appropriately timed, intervention strategies. In such fashion it may be possible to work toward attaining for the partially-sighted in the field of communicative competence what Neilson has been attaining for them in the field of spatial mobility. Were we to begin to realize such aspirations then we would have begun to serve the blind and partially-sighted child. Otherwise we are in danger of continuing to need the blind more than they need us.

Chapter 11.

PATTERNS OF INTERACTION BETWEEN THREE BLIND INFANTS AND THEIR MOTHERS

Charity Rowland

INTRODUCTION

The early communicative ability of visually-impaired children has received little attention until recently, probably because visual impairment *per se* has not been regarded as an impediment to the eventual acquisition of language skills. Although speech problems are more prevalent among blind than sighted children (Miner, 1963; Graham, 1966; Elstner, Chapter 3), the linguistic ability of the average blind child without concomitant handicaps has been reported on a par with the sighted child of the same age (Fraiberg, 1977). Burlingham (1961) found that an initial delay in vocabulary acquisition had been surmounted by school age, and found no deficit in syntactic abilities among blind children.

The lack of language problems associated with visual deficits is surprising, given that the blind infant typically displays significant delays in gross motor development, cognitive development and psycho-social development. It is only recently that attention has been focused on the early stages of language development, including the pre-verbal abilities of blind children.

Fraiberg (1977) described the average blind infant as communicatively rather unresponsive, with a restricted range of facial expressions and a suspected low rate of spontaneous vocalizations. She described the pre-verbal communication system of the blind infant as a system of "smile" and "hand" language that substitutes for the "eye" language of the sighted infant. The reported research investigated such suspected behavioural differences between blind and sighted infants through the micro-analysis of communicative behaviours of pre-verbal blind children and their mothers.

The study was guided by convergent trends in the recent literatures in language acquisition and developmental psychology. The first trend derives from an abundance of developmental research (Lewis and Rosenblum, 1977; Schaffer, 1977), that describes the extremely sophisticated receptive and signalling abilities of the human neonate that are evident in vocal and visual exchanges. The second trend derives from the revival of interest in a pragmatic approach to language development - one which ascribes the functional properties of language to certain pre-verbal behaviours (Dore, 1974, 1975; Halliday, 1979). A request, for instance, may be realized before the acquisition of formal language, through non-verbal behaviours such as pointing, visual regard or fussing. Early play activities and turn-taking rituals especially are considered important precursors to formal language (Bruner, 1974/5). In the words of R. Clark (1978, p. 234), language is considered a "progressive complication of the basic communicative function".

In a longitudinal, correlational study with empirical implications for this approach, Bates et al. (1977) found several good predictors of language development in the pre-verbal abilities of sighted children aged 9-13 months. These predictors included conventional gestures, such as pointing and showing, symbolic and combinatorial play, imitation and tool use. The authors interpreted their data as support for a common substrate for both pre-linguistic communication and language - a substrate that may be described as a capacity for communication through the use of conventional signs. Such studies as this formed the theoretical perspective that guided the behavioural observations of this study.

The four main research questions addressed by the study were:

1. What are the potentially communicative behaviours produced by blind infants and their mothers, and at what rates are these individual behaviours produced?

2. To which maternal behaviours do the blind infants seem to be responsive or non-responsive, as evidenced by temporal relationships between maternal and infant behaviours?

3. To which behaviours do the mothers of blind infants seem to be responsive or non-responsive, as evidenced, again, by temporal contingencies between behaviours?

4. Finally, do blind infants appear to adhere to the same course of development in early

communicative skills as Bates et al. (1977) described for the sighted infant?

METHOD

Subjects

The three subjects described here were congenitally totally blind. All three infants were female and were enrolled in a pre-school programme at a university affiliated Child Study Center (CSC) in Oklahoma. The children, Amy, Maria and Tanya were 11, 15 and 16 months of age, respectively, at the start of the six-month project. Amy and Maria lived close enough to the Child Study Center to attend hour-long individual sessions twice a week. Tanya attended the Center for longer individual sessions once a month and attended local special education classes twice a week. The reported research was conducted independently of these educational programmes, except that the films of the children were made available to their teachers at the Center. Although none of the subjects suffered from concomitant sensory handicaps, Amy and Tanya were severely developmentally delayed. The three infants are profiled in Table 11.1. In the brief descriptions below, the various developmental milestones are listed. For the purpose of comparison, these are followed in square brackets by age-equivalents for sighted children taken from the Callier-Azusa Scale (Stillman, 1978).

Amy was eleven months old at initial observation. She had no useful vision, suffered from generalized hypotonia and was developmentally delayed in all areas. Amy sat only with support [4 months], had poor head control, and would hold objects only passively, and for no more than a few seconds [3 months]. She seemed happy to be left alone, playing with her hands and babbling. Interestingly, she demonstrated excellent head-turn and eye-orientation to auditory cues [5 months]. By 17 months of age, she was playing with her hands at midline [4 months], and would play independently with toys. She could sit unsupported in a high chair, tuck her legs under her and rock in a crawling position [8 months] and move around the floor a little by rolling and scooting [6 months]. Her auditory localization skills were excellent [12 months] and manual exploratory behaviour was becoming more purposeful and frequent [8 months].

Table 11.1: Subject Profile

	Amy	Maria	Tanya
Birthdate	12.77	7.77	6.77
Age at Initiation of Project	11 months	15 months	16 months
Family Income	Low-middle	Low	Low
Home	Urban	Urban	Rural
Ordinal Position in Family	2nd of 2	1st of 1 (but 4th of 4 under 21 yrs. in extended family)	3rd of 3
Others in Home	Mother, father, 1 sibling	Mother, 2 aunts, uncle, grandmother, various other relatives move in/out	Mother, 2 siblings
Most Recent Visual Assessment	Responds to bright lights (10 months)	None (10 months)	No visual response (13 months)
Visual Diagnosis	Visual impairment; cortical basis	Congenital anophthalmia	Bilateral optic hypoplasia
Age at Diagnosis of Visual Impairment	6 months	Birth	Prior to 9 months
Concomitant Handicaps	Generalized hypotonia	None	None
Age at First Evaluation by CSC	10 months	3 months	9 months
Vision at Time of Referral to CSC	No consistent response, may see shadows	No visual response	No visual response
Age at Onset of Therapy	11 months	4 months	10 months

She vocalized loudly and fairly frequently; she seemed to understand a few verbal phrases [10 months] and responded to vocal intonation [3 months]. Amy's mother was highly anxious, painstaking in her application of recommended programmes and at the start seemed over-involved with her infant. Her behaviour levels were very high except for vocalization, and she produced a high rate of behaviour combinations. As her child became more independent and competent, however, Amy's mother managed to disengage herself to a certain extent.

Maria was 15 months at initial observation. Born without eyes, her blindness was evident from the start, and educational programming began at four months. Maria was by far the most advanced of the subjects in terms of social, motor and language skills; she was a confident, insatiably sociable baby. At the start of the project, she was trying eagerly to stand up and walk (although she did not crawl) and she would stand unassisted momentarily [10 months]. She imitated some words as well as non-linguistic vocalizations such as coughing and sneezing [12 months]. She could touch several body parts and wave good-bye on command [18 months]. By the end of the project, at the age of 21 months, Maria had taken as many as six steps by herself [11 months] and had been 'cruising' around the house for several months [10 months]. She had a vocabulary of about 20 words which she used in up to three-word combinations [24 months].

Maria's mother was a 16-year old high-school student when her baby was born. She was a warm, effusive girl, who continued to live with her own family after the birth of her child. She did not seem very attentive to professional recommendations, preferring to interact more spontaneously with her daughter. An environmental variable that set this infant apart from the other subjects was the large size of the family. Maria interacted virtually ceaselessly with a relatively large number of people. This family situation, combined with the fact that her handicap was evident at birth, no doubt contributed to her rapid development. When she was four months of age, Maria's mother and her grandmother began receiving training in tactile, vestibular, locomotor and language stimulation for Maria. Some of the training was then passed on to other members of the large extended family. Thus, effective interaction patterns that were appropriate to Maria's sensory abilities were established early on with a relatively large number of partners. (Amy and Tanya, in contrast, were not even diagnosed as visually-impaired until they were six months of age.)

At 16 months, Tanya was developmentally delayed in all areas and showed no visual response. She was a passive, contented baby who was able to sit unassisted [7 months] and had once sat herself up [8 months]. Once in sitting position, however, she tended to engage in self-stimulatory behaviour. She could push herself up into a crawling position and let herself down, and her tactile exploration was proceeding well. By the end of the project (at 22 months), Tanya had begun to move around the house by rolling [6 months]. She could sit herself up, lie back down, and rock back and forth in a crawling position [8 months]. She explored faces very carefully with her hands, and searched well in any direction both to a sound cue [12 months] and in quest of temporarily abandoned noiseless toys [9 months]. Her range of vocalizations had increased, and she had begun to say *mama*, but only imitatively [12 months]. At the start of the project, Tanya's mother was quite restrained in vocalization and touching behaviour. Her interactions with Tanya tended to focus on inanimate objects and her general behaviour level was low. By the end of the project, she had become much warmer and more engaged. Her touching and vocal behaviour had increased, while her production of noise using inanimate objects had decreased.

Procedures and Analysis

Films of mother-infant interactions were made in the subjects' homes at regular intervals over a six-month period to document the development of communicative skills within each dyad. Mothers were instructed to play with their children in as natural a manner as possible during filming. Approximately one-half of the filmed sessions were structured by the introduction of a standard set of toys not available in the subjects' home. The remaining sessions did not involve inanimate objects. The films were analyzed at two-second intervals for seven categories of infant behaviour and three categories of maternal behaviour, comprising a total of 42 subcategories. The coding system is described below.

Code Development

The observational coding system was developed from a combination of theory, intuition and practice on the preliminary data. The code was revised frequently to accomodate the first sets of filmed data as they became available for analysis. The rationale for the code developed from the following considerations:

1. The communicative behaviours of mother and infant were of primary interest.

2. From the perspective of the blind infant, many of the potentially communicative behaviours of the mother (such as facial expression and visual regard) are functionally non-existent. Therefore, the scoring of maternal behaviours was limited to those observable behaviours that could be sensed by a sightless infant. (No doubt the infants also responded to certain other maternal stimuli such as breath, body temperature and odour - but since these variables were neither observable nor subject to the mothers' voluntary control, they were not coded.)

3. From the maternal point of view, however, almost any infant behaviour might be considered expressive, so that almost all categories of gross infant behaviour were coded.

4. Initially it had been hoped that both verbal and non-verbal infant behaviours would be codable. When only one infant demonstrated any verbal behaviour, special attention was paid to the presence of the conventional pre-verbal gestures. However, the number of conventional gestures was also so low, that it quickly became obvious that a more molecular level of analysis was required than had originally been anticipated. Thus, attention came to be focussed upon more idiosyncratic expressive activities of the infants.

The coded behaviour categories appear in Table 11.2. A minimum of 80 per cent inter-observer agreement was achieved between two observers for each behaviour category for each subject. Data were first analyzed for the frequency of behaviours. Many subcategories (the majority) did not occur sufficiently frequently to warrant further analysis. Where subcategories could be meaningfully collapsed into larger categories, this was done (for instance, linguistic and non-linguistic vocalizations were collapsed). Where collapsing subcategories was not feasible, the low-frequency behaviour categories were excluded from further analysis.

Table 11.2: List of Coded Behaviours

Infant	
A.	Non-vocal Sound
B.	Vocal Sound
	1. linguistic
	2. non-linguistic
	3. imitation of maternal vocalization
C.	Head Gestures
D.	Facial Expression
	1. positive
	2. negative
E.	Manual Activity
	1. spontaneous gesture
	2. elicited gesture
	3. exploration of space
	4. reach for mother
	5. reach for object
	6. release mother
	7. release object
	8. explore mother
	9. explore object
	10. manipulate mother
	11. manipulate object
	12. hold mother
	13. hold object
	14. withdraw hand from mother
	15. withdraw hand from object
	16. push away mother
	17. push away object
	18. touch self
F.	Whole Body Movement
	1. approach
	2. avoidance
G.	Stereotypic Behaviour
	1. with object
	2. with self
	3. self-abusive
Mother	
H.	Tactile Behaviour
	1. caress
	2. restrain
	3. direct
I.	Vocal Sound
	1. linguistic
	2. non-linguistic
J.	Non-vocal Sound

RESULTS

Communicative Repertoires of the Infants

Frequency data for the individual behaviour categories of mothers and infants have been described in an earlier paper (Rowland, 1981). Table 11.3 presents the proportion of scored intervals containing a few selected behaviours for each pair of subjects. Highlights of these data follow.[1]

Table 11.3: Comparison of Pairs on Occurrence of Selected Behaviours: Proportion of Intervals Containing Each Behaviour

	Infant Behaviours	Amy	Maria	Tanya
[b]A	Non-vocal Sound[a]	.17	.26	.25
B 1,2,3	Vocalization	.29	.23	.19
D 1	Positive Facial Expression	.08	.23	.30
D 2	Negative Facial Expression	.07	.03	.00
E 1	Spontaneous Manual Gesture	.01	.06	.09
E 3	Explore Space	.03	.17	.00
E 11	Manipulate Object[a]	.19	.31	.27
E 9	Explore Object[a]	.06	.04	.10
E 8	Explore Mother	.00	.02	.05
E 5	Reach for Object[a]	.01	.20	.17
E 18	Touch Self	.35	.03	.10
	No Manual Activity	.46	.24	.33
	Maternal Behaviours	**Amy**	**Maria**	**Tanya**
H 1,2,3	Touch	.87	.53	.67
I 1,2	Vocalization	.44	.66	.56
J	Non-vocal Sound[a]	.56	.24	.30
	Vocal Imitation of Infant	.01	.03	.00

Note: a. Proportions generated from toy sequences only.
Note: b. Numbering system references the equivalent coded behaviours from Table 11.2.

Infant vocalizations occurred in at least 19 per cent of all intervals across subjects. Significantly, none of the mothers considered their infants to be particularly quiet, and all mothers reported high rates of vocalization by their infants when they were left alone. Only Maria, however, who was by far the most advanced in all developmental areas, produced any linguistic vocalizations. Facial expressions (positive and negative combined) occurred in at least 15 per cent of intervals across subjects. Independent manual activity, which had been expected to be relatively frequent, was completely absent in at least 24 per cent of intervals across subjects (see Table 11.3; Item: No Manual Activity). Spontaneous manual gestures, which included idiosyncratic movements of hands or arms, occurred in an average of 5 per cent of intervals across subjects. Examples of these gestures appear in Table 11.4. No conventional gestures such as giving or reaching as a request were observed in the infants.

The mothers exhibited high rates of touching, which were undoubtedly related to the postural maturity of their respective infants. Amy's mother touched her daughter, who was unable to sit unsupported, almost 100 per cent of the time. Maria's mother touched her daughter, who had good locomotor skills, least frequently (about 50 per cent of the time).

Table 11.4: Examples of Spontaneous Manual Gestures

Subject	Age (months)	Examples
Amy	11	Fingers on left hand play - hand moves slightly as mother squeezes ball at her
	11	Right hand, with index finger extended, waivers as she cries
	14	Pats stomach
	17	Throws arms and head back, starting to vocalize in protest
Maria	15	Right arm darts out suddenly as she laughs
	16	Waves and claps hands excitedly
	16	Lifts hands to face
Tanya	16	Brings arms up as mother shakes slinky toy
	17	Arms go up, hands go to head, brush head, arms go down, but stay extended (as she smiles)
	18	Bats arms, claps hands

The mother's vocalization rates were also high (occurring in at least 44 per cent of scored intervals), but the mothers rarely imitated their infants' vocalizations. Significantly, Maria's mother was most likely to imitate her infant's vocalizations, which were frequently linguistic.

Directions of Effects

Following the frequency analyses, the sequences of behaviours for each subject pair were analyzed for interdependencies over time using a lagged conditional probabilities programme developed by G. Sackett (1979, 1980). This nonparametric technique compares the observed (or contingent) probability of a target behaviour, given the antecedent occurrence of a criterion behaviour at any specified time lag, with its expected (or chance) probability of occurrence over an entire series of sequential observations.

This 'lag' technique is extremely costly and easily produces unmanageable amounts of data. Furthermore, 'fishing expeditions' into the dependencies between large numbers of behaviours produced by interacting individuals are bound to yield numerous chance relationships. Therefore, the 'lag' analyses were used only to investigate pairs of behaviours that were expected to be highly temporally related, either by virtue of the theoretical assumptions of the research, or as a result of actual observations of the mother-infant interactions. Thus, a very limited set of behavioural contingencies was examined. In this paper, discussion will centre around the analysis of temporal relationships between Infant Smiles, Gestures, and Vocalizations and Maternal Touch and Vocalizations (see Table 11.3).

In the sighted mother-infant pair, behavioural reciprocity, or mutual responsivity, is observed at a very early age. Condon and Sander (1974) found that "micro-kinesic" behaviours of neonates were responsive to maternal speech; Tronick, Als and Brazelton (1975) found a conversational quality in the vocal exchanges of three-month old infants and their mothers; Stern, Jaffe, Beebe and Bennett (1975) discuss mutual reciprocity in the visual and vocal exchanges of mothers and infants. Although we cannot concisely quantify or compare the degree of behavioural reciprocity displayed by the mother-infant dyads of this study, it is clear that the infants affected their mothers' behaviour much more strongly and systematically than the mothers affected the infant's behaviour. When we examine the probabilities of specific infant behaviours following specific maternal behaviours at the immediately succeeding interval, we see a striking lack of responsiveness of infant behaviour. A similar analysis of the probabilities of maternal behaviours following specific infant behaviours at the immediately succeeding interval revealed that mothers responded rapidly and frequently to infant behaviours and particularly to Infant Smile. In order to test the consistency of these immediate or lag-1 effects, two statistics, called the Magnitude and Z_{sum} were computed for each subject pair across the first ten intervals (20 seconds) following a given behaviour. Magnitude describes the extent to which contingent probabilities exceed chance in either direction, averaged over a specified number of lags. The larger the Magnitude, the more predictable is the change in the frequency of the contingent event, given a specified antecedent event. The Z_{sum} describes general trends in the direction of change: a large positive Z_{sum} implies a reliable excitation of the contingent behaviour, while a negative Z_{sum} implies an inhibition of the contingent behaviour. The computed statistics for these temporal relationships appear in Table 11.5.

The upper half of Table 11.5 displays statistics for the contingent probabilities of Maternal Touch and Maternal Vocalization following three different infant behaviours (Vocalization, Gesture and Smile). For each subject pair, the Magnitude of Maternal Vocalization was highest following Infant Smile. The Z_{sums} for Maternal Touch and Vocalization following Infant Smile are uniformly positive and significant ($p < .001$), indicating a reliable excitation of maternal behaviours in response to Infant Smile. For Amy and Tanya, the maternal response following Infant Vocalization was of very low Magnitude with non-significant Z_{sums}. For Maria, however, the Magnitudes of maternal behaviours following Infant Vocalizations were higher, and the Z_{sums} positive and significant ($p < .001$). The sharp contrast in maternal response following Maria's vocalizations may reflect the fact that many of her vocalizations were actual words, while the other infants produced only non-linguistic vocalizations. Interestingly, the mothers of Amy and Tanya, who did not have infant words to respond to, did appear to be more responsive than Maria's mother to Infant Gestures, as evidenced by the significant Z_{sums} associated with Maternal Touch and Vocalization following Infant Gestures.

Table 11.5: Magnitude and Z_{sums} of Crosslagged Functions[a]

Criterion Behaviour	-->	Target Behaviour	AMY Magnitude[b]	AMY Z_{sum}[c]	MARIA Magnitude	MARIA Z_{sum}	TANYA Magnitude	TANYA Z_{sum}
Infant Vocalize	-->	Mother Vocalize	.53	+1.24	1.84	+5.23***	.83	+1.89
Infant Vocalize	-->	Mother Touch	.66	+1.84	2.69	+7.65***	.49	- .11
Infant Gesture	-->	Mother Vocalize	2.29	-6.52***	1.17	+2.27	1.56	+4.44***
Infant Gesture	-->	Mother Touch	1.04	+2.63**	.78	+1.31	1.21	+3.45***
Infant Smile	-->	Mother Vocalize	2.92	+8.31***	3.14	+6.88***	2.76	+7.86***
Infant Smile	-->	Mother Touch	1.40	+3.99***	3.80	+10.82***	2.67	+7.60***
Mother Vocalize	-->	Infant Vocalize	.65	-1.08	.53	+ .71	.75	+1.10
Mother Vocalize	-->	Infant Gesture	.88	-1.72	.98	+2.76**	.83	- .49
Mother Vocalize	-->	Infant Smile	1.04	-2.97**	1.00	+ .23	1.35	+3.51***
Mother Touch	-->	Infant Vocalize	.72	- .84	.60	+ .05	.83	- .46
Mother Touch	-->	Infant Gesture	1.09	+ .69	.55	- .72	.87	-2.28
Mother Touch	-->	Infant Smile	.96	-2.19	.65	+ .59	2.70	-7.69***

Note: a. Contingent probability of target behaviour following criterion behaviour, lagged from the onset of the criterion behaviour across a series

Note: b. $\text{Magnitude} = \sum_{1}^{n} |z| / n$

Note: c. $Z_{sum} = \sum_{1}^{n} z / \sqrt{n}$ of 10 2-second lags.

** $p \leq .01$ (two-tailed)
*** $p \leq .001$ (two-tailed)

The lower half of Table 11.5 displays Z_{sums} and Magnitudes for the contingent probabilities of three infant behaviours (Vocalization, Gesture and Smile) following Maternal Vocalization and Maternal Touch. Only four of the displayed Z_{sums} are significant beyond the .01 level, and two of these are negative, implying an inhibition of the contingent infant behaviour. The pattern of infant behaviours following Maternal Vocalization is of particular interest. Following Maternal Vocalization, the Magnitudes for Infant Smile were uniformly greater than for Infant Vocalization or Gesture, indicating that the Smile is the most likely response to Maternal Vocalization. Furthermore, the Magnitudes for Infant Vocalization were uniformly lower than those for either Smile or Gesture following Maternal Vocalization.

These temporal functions demonstrate two important anomalies in the observed mother-infant interaction patterns. First, in terms of direction of effects, it is clear that the infants (admittedly unintentionally) achieved a great deal of control over their mother's behaviour, while the reverse was not true. Stated in other words, the mothers were much more responsive than their infants. Second, the lack of mutual responsiveness involving vocal behaviour contrasts sharply with the conversational quality of vocal exchanges found in sighted mother-infant dyads (Bateson, 1975). The lack of responsivity of Infant Vocalizations is surprising, given the fact that strong emphasis was placed on the reinforcement of vocalizations in the home programmes recommended to the infants' parents. Perhaps the deviation in vocal behaviour reflects differences in temporal organization rather than in rate of production. These infants did not seem to vocalize when they were expected to - neither in response to maternal behaviour nor to stimulation. Indeed, the mothers' attempts to encourage vocalization were often met with silence.

Silence, or listening, should be an especially important behaviour for a blind infant. First, auditory information is virtually the only information available about the environment that exists beyond arm's reach of the non-ambulatory blind infant. Second, it is very difficult to process competing auditory information. Listening may be so critical to the interpretation of the distal environment that it would be maladaptive for the blind infant to clutter the auditory environment with her own vocalizations. Thus, when the mother vocalizes, the infant's undivided attention, reflected by silence, may be the safest response. Solitary situations, on the other hand, when the environment does not require close attention, may be 'safer' situations for vocalizing. Significantly, all three infants were reported to vocalize at a high rate when left alone.

Pragmatic Perspective

In addition to the microanalysis described above, a more global assessment of the infants' pre-verbal behaviours was achieved through the pre- and post-project administration of the maternal interview devised by Bates et al. (1977). This interview documents the presence or absence of gestural communicative behaviours as well as play, imitation and language skills.

Table 11.6 presents the pre- and post-project communicative skills for the three subjects. Clearly all three subjects displayed most of the normal mechanisms for expressing pleasure and displeasure. They also engaged in some vocal imitation and developed limited receptive vocabularies. In addition, all infants displayed repertoires of non-conventional idiosyncratic manual gestures, most of which were associated with affective states. However, only Maria began to produce words spontaneously and communicatively and only Maria produced any conventional gestures. These conventional gestures, however, developed as tricks. They were prompted by commands from adults (*Wave bye-bye* and she would wave; *Are you hungry?* and she would rub her tummy). The gestures were invariably rewarded with laughter and praise - but they were neither spontaneous nor clearly referential.

Many schemes apparently associated with language development in normal children were absent. Bates et al. (1977) had found that combinatorial and symbolic play were highly correlated with the gestural complex. Only Tanya displayed true combinatorial play and none of the infants engaged in symbolic play. A delay in symbolic play would be expected given the self/other confusion typical of visually-impaired children (Fraiberg and Adelson, 1973). Giving and showing, which normally form the basis of the early games and turn-taking rituals that Bruner (1974/5) considers precursors to the joint regulation of verbal exchanges, were virtually absent in these subjects. Only Maria had started giving by the end of the project.

Table 11.6: Pre- and Post-Project Scores on Communicative Skills Interview[a]

	Amy		Maria		Tanya	
Pre- and Post-Project Ages:	0;10	1;4	1;2	1;9	1;4	1;10
Gestural Communication						
Points						
Shows						
Gives				X		
Expresses Desire:						
Cries/Whines	X	X			X	X
Agitates					X	X
Reaches		X	X	X	X	X
Special Sound	X	X	X	X		
Word				X		
Moves to Object				X		
Expresses Dislike:						
Cries/Fusses	X	X	X	X	X	X
Agitates		X				
Special Sound		X			X	X
Pushes Away		X			X	X
Averts Head		X			X	X
Shakes Head				X		
Word				X		
Shows Off			X	X		?
Laughs with Others	X	X	X	X	X	X
Repeats Behaviour for Laughter				X	X	X
Non-conventional Gestures[b] in Filmed Sequences	9	24	13	18	4	47
Conventional Gestures[b]	0	0	2	12	0	0
Play/Imitation:						
Likes Music			X	X	X	X
Dances to Music				X		
Sings to Music			X	X		
Combinatorial Play				?	?	X
Pretends						
Imitates Vocalization		?	X	X	X	X
Imitates Gestures			X	X	?	X
Imitates Activities			X	X	?	X
Games Played[b]	0	0	5	10	2	5

Table 11.6 (cont'd)

Pre- and Post-Project Ages:	Amy 0;10	1;4	Maria 1;2	1;9	Tanya 1;4	1;10
Language						
Understands "no"			X	X	X	X
Responds to "where is"			X	X		X
Responds to "go find"				X		
Excitement Response to Pleasant Words			X	X	X	X
Negative Response to Unpleasant Words				X		X
Touches Named Item			X	X		
Words Comprehended[b]	0	3	10	60	5	9
Words Spontaneously[b] Produced	0	0	10	42	0	0

Note: a. adapted from Bates et al. (1977).
Note: b. pre-score includes different gestures produced in four films from first observation; post-score includes all new gestures produced in subsequent films.

Pointing (an especially good predictor of language development according to Bates et al. (1977)), and reaching-as-a-request, which are both visually-guided behaviours, were of course also absent.

Both Mulford (Chapter 9) and Urwin (Chapter 13) discussed the difficulty in directing another person's attention to a distal object without the benefit of the non-verbal mechanisms available to the sighted child. Parallel to Mulford's observations on the establishment of reference, it was noted in this study that the capacity to direct attention to self developed first. All three infants were capable of attracting attention to themselves, but none of them were capable of intentionally direction attention. Thus, once the attention of the mother had been attracted, it was up to the mother to initiate the 'topic' or content of an interaction. Once her mother initiated an interaction, Maria was then able to sustain it through a series of 'turns' in a typical turn-taking routine. Amy and Tanya, however, would fill only the first turn, and then would stop. They did not seem to be able to maintain an interactive ritual, but had to be primed for each turn.

DISCUSSION

Bates et al. (1977) suggest that the gestural complex involves the use of conventional signals that have communicative function and external reference. Perhaps the absence of conventional gestural performatives in these visually-impaired subjects reflects delayed acquisition of the construct of external reference. Studies of the cognitive development of blind children (Kephart, Kephart and Schwarz, 1974; Hartlage, 1976; Lopata and Pasnak, 1976) suggest that cognitive delays may reflect experiential deficits secondary to blindness, rather than visual deprivation per se. One source of experiential deficit that may be assumed to impact seriously on cognitive and language development is the substantial lag in locomotor abilities often suffered by blind children. The pre-mobile sighted child may passively observe and absorb the concepts of self, other, agent, action, object and the relationships between them. The pre-mobile blind child has difficulty determining where she ends and another person or object begins; she may not realize that another entity exists at all if it is beyond arm's reach or if it is silent. Self/other confusion and delayed person- and object-permanence no doubt impact seriously on the acquisition of distal referencing abilities. It seems logical that the blind infant would require more active, exploratory experiences which are dependent upon an advanced level of locomotor ability to acquire the concepts and relationships critical to dual-orientation and to the establishment of distal or joint reference. I would suggest that Maria's relatively advanced locomotor abilities were critical to her advanced abilities in cognitive and communicative areas.

Just as in motor development, the blind child often goes directly from sitting to walking, unable to explore the distal environment at all until posturally mature enough to walk, so she seems to make a leap in communicative development, going directly to language as the first means of distal reference. Coordinating an unseen and unreachable adult with an unseen and unreachable object would be difficult without at least primitive referencing strategies. With neither conventional indicating gestures nor visual regard as an early means of distal reference, it becomes even more critical that early vocalizations be consistently reinforced and shaped - first into conversational patterns and eventually into language.

The uncommunicative quality of the vocal patterns observed in these three blind infants may reflect their mother's weak responses to their vocalizations. A consistent maternal response to infant vocalizations seemed to be lacking in the environments observed in this project. Given that vocal-verbal behaviour will probably be the first recognizably referential behaviour available to a blind child, close attention should be paid to the patterning of parental vocalizations and responses to infant vocalizations as a potential intervention strategy. Specific clinical recommendations for such a programme will be included in a forthcoming paper.

NOTES

1. The data were originally analyzed in three phases, each phase representing two month's worth of data per subject. The data presented here are collapsed across all three phases due to space limitations. Statements that appear in the Results section hold true when data is considered on a phase-by-phase basis as well as when collapsed across phases.

Chapter 12.

COGNITION, INTERACTION, AND DEVELOPMENT, WITH SPECIAL REFERENCE TO EDUCATION OF THE HANDICAPPED CHILD

Ton van der Geest

INTRODUCTION

In her paper Charity Rowland (Chapter 11) is mainly concerned with the presentation and discussion of the results of her investigation into mother-blind child interaction. She did not consider more theoretical and practical matters concerning interaction, language acquisition, and education. I will try therefore to address the context and type of problems in which the investigation of mother-child interaction, and in this special case the interaction between blind children and their mothers, makes sense. Rowland's work illustrates some of the problems typical of interaction research which I would like to discuss further. I will also present some opinions on the question of how to put into practice the results of language acquisition research.

LANGUAGE ACQUISITION AND MOTHER-CHILD INTERACTION

Three theories of language acquisition have been recently discussed in depth by Clahsen (1981). The first theory he treats is based on universal grammar. Within this theory it is essential that the child have an innate mechanism at his disposal that determines the form of a possible human language and furthermore an evaluation yard-stick by which the child is able to select that grammar that is both compatible with the primary linguistic data and as simple as possible (mentalistic theory). Interactive theory, the second treated, holds that the acquisition of syntax is significantly influenced by the form of verbal interactions between child and mother. The third theory Clahsen discusses is cognitive theory. Certain cognitive operations are here a condition for the acquisition of language. Linguistic learning processes are essentially determined by the cognitive complexity of the linguistic structures to be learned.

Mentalistic linguistic theory is rejected by Clahsen on, in my opinion, valid grounds and I refer to his work for the detailed arguments. The interactive theory can only be accepted in so far as mother-child interaction is one of the essential conditions that enable the child to acquire his language. It is to be rejected - as Clahsen argues - since this approach does not explain the learning processes that lead to the acquisition of syntax. This problem can, according to Clahsen, probably only be resolved by the cognitive theory as deduced from Piaget's theory (Sinclair, 1970) and as worked out by Slobin (1973).

Apart from the question whether Clahsen's evaluation of the theories is correct or not, it is clear that the study of mother-child interaction can be motivated extrinsically. An analysis of this interaction can be of great help in those cases in which languages may develop deviantly, especially where the child is handicapped with deafness or blindness. Since the quality of the primary linguistic data at least determines to a very large extent how prosperously language develops, it can be concluded that actual knowledge of mother-child interaction, in the case of both the normal and the handicapped child, can be applied in order to influence development positively.

Clahsen's rejection of the interactive theory can also be questioned. Firstly, he does not himself investigate mother-child interaction but only the development of syntactic complexity in child utterances. So his conclusions are based only on the literature referred to in his discussion of the theories.

Secondly, it has been shown that cognitive complexity is not fully independent of the way in which mothers and children interact, for example in the work by Brown and Hanlon (1970), Bruner (1974/5), Miller (1976), Van der Geest (1977, 1978), Miller and Weissenborn (1979) and Van der Geest and Heckhausen (1981).

Thirdly, it must be emphasized here that it is not necessarily correct to assume that one theory alone must be able to explain such complex processes as those underlying language acquisition. It is, for example, easy to see that, in more than one respect, cognitive and interactive theory may be complementary. If we accept, for example, that a cognitive theory of language acquisition must be based on Piaget's theory of intellectual development, then we have to accept not only the cognitive processes within the child's mind (the child's activity) but also the interactive aspect of Piaget's theory in which it is emphasized that what the child learns is the product of the interaction between the active child and his environment. This implies that how the child's environment is structured is one of the two relevant factors of development. Furthermore, it can be shown that the cognitive prerequisites in the child's development are directly correlated with the linguistic structuring of the dialogue by the mother. This means, in my opinion, that mother-child interaction is not only one of the essential conditions for language acquisition but also is intrinsically relevant to the processes of language acquisition itself.

Rowland's paper may illustrate this relevance. She reports some remarkable differences between mother-child interaction dependent on whether the child develops well or not. The infant behaviours "non-vocal sound", "manipulate toy", and "reach for toy" and the mother behaviours "vocalization" are positively related to development. The proportions of intervals for these variables reflect fully the development of the three children Rowland investigated (see Table 11.3). The infant behaviours "touch self" and "no manual activity" and mother behaviours "touch" and "non-vocal sound" are negatively related to child development. There are, furthermore, some interesting differences in the interactions. In the prosperous interaction, there are not only systematic mother reactions to the child's vocalizations which are absent in the other interactions, but there is also a systematic child reaction to the mother's vocalizations in the well-developed interaction. I do, however, miss a discussion of the impacts of these relevant results in Rowland's paper.

METHODOLOGY OF THE INVESTIGATION OF MOTHER-CHILD INTERACTION

In interaction and communicative research, both category systems and sign systems can be applied. If nothing or relatively little is known about the topic, than a sign system should be applied. In such a system as many aspects as possible are investigated;

instead of categories of aspects, elementary aspects should be investigated. In this way one is able to deduce what kinds of aspects are relevant for the topic under investigation and what aspects can be grouped into one category. Thereafter category systems can be applied in order to have a larger amount of data pertinent to the individual variables. Linguists prefer working with sign systems. Labov and Fanshel's (1977) work is a good example in this respect for showing how such initial detecting work proceeds. Social psychologists normally prefer category systems but this is not only based on previous work with sign systems but in fact mostly on intuition.

Although a lot of research on mother-child interaction has been done in the last five years, we have to admit that still only a little is known about how they actually interact. The results of most studies reveal only that interaction is relevant to language development, not, however, the form interaction takes and how it influences language acquisition. There are a few exceptions (e.g. Van der Geest, 1977) but such studies can be criticized on other grounds (see Brown, 1977; McTear, 1978). The main objection to my paper concerns the 'direct observation - indirect interpretation' controversy as discussed for example by Fiske (1978) and Van der Geest (1981). In almost all experimentally, psychometrically and statistically oriented designs, the direct observations are not described; instead, only an interpretation of the results of statistical analysis is given. Only when the observation of interaction is reported, are we able to examine whether two subsequent actions of two partners are related to each other or are independent, and, if they are related, on what level.

Relations between two events that are in principle independent, cannot be determined through statistical analysis. We can only infer that a relation may exist between two types of events. This is essentially what McTear (1978) criticizes in my paper. Especially in cases in which we are trying to discover regularities first or to detect the central variables in a new area of research, it makes sense to restrict one's activities initially to mere observation. As I have already mentioned, the study of mother-child interaction with respect to language acquisition is still in its infancy. This is even more the case for the study of special cases of interaction involving, for example, blind or deaf children. For deaf children I know of only one observational study (Tervoort, 1981); for blind children Rowland's study is the only one to my knowledge. The state of the art of interaction research with respect to language development has to lead, in my opinion, automatically to observational research. These two points, that is that, at least at the initial stage of research, (1) category systems should be avoided, and (2) observational, rather than statistical studies should be carried out, will be discussed in more detail in relation to work with blind children.

Category Systems

Concerning the behavioural variables used in the analysis, it can be deduced from the section "Procedures and Analysis" that Rowland used a category system: 7 child-behaviour categories, 3 mother-behaviour categories, and a total of 42 subcategories. As neither categories nor subcategories are mentioned in the text, we may only guess that they have been extracted from interaction research with the sighted child. This is, however, problematic for more than one reason. Besides the fact that postulated categories in new research areas should be avoided, in this very special case we must determine whether the categories of interaction with the sighted child, are relevant for interaction with blind children. The results of Rowland's study are already evidence enough to conclude that there are systematic differences between these two types of interaction.

This conclusion may also be the solution to the problem in Piagetian theory with respect to cognitive development in the sighted, deaf and blind child. From Furth (1966) and Oléron (1957) it is clear that deaf children develop almost normally. This is in sharp contrast to cognitive development in the blind child, which, at least at the transitional stage from pre- to concrete operations, is enormously (almost four years) retarded (Hatwell, 1960, as cited in Sinclair de Zwart, 1969). If it is accepted from both Piagetian research and from research in language acquisition (e.g. Clahsen, 1981) that cognition is a kind of pace-maker for language acquisition, it follows necessarily that for blind children there must be an enormous delay in language development. This does not, however, always appear to be the case, as may be evident from the blind child, Maria, in Rowland's data and from the work of Urwin (1978b), and Fraiberg (1977). We are, therefore, in the awkward situation of looking for an explanation of this Piagetian paradox. An explanation that would make sense is to assume that cognitive development in the blind and normal child takes different routes. The assumption is plausible if we allow that cognitive development is a result of interaction between the active child and its environment and that the quality of the blind child's environment is essentially different from that of the sighted child. The delay found in the cognitive development of the blind child, may be nothing more than an artifact of the false assumption that blind children develop cognitively along the same routes as sighted children. If it is assumed that they develop along different routes and that cognition is a necessary prerequisite of language acquisition, we may conclude that different aspects of communicative behaviour are relevant to investigation. It is therefore questionable whether the categories in Rowland's study are fully adequate for the problem she investigated.

Observational vs. Statistical Analysis

Rowland draws conclusions with respect to interaction on the basis of statistical analysis, instead of on the basis of observation. If I understand Rowland correctly, she analyzed the supplement behaviours of mother and child in order to conclude whether a type of sequence (e.g. A,B) occurred more frequently than can be expected on the basis of probability. It was not investigated whether or not in each occurrence behaviour A and behaviour B were interrelated in substance.

On the contrary, she accepted as subsequent behaviour a behaviour that occurred as much as 20 seconds later (more or less the time span an athlete needs to cover 200 yards). It is also allowed that, between A and B, other behaviours that are relevant for the interaction analysis occurred. Even if this is not the case, the problem remains unsolved whether A and B are only subsequent to each other or whether they are interdependent. It is unclear whether coincidental events should be regarded as systematic or not. In my opinion the statistical procedure of 'lagging' leads to severe problems in interpretation, since it implies that behaviours which are subsequent to one another also interact with one another (see title of Rowland's paper).

Another methodological point concerns the fact that the same categories are used not only for three children that are very different from each other in terms of development, but also for the same child during six months of observation. From the description of the children and from Table 11.3, it appears that the three children developed rather well during this period so that we may guess that other types of behaviours came into the foreground. By this very fact some effects of interaction and development may become invisible if the frequencies that are analyzed statistically concern the number of occurrences in the data of the whole period.

A longitudinal investigation of mother-child interaction has confirmed this point. Twelve children were studied in the age range from 1;0 to 2;1 (Van der Geest and Nörenberg, in prep.). In this investigation we subdivided the children into two groups: six quick and six slow developers, and looked for interactive differences between the two groups. We found that (1) different communicative variables played a role in the adaptation of the mother to the child's communicative level in the two groups; (2) children 'preferred' different variables in their communications with their mothers; (3) many variables described in earlier investigations did not discriminate between the two groups of interactions; (4) only after a division of the children into four groups and analysing each session separately were we able to demonstrate that linguistic variables are only discriminating with respect to mothers' adaptation and children's preferent usage during a very short time span. I hope that such developmental questions as raised here will be answered in the (planned) fuller publication of Rowland's investigations.

ADAPTABILITY OF MOTHERS

Apart from these critical remarks, with respect to research methodology, we can say that many of the results and interpretations of these results are interesting for the description of communicative development in blind children. The results show that there are obviously great differences between interactions with sighted and with blind children; and that these differences can not only be explained as delay; the high rates of touching and reactions of the mothers to the infant smile seem worthwhile mentioning here. As can also be observed in mother-sighted child interaction, the infants affected their mothers' behaviour much more strongly and systematically than the mothers affected the infant's behaviour. I would interpret this fact rather as an adaptive quality of the mother than as an influencing capacity of the child. It is the child's contribution to produce those behaviours that are attractive for the mother to react to. It is the mother's creative contribution to pick up on this child activity and to reinforce it by appropriate communications and reactions. The fact that the child does not react so often can perhaps be explained by the fact that (1) the child does not have a teaching task; (2) the child has only a very small reaction repertoire at his disposal; (3) reacting is much more difficult than behaving if the context is not restricted by ongoing interaction.

FURTHER RESEARCH

Before any conclusions are drawn for educational programmes with the blind, a more detailed description is necessary of interaction in mother-blind child pairs. I can only repeat my belief that a more observational approach would have been more effective in describing the interactional and developmental processes adequately, and that only on the basis of such observational data can therefore well founded recommendations for intervention be made. Prevalent clinical practice leads me to fear that statistically established categories will lead to the setting up of diagnostic tests and on these tests recommendations for intervention and treatment will be based. This is common practice, although tests measure the products and not the processes leading to these products and therefore do not deliver indications for treatment of the individual case. In my opinion, shared also by Fiske (1978), it is better to investigate behaviour with a minimum of postulates and theory and to find out what kinds of behaviours are critical. Instead of applying tests, one should diagnose by the observation of behaviour (with the help of critical variables) because observation leads to knowledge of the facts, the underlying processes, and the system. Instead of a standardized programme we need an intervention method to influence the processes of the system.

In order to come to grips with what is going on in mother-blind child interaction and with the question of how cognition and language develops in a sightless child, the basic investigation of interaction between a blind child and a blind mother may be of great help, especially in so far as diagnosis and intervention are concerned. The argumentation with respect to this belief must, unfortunately, be indirect, and derives from research with the deaf child.

From many investigations with deaf children (e.g. Tervoort, 1972) it appears that congenitally deaf children who have deaf parents have generally greater language capacity in both the deaf's sign language and in the oral language of the environment than deaf children with hearing parents. One could argue that deaf parents have a better understanding of the deaf child's communicative problems and will be, therefore, more efficient language trainers with respect to the language acquisition of the deaf than hearing parents are. It would make sense, therefore, to investigate this typical interaction and this typical language development in order to detect how the language learner situation is structured optimally and how parents interact optimally with respect to development. It seems reasonable to me that the same would apply to the blind child.

Chapter 13.

DIALOGUE AND COGNITIVE FUNCTIONING IN THE EARLY LANGUAGE DEVELOPMENT OF THREE BLIND CHILDREN

Cathy Urwin

Like several contributions to this volume, this chapter is about the earliest stages of language acquisition, and the developments which enable blind children to use language in the first place. It presents findings from an intensive longitudinal study of three congentially blind infants (Urwin, 1978a), with the aim of challenging two assumptions which are frequently made about blind children's development. The first of these is that certain aspects of development, in language and cognition, are necessarily delayed in blind children. The second is that acquiring language is relatively 'unhelpful' in the development of cognitive functioning. Finally, the chapter probes the question of how far, if at all, studying blind children's language development can throw light on the normal process.

RECENT RESEARCH INTO LANGUAGE ACQUISITION IN SIGHTED CHILDREN

My starting point is recent work with sighted children which has been discussed or referred to elsewhere in this volume (e.g. in Mills' introduction, and in the contributions from Rowland and Van der Geest). This work argues for a relationship between infant development and the earliest stages of language acquisition, and very broadly can be divided into two major lines of approach. One has concentrated on semantic aspects of language and proposes that cognitive schemes established in infancy provide the conceptual input for children's earliest utterances (e.g. Bowerman, 1973; Brown, 1973; Edwards, 1973; Nelson, 1973). Here, probably the most influential approaches have drawn on Piaget's (1951, 1953, 1955) theory, to argue, for example that the development of sensorimotor intelligence contributes to constraints on the kinds of words acquired through the single word stage and to systematic changes in their usage (Bloom, 1973), and that its terminal achievements account for apparent universals in the conceptual relations underlying the first word combinations (Bowerman, 1973; Brown, 1973; Edwards, 1973; Slobin, 1973).

The other major line of approach has been primarily concerned with communication and functional aspects of language, and has aimed to demonstrate a developmental continuity between pre-verbal and verbal communication, for example by Bates, Camaioni and Volterra (1975), Bruner (1975, 1978), Carter (1974, 1978), and Halliday (1975). Here, the theoretical frameworks have been far more diverse, varying from applications of different versions of Speech Act Theory (Bates et al., 1975; Bruner, 1975), through Halliday's (1973, 1975) own functional theory, to Carter's (1974, 1978) descriptive study of the evolution of one child's gestural communication system. There are a number of unresolved problems with this work, some of which centre around moving beyond speculation or reasoning-by-analogy in accounting for the origins of syntactic structure in communicative terms (for critiques, see, for example, Schaffer, 1977; Dore, 1978). But as far as the initial entry into language is concerned, the concensus is sufficient to establish that, before they begin to speak, sighted children have already consolidated simple communicative procedures for initiating interaction, making demands and directing the behaviour and attention of others. Once they begin to acquire standard words, these procedures persist as accompaniments to children's early utterances, and serve to convey the particular communicative effects which they intend (Carter, 1974; Bates et al., 1975; Bruner, 1975, 1978; Dore, 1975). Thus, the communicative functions first expressed with words are related to those already available to the child, a finding which is taken to endorse the general notion that the "very nature" of the child's pre-speech communication system may be such as to aid the passage through to language (Bruner, 1978).

IMPLICATIONS FOR BLIND CHILDREN

Now whether one emphasizes the propositional content of children's utterances or the communicative functions served by using them, both these lines of approach lead to the prediction that blindness will pose considerable problems for infant development and that this will have consequences for the emergence of language. Piaget's theory, for example, on which many semantic approaches have relied, is often interpreted as giving vision a primary role (Cromer, 1973), and indeed Piaget's own writings imply that lack of vision will "slow down" cognitive development in infancy (Piaget and Inhelder, 1969). If this view is correct, we might anticipate that blind children will be initially delayed in acquiring words and in forming word combinations, and/or there will be restrictions in underlying meaning relations in both the single word period and afterwards (see Landau (Chapter 7) and Werth (Chapter 8)).

But the sighted child literature predicts perhaps even greater constraints on blind children's learning to use language to communicate. Despite their differing theoretical frameworks, the majority of pre-verbal communication studies in sighted children have concentrated on just those communication systems which blind children lack. These include the use of eye-to-eye contact in the regulation of early reciprocal exchanges between mother and child (Bruner, 1975; see also Brazelton, Koslowski and Main, 1974; Stern, 1974), the use of the visual system in monitoring mutual attention to distal objects and events, a capacity which is said to provide the basis for establishing a shared frame of reference (Bruner, 1975, 1978; see also Collis and Schaffer, 1975), and the use of gestures such as indicative pointing and reaching-in-demand. Along with 'showing off' to gain adult attention and 'give and take games' with objects, these gestural procedures typically emerge in the last quarter of the first year (Carter, 1974; Bates et al., 1975; Bruner, 1975, 1978; see also Trevarthen and Hubley, 1978). The availability of these procedures is assumed to contribute to what are dominant language functions in many sighted children in the early stages, using words to name and to make requests for objects. Thus one would again expect that the absence of these and other visually-based communication means would delay the onset of language, and/or restrict the kinds of communicative functions which blind children are able to express.

If we look at the available evidence on blind children's development there is apparently considerable support for these predictions. The work of Fraiberg (1977), Adelson (Chapter 1) and other clinical investigators (e.g. Burlingham, 1961, 1964;

Wills, 1970), emphasizes the severe problems which blindness poses for development in infancy, in both cognitive functioning and social interaction. Although clinicians and educators are well aware of the relatively high incidence of language problems among school-age blind children (see Urwin, 1978b; Elstner, Chapter 3), up until now there has been surprisingly little work on the language of younger children. But what evidence there is suggests that problems with semantic and/or communicative aspects of language are extremely common, even in children for whom there is no reason to suspect additional neurological damage. For example, many blind children are initially delayed in acquiring their first words, and may not immediately use them spontaneously in communication. They may repeat them to themselves in their own play, and fail to produce them to initiate interaction, requiring some prompt to imitate on the part of the parent until well into the third year (Wood, 1970). Though other children acquire their first words within the sighted age range, social words and phrases often markedly predominate over words for referring to objects, such that the children appear to be showing an extreme form of a language acquisition strategy which, for sighted children, Nelson (1973) has characterized as "expressive". In some cases the child's language may remain tied to his or her body movement or to familiar social routines for a prolonged period, and a reliance on phrases acquired wholesale is often coupled with a marked propensity for imitation and/or echolalia. Even the group studied by Fraiberg (1977) and Adelson (Chapter 1), who had the advantage of clinical intervention, showed some delay in using words to name objects and in the production of the first word combinations. These delays, Fraiberg and Adelson suggest, were due to constraints on the development of sensorimotor intelligence and the emergence of representation in the Piagetian sense, the latter being delayed in all the children in the sample.

This position is consistent with the semantic approaches to sighted child language discussed above, and concentrates on the origins of the propositional content of children's utterances. But naming objects is generally, of course, also a communicative act, frequently accompanied by gesture in sighted children. Blind children do not, apparently, point spontaneously to distant objects. This raises the question of the implications of the absence of particular pre-verbal procedures.

Consistent with this, there is evidence suggesting that the use of words to make requests, particularly for objects, is slow to emerge in blind children. Wills' (personal communication) observations, for example, suggest that requests based on internal need states, such as demands for food or body action, are likely to emerge considerably earlier than demands for things in the external world. This would again support the assumption that young blind children are constrained by the absence of gesturing in the pre-verbal period and/or by lack of knowledge of the permanent existence of objects. In addition, there is one developmental delay which Adelson (Chapter 1) and Fraiberg (Fraiberg and Adelson, 1975; Fraiberg, 1977) have proposed is universal in blind children: a delay in the acquisition of I as a stable pronoun and, by implication, the ability to use you to refer to the other party in interaction. Fraiberg and Adelson propose that this delay is related to a delay in a more general developmental process, the capacity for self representation. Pronominal reference is, of course, a later development than the ones discussed so far. But the claim is nonetheless in line with the assumption that blindness inhibits the development of reciprocal interaction and/or independent action in infancy, and that this has cumulative implications for language development.

Broadly speaking, then, these observations are consistent with predictions drawn from the sighted child literature. They would thus seem to support the theoretical assumptions underlying that work, and the priority it explicitly or implicitly assumes for vision. But for children who do not have vision, it would be an extremely negative conclusion to leave the matter there. It is all too easy to assume that difficulties are an inevitable consequence of blindness. Furthermore, there are many dangers in relying entirely on theories of sighted children's development in understanding the development of blind children.

Firstly, the theories of 'normal' development with which one begins may be wrong or in some ways inadequate, even in their own terms. For example, there is currently considerable dissatisfaction with the way Piaget's theory has been applied to the study of language acquisition in sighted children (see, for example, McShane, 1980; Elliot, 1981), and the theory itself is increasingly being criticized for its neglect of social aspects of cognition (see Donaldson, 1978; Walkerdine and Sinha, 1978;

Walkerdine and Corran, 1979). Secondly, if a theory of 'normal' development already gives priority to vision, then that theory itself cannot tell us what alternative routes may be available to blind children, nor what form adaptation to the absence of vision might take. Nor will it explain why common 'anomalies' should take the particular form that they do.

To answer these questions we have to uncover the processes of adaptive development. This may best be achieved by taking a closer look at what blind children actually do. The next section describes the development of three congentially blind children whose language and overall development has progressed extremely well, even when compared to the children in Fraiberg's sample. This provides an opportunity for demonstrating what can be achieved by blind children, questioning many assumptions as to the necessity of developmental delay. In itself this may have important implications for the kinds of guidance which it is appropriate to give to parents of other blind children. But in so far as these children's development contradicts the predictions drawn from the theories of development in sighted children, we may also be required to reexamine the adequacy of these theories, even for sighted children.

A LONGITUDINAL STUDY

The three children are all legally blind and have no additional neurological damage. Jerry and Suzanne are both totally blind through optic atrophy, but Steven has a little sight in one eye, in which he has glaucoma and aniridia. Though extremely limited, this vision gave Steven considerable advantages. Nevertheless his early communicative behaviour and language showed many characteristics differentiating him from fully sighted children.

The three children were observed, video- and audio-recorded in the home in interaction with one or other of their parents at regular intervals. The research methods, described more fully elsewhere (see Urwin, 1978a), included a descriptive analysis of the development of communicative exchange between each mother-child pair, and a longitudinal analysis of each mother's own use of speech. By and large, cognitive development was assessed through observations of the children's spontaneous play with objects. Jerry and Steven were followed through a large part of the pre-verbal period and the one-word stage to the point at which they began producing their first combinations. The studies were closed at approximately 20 months in both cases. Suzanne was followed through the first 14 months by Dr. Michael Tobin who has made his video- and other records available to me. I myself began following Suzanne when she was 15 months old, and made monthly recordings until 22 months. Further extended recording sessions took place at two years and two years three months. Unlike Steven and Jerry, who are both first born children, Suzanne has a sister, Elaine, who is two years older and sighted. Elaine was present for a large part of each recording session.

The relatively satisfactory development of these children, when compared to that of the blind child population as a whole, was largely due to the opportunities for social interaction and active exploration provided by the parents. Though there were considerable differences in the children's home environments and in the parents' beliefs about children's development (see Urwin, 1978c), the interactions between the three children and their parents nevertheless had many features in common. Of these, the most crucial concerned the extent to which all the parents made use of non-visual communication systems themselves, and discovered alternative cues to the infants' attention, involvement and intention.

In the early months, for example, in spite of the absence of or (in Steven's case) reduced eye-contact, all the mothers would watch their babies' faces intently, 'mirroring' changes of facial expression and the effect of body movement in their voices. They also used touching, stroking, tickling and grosser forms of body play extensively, elaborating their own routines or adapting versions of well known games such as "pat-a-cake", "ride-a-cock horse" and even "peekaboo". As I have described elsewhere (Urwin, 1978c), the parents would use the predictability inherent in these games to build up expectancies, encourage anticipation, and eventually to 'push' the babies towards taking more active roles. By the end of the first year all three infants were capable of dictating the 'next step' in these games, using their own bodies to control their parents' actions and reactions, and accompanying these procedures with distinctive prosodic marking.

Vocalization, too, was another area which these parents encouraged. In all three cases the mothers would not only talk to their infants, but also mark, question, imitate or otherwise respond to their babies' pre-verbal vocalizations, prompting them to vocalize in turn. In contrast to some of the mother-child pairs described by Rowland (Chapter 11), by the last quarter of the first year each of these infants would collaborate in and prolong vocal imitation sequences and quasi-dialogues, the children showing an exquisite control over the adults' following responses (see Urwin, 1979). Jerry, for example, would keep in contact with his mother for as long as 20 minutes at a time while she got on with the housework in the next-door room.

Despite the absence of vision, these children thus showed an ability to allocate 'turns' in interaction (see McGurk, Chapter 10), and to control the other's actions which was well on a par with sighted children. Their ability to manage body-play routines, for example, emerged over the age range when sighted children begin to 'show off' to court adult attention and to use gestures (Bates et al., 1975), and may thus be regarded as parallel developments. In the emergence of language and its early development, similarities with sighted children were again striking. As is consistent with the evidence discussed above on continuity of a function between pre-verbal and verbal communication in sighted children, each of the children's early words used in communication were initially accompanied by pre-existing vocal and/or action procedures which conveyed particular communicative intentions. These included demands for body-action, protests or requests that a particular game be repeated, and in the vocal sphere the pre-verbal vocal 'dialoguing' paved the way for an unusually early mastery of basic conversation-maintaining procedures. These included the use of rising intonation to prompt replies and various devices for opening and closing encounters (Sachs, Schegloff and Jefferson, 1974; Urwin, 1979). As for the children's lexical development, in each case their first words originated in affective or routinized interaction contexts in which he or she had gained some measure of active control. Again this is typical of many sighted children (see, for example, the data reported by Bowerman, 1978 and Ferrier, 1978). Though not all kinds of over-extensions observable in sighted children could be identified (see Urwin, 1979) through the single-word period, these children nevertheless extended early acquired words into new contexts including those involving objects, thus shifting the locus away from their own bodies. At around 18 months their vocabularies expanded rapidly and they began to produce their first word combinations. In each case these developments occurred with the beginnings of pretend play and changes in search behaviour which indicated that the children knew of the continued existence of objects apart from their own actions and independent of specific locations.

Such close parallels with sighted children's developments clearly challenge the assumption that the emergence of representation is necessarily delayed in blind children. However, it was not the case that there were no areas of relative restriction for these children. For example, since they could not look towards their mothers, before the emergence of language their ability to initiate interaction was somewhat restricted. Thus the play exchanges described above still depended on physical contact up to the end of the first year, and hence on the parents' prior decisions to put themselves at their infants' disposal. Limitations in the means available to the blind infants to initiate interaction have been commented on by Fraiberg (1977), and Wills (1970). But for these children, situations which involved the mothers and children having to attend to distant objects and events also posed significant constraints. In this the difficulties were as great for the parents as for the children. The sighted child literature, as mentioned above, has made much of the potency of visual gaze as a cue to the child's attention to distant objects (Bruner, 1975, 1978; Collis and Schaffer, 1975). In contrast, cues associated with listening are far more ambiguous, such that it was comparatively rare for the mothers to perceive and comment on things that the infants might have been listening to unless they were producing the sounds themselves. By the same token, of course, the infants were limited in gaining access to the objects of others' attention. Similarly, where sighted children may use gestures such as reaching in demand and indicative pointing to direct attention towards distant objects, this kind of gesturing did not, apparently, emerge spontaneously in these children. Nor did they offer and exchange objects without deliberate training on the part of the parents.

Constraints on initiating interaction and on establishing mutual attention to distant objects and events at first restricted the children's use of language. For example, in the two totally blind children, using language to initiate particular forms of play, as distinct from using it to sustain or restart some game already underway, did not emerge until well into the second year, after a period in which they learned to use movements from well established routines to control the parents' actions and reactions across the space between them. Once language began, of course, a relatively unambiguous means for initiating interaction was available to them. Perhaps related to this, by the end of the single word period all the children had amassed a large number of names of significant people. These the totally blind children used particularly frequently . Suzanne, for example, would call out to the people present and even to the children next door when she heard them playing in the street. But by the time they began to combine words, none of the children were observed producing utterances which referred explicitly to other people as agents of their own actions (as would be expressed in utterances of the form *Mummy push* or *Mummy go*, for example). This is not an early development for sighted children either, nevertheless Greenfield and Smith (1976) report that the two children in their longitudinal study had begun to refer to others' agency by the end of the single word period. Nor did the blind children comment on other people's possession of objects at this stage, though they referred to their own.

Related constraints appeared in the way these children named objects. In acquiring names of people, of course, they were acquiring words for objects which were capable of answering back. In contrast, relatively few inanimate objects in their environments produced sounds without being acted on. All three children would name familiar objects, sound-producing or otherwise, when they contacted them physically, or in Steven's case, when they came within his limited visual range. But at this time none of the children would name or refer to objects remote from themselves. Nor did they make requests for them. Steven began to demand objects at around 18 months, but these demands were restricted to particularly familiar things when he could see them. Jerry had not begun to demand objects by the close of the study. Suzanne's first requests for objects emerged at around 21 months, when they were extremely infrequent and handled with questions of the form *Where's X?*. This was in spite of the fact that a semantic analysis of her language at this time provided examples of each of the two-term semantic relations which Brown (1973) has argued are related to, and depend on, the emergence of representation.

A superficial inspection might suggest that at this time these children's language showed the restrictions relative to sighted children which are common amongst the blind child population as a whole, and which have been described above. But here the kinds of explanations which can be derived from the sighted child literature are of relatively limited value. A simple explanation in terms of a 'delay' in some general cognitive process, for example is clearly inadequate for these children. Their language development in other areas was well on a par with that of sighted children; their search behaviour and other activities involving objects indicated that they knew of the permanent existence of objects, and further developments in social play indicated that they had some understanding of reversible roles and other people's agency (Urwin, 1978a, 1978c). Moreover it is misleading to assume that similar functions for language, such as naming and making requests for distant objects, necessarily represent equivalent developmental achievements in blind and sighted children. In sighted children of this age this behaviour is largely or entirely elicited by things which are in view or by visual props in the immediate context, such as cues which indicate their habitual location (Huxley and Urwin, unpublished data). In contrast, blind children are excluded from much that is going on around them. For them to name and request objects is perhaps more akin to sighted children's referring to things which are absent or concealed, with the minimum support from the immediate context. This use of language is not observable with any degree of frequency in the early stages, suggesting that apparently similar phenomena may represent more complex developmental achievements on the part of blind children.

It is in just such areas, however, that language can provide blind children with many advantages, enabling them to achieve what sighted children achieve with gesture in the pre-verbal period, and to refer to and seek information about events to which they have little or no direct access. But another limitation with the sighted child literature now becomes apparent. Though the absence of some communication system in infancy, such as the use of gesture, may well have contributed to the blind children's difficulties, there is nothing in that literature which explains how these difficulties can ever be resolved. To understand this, we again have to look at the blind children themselves. This was possible for Suzanne since she was followed to an older age.

SUZANNE'S LATER DEVELOPMENT

For Suzanne, the answer is somewhat paradoxical. For her the resolution of early restrictions, relative to sighted children, was greatly aided by the entry into language itself, or more properly, the opportunities which this created for dialogue with other people. Here there were a number of ways in which Suzanne's mother's own use of speech appeared particularly suited to extending the child's access to the surrounding context. This can be illustrated particularly clearly by looking at interaction sequences invovling mutual attention to objects, and at the significance of Suzanne's ability to name them for herself.

As mentioned previously, the research methods used in this study included an analysis of each mother's speech to her child. In many respects, as applied in all three cases, Suzanne's mother's speech showed just those syntactic, semantic, and functional characteristics which have now been described many times for mothers speaking to their sighted children (e.g. Snow, 1977a). In addition, her speech showed a predominance of various dialogue-sustaining devices, such as the use of expansions and incorporations, which Cross (1977) found correlated with rapid speech development in sighted children. However, there were also some significant differences, which again applied to the other two mothers. Compared to the two mothers of sighted infants studied longitudinally by Snow (1977b), these mothers talked relatively more about the 'child' and relatively less about objects and events in the 'outside world' for much of the pre-verbal period. This partly reflected the extent to which the mothers of blind children used their own speech to frame their babies' body actions and facial expressions, feeding back their effects on those who watched them, as described above. But it may also have been due to the relative paucity of cues to the blind children's attention to distant objects and events, such as looking and gesture itself.

Nevertheless, the mothers of the blind infants could refer to objects which the children were investigating close at hand. This Suzanne's mother did particularly frequently, which allowed the child to become familiar with the names of particular objects. At the same time the process also marked the fact that these objects were accessible to the mother as well as to the child herself. In consequence, as soon as Suzanne began to name objects and the mother to acknowledge this verbally, language itself provided Suzanne with a means for establishing that her proximal space was shareable with other people, despite her lack of vision. This change in the child's initiatives had important implications for changes in the mother's contribution to the interaction. Apart from the fact that she was now answering verbal initiatives, Suzanne's using object names appropriately made it indubitably clear to the mother that the child knew of the things to which these words referred. Coupled with the observable changes in Suzanne's searching for objects which occurred over the same period, this led the mother to refer more frequently to familiar objects when they were beyond the child's range of touch. For example, she began to use the names of familiar objects in *Where's X?* questions to prompt the child to explore the space around her: *Where's the car?, Where's your dolly, Suzanne?, Find your dolly for Mummy,* and so on. Prompting the child's action, the mother's language again drew attention to a shared space. Reversing the procedure, it was this question form which the child appropriated to express her first requests for objects.

Yet the ability to articulate demands itself added a new dimension to the interaction. Over the same time period, Suzanne was becoming increasingly mobile. Besides bringing her into direct contact with more objects which were further afield, this also opened new contexts in which talk could take place. Though the mother named new objects with which the child came into contact, she became less likely to respond to the child's requests for objects by actually providing them. Rather, she would prompt the child to get them for herself by specifying their location relative to the child, or to familiar landmarks for which she now had names: *This way, That way, It's on the table, It's in the bedroom,* or *It's by the door.* Thus, by taking what the child said as a starting point and relying on her understanding of familiar words, the mother's language linked the child to the surrounding context. Again the child took over many of the mother's location markers, such that she was using terms such as *in* and *on* frequently and appropriately by the end of the study, to refer to places outside her own body.

Apart from contributing to her ability to talk

about objects and locations, dialogue with her mother also facilitated Suzanne's using language to refer to other people's actions and possession of objects. Looking at the origins and emergence of Suzanne's references to her sister, Elaine, illustrates this particularly closely.

As mentioned above, Elaine was present for a large part of each recording session. During this time Suzanne's mother would consistently refer to her in her speech to Suzanne, keeping her comments within the kinds of things Suzanne was likely to understand. Increasingly these references came in response to verbal initiatives from Suzanne as, from 18 months onwards, she began to call out to her sister by name, often as she produced some sound which caught her attention. The mother would comment on what Elaine was doing, thus providing a basis from which Suzanne could interpret the significance of particular sounds. From the end of the second year the kinds of activities in which the two children engaged became more obviously similar. They played with many of the same toys, for example, such that references to Elaine in the mother's speech began to include statements or explanations about Elaine's actions on familiar objects. By the third year the mother was obliged to sort out some competition between the two sisters. Many of Suzanne's requests for objects, for example, were prompted by her recognizing what her sister was playing with, either by the sound of the thing itself, or through understanding what Elaine was saying. The following example shows how, at the close of the study, Suzanne was now using language to establish mutual attention to objects, to refer to objects distant from herself, and to distinguish her own and the other's access to them. Reconstructing the language which the mother used habitually to 'keep the peace' between the two sisters, Suzanne marks the relation of possession. Perhaps at the same time she is coming to terms with notions of sharing (Suzanne 2;3).

Example 1. Suzanne: *Elaine's got the case.*
Mother : *Elaine's got the case, yes.*
Suzanne: *And I got the hairdrier, naughty old hairdrier!*

Suzanne's ability to refer to Elaine and her actions was, of course, related to the fact that her sister's activities were predictable and very similar to her own. Yet at the same time, though consistently drawing attention to this relationship, the mother's language helped to provide the bridge. Once again, the use of language enabled Suzanne to penetrate contexts which were not immediately accessible to her. In this way the acquisition of language facilitated her building a model of her world.

A further example is an instance of fantasy play in which Suzanne uses language to reconstruct an episode which took place shortly beforehand. It illustrates how language can provide blind children with a powerful tool for understanding what is going on around them, and also serve as a medium for representing a distinction between 'self' and 'other'. Here Suzanne reproduces variations in tone of voice and discourse content to take up the positions of her mother, her sister and herself. In doing so she uses the pronouns *I* and *you*. Though she was not followed for long enough to plot the emergence of the *I/you* distinction in all its grammatical manifestations (this is not normally expected in sighted children before the middle of the third year, see E. Clark, 1978), this example and the one above indicate that she was already beginning to achieve what poses considerable problems for most blind children (Fraiberg, 1977).

Example 2. Elaine is bouncing on and jumping off the settee. Suzanne (2;3) apparently appreciates something of what she is doing and in her own way attempts to copy her.

Suzanne: *'Laine, I'm* [laughing] *Whoops!* [she deliberately throws herself on the floor] *I fell over.*

The mother interferes and warns Elaine and then smacks her to discourage her exuberance. Shortly afterwards Suzanne laughs and apparently reconstructs the scene for herself.

Suzanne: *You's fall over!* [in her own voice]

Using a severe intonation, she then reproduces something of her mother's language.

Suzanne: *Now watch it! You asked this!*

The episode ends with a mock cry, presumably as a representation of Elaine, and further laughter from Suzanne.

Thus, by the close of the study, at two years three months, the early restrictions in Suzanne's language relative to sighted children had apparently been resolved. She was naming and requesting objects frequently, referring to places beyond her range of touch, commenting on other people's possession of objects and on their actions where those actions where familiar to her. Though her mode of access to the environment and her sensory experience is different from sighted people's in crucial respects, the entry into language has given her a means both for extending her own awareness of what is going on around her and also for sharing in those events with other people. In a very real sense dialogue has provided a bridge to others, objects and the surrounding context, giving her a handle on the outside world.

CONCLUDING DISCUSSION

It is usually assumed that studying the development of children with such an apparently clearcut handicap as lack of vision will throw light on the processes involved in 'normal' development. The general method is to start with some theoretically based assumptions about the importance of vision or visually based systems to sighted children, using these assumptions to make more or less specific predictions about the likely consequences of blindness. Comparative studies are then undertaken with the aim of supporting or disconfirming the original theory. In practice, the original assumptions lead to the prediction of difficulties or delays for blind children. Since this is what is generally found, unfortunately the comparative studies rapidly reduce to demonstrations of the importance of what blind children lack, namely vision, to the children who have it, namely the sighted.

This chapter began in this tradition, by drawing predictions about the likely consequences of blindness for the emergence of language from recent work on sighted children. But particular limitations in such an approach may now be apparent. Apart from the fact that it tends to foster a totally negative view of blind children's development, or the assumption that they are like sighted children with 'something missing', such a framework can tell us little about what is involved in adapting to the difficulty. As a consequence practical implications must be speculated upon afterwards, rather than following directly from the research itself.

This might suggest that we should abandon the idea of using studies of handicapped groups to enrich our understanding of the 'normal' process, and that comparative work can do little to help blind children themselves. One might argue that, if our primary concern is understanding how blind children acquire language, we should give priority to this population, concentrating on the uses which may be made of senses which they have rather than on those which they lack, and on the functions which language might serve for them. This could provide more adequate criteria for what constitutes developmental progress for blind children, and have implications for intervention as a direct outcome of the research itself. For example, one might use factors found to be associated with relatively satisfactory progress within the blind child population as the basis from which to design enrichment programmes.

However, in so far as blind and sighted children are growing up to speak 'the same language', some kinds of comparisons between the two populations are essential for clinical purposes, and it is, after all, only through processes of comparison that the notion of alternative routes in development can become tangible. But further than this, it is my contention that it is through examining alternative routes that the study of blind children can shed most light on the 'normal' process. This can be illustrated particularly clearly by looking at children whose development contradicts predictions drawn from the sighted child literature, as has been the case with Steven, Jerry and Suzanne. What does the relatively satisfactory development of these children do to the status of the original theories?

The issues raised by these three children's development are complex, less a question of simply proving the sighted child theories right or wrong than of revealing areas of inadequacy and inconsistency. For example, the close parallels between the development of these blind children and that of sighted children, in pre-verbal communication, the emergence of representation and broad features of language development, challenges any claim that lack of vision necessarily results in developmental delay. But this does not mean that vision is not important to sighted children. Rather it suggests that there is a problem in the way in which its role is usually conceived. Similarly, the notion of continuity between pre-verbal communication and early language is not disputed by these children's development. Indeed, the persistence of communicative procedures which were relatively idiosyncratic, or which are unlikely to be found as extensively in fully sighted children, provides fairly strong support for continuity of function. But clearly the relationship will have to be posed in a new way if we are to account for how it is that blind children discover functions for language, such as requesting objects, which were not available in the pre-verbal period. On the relation between cognitive development and language acquisition, the third major area touched on in this chapter, these children's development is consistent with the notion that cognitive change is integral to the emergence of language, as has been argued for sighted children. However, the gains in Suzanne's understanding which were made possible, but not totally determined, by the entry into language itself are not easily encompassed within traditional approaches to the relation between language and thought. This suggests that a new way of posing the relationship is necessary.

Understanding the alternative routes discovered by these children does not, however, simply indicate areas of inadequacy. In this case it has more specific implications for theoretical changes, or suggests areas where future research might be profitably directed. For instance, on the question of the role of vision, the problem may lie in assuming that any system has a necessary priority, functioning independently of others, as if they constitute separate faculties. Considering the three infants' interactions with their parents, for example, it was true that the mother's use of alternative systems led them to talk more and to use more physical contact than is typical of mothers interacting with their sighted infants (see Urwin, 1978a). More striking were the ways in which they used non-visual systems simultaneously or interchangeably, and established correspondences across different sensory/communication systems, as in the ways in which they used their voices to match the babies' facial expressions, and mark body movement. Ultimately, it is this potential for multiple access to and encoding of reality which makes it possible for children lacking one kind of sensory experience to acquire the language used by all. This suggests that further research should concentrate not on the senses in isolation but on the relations between them and on their potential substitutability. Though concerned with rather different questions, the work of McGurk and MacDonald (1977) and Mills (Chapter 5) on visual/auditory illusions and Landau's work (Chapter 7) on the blind child's use of sighted terms represent exciting examples in this direction.

Similar issues are raised by the question of how to account for the later emergence of language functions which are established pre-verbally through gesture in sighted children. Reflecting back on the sighted child literature, it now appears that the limitations may at least in part be due to a tendency to conflate form and function in development, and to disregard implications of actually acquiring words for changing the child's communication system. In the desire to demonstrate continuity, investigators have concentrated on the insertion of linguistic forms into pre-established communicative means, for example, on the use of indicating gestures followed by the use of indicating gestures plus standard words. These communicative acts are clearly related. But to assume that they are identical ignores the fact that the acquisition of words allows for a separation between form and function less available to the pre-verbal child, which may itself pre-empt further developments. What, for example, is the significance of the child's beginning to use the same word in a variety of communicative contexts, or different words to achieve similar ends? It may be that a closer examination of the diversification of the child's system may throw light on what 'lifts' the child out of pre-verbal communication into language proper. Furthermore, apart from providing a 'distance' from external reality, the insertion of words may change the nature of the child's interactions with other people dramatically. The implications of this were particularly marked in Suzanne's case, since it was through entering into verbal dialogue that she discovered new functions for language.

In attempting to argue for a relationship between language development and cognition, the sighted child work, discussed above, has relied on arguing for a correspondence between two-term semantic relations and underlying conceptual structures. Apart from the problem of accounting for the mapping mechanism which unites linguistic and cognitive structures (see Elliot, 1981), this argument is in accord with a more general tendency to assume that one is a reflection of the other, or that language and thought are in some way isomorphic. Yet language does not only map concepts or refer to things in the world. Meaning in language is also carried by connections or associations which operate between words themselves. That is, language allows for establishing connections across or between contexts, for marking relations of similarity, correspondence, difference, and so on, a process which may itself bring into being new orders of meaning. It was through establishing such connections that Suzanne was led to understand what was unknown to her, as the mother used language to make the wider context accessible to the child by setting it in relation to what was already known.

Suzanne's development represents only one possible alternative route through which blind children can resolve early restrictions related to their limited access to the immediate context. Though using language to establish links across contexts is clearly particularly advantageous to blind children, it is important to recognize that the process described is not confined to blind children, or even only to children. It is, for example, integral to using language in teaching or explanation (Ortony, 1979). Walkerdine and Corran (1979), for example, have described strikingly similar procedures used by teachers helping children grasp mathematical concepts in a classroom situation. They have shown how the teacher begins with what is familiar to the child, and uses language to set up connections or correspondence across numerical groupings. This process both focusses the child's attention on the common underlying relation, and at the same time allows him or her to become aware of deficiencies or inadequacies in the previous assumption or explanation.

Such a viewpoint gives language, or rather the possibility which this creates for dialogue with others, a progressive role in the child's thinking. It is in marked contrast with the assumption underlying much of the earlier work on blind children's language carried out in educational establishments (e.g. Cutsforth, 1951). As I have argued elsewhere (Urwin, 1978b) the preoccupation with 'verbalism' and the lack of a framework for conceptualizing the advantages of language to blind children may have been major factors contributing to the paucity of work on how blind children actually acquire language. It is perhaps time to focus more attention on what blind children may gain through acquiring language, with respect to both their opportunities for social interaction and for their understanding of the wider environment. Further studies of parent-child discourse in the early stages would seem a useful point at which to begin.

Chapter 14.

THE INVESTIGATION OF VISION IN LANGUAGE DEVELOPMENT

Michael Garman

In the preceding chapter by Cathy Urwin we have a balanced and careful consideration of early language development in the blind child as seen in the context of some recent proposals on cognitive functioning in relation to language development in the sighted child. It is a paper that invites some reflective discussion, I think, and I shall take up three points for this treatment. First, though, I have to make it clear that I am commenting as a linguist with a special interest in language development, including language disability in children, but that I speak from no first-hand contact with the language of the blind child.

The first point concerns the possibility that we might treat language acquisition by blind children as a testing ground - specifically, in this case, for cognition-language relationships in early language development. It is easy to see that specific predictions might be made about difficulties in language acquisition by the blind child, given what we currently think about the situation in the sighted child; and the success of such predictions in relation to the data might certainly be taken as a useful test of our knowledge. To take a very crude example: if reciprocal gaze between child and adult is crucial to the establishment of (proto)conversational interchange (Bruner, 1975), and if conversational units are the building blocks of language acquisition (Dore, 1979), then we might expect blind children to be at a disadvantage. Studies like Urwin's suggest that we may indeed find some disadvantages of blind children, but that there will also be many overall similarities with sighted children. The important question for us, then, is, how are such findings to be interpreted? When we find specific and reliable difficulties, we can perhaps conclude that they are indeed the result of blindness (although this statement may well be too simple). Faced with reliable similarities, on the other hand, we might conclude either that what we thought was crucial to language acquisition is not so crucial, after all, or that indeed it is crucial, but that blind children have compensated in some way. The upshot of the latter interpretation is that our prediction survives in spirit, even though it is apparently challenged. Following this up for a moment, it may lead us to consider a view of human language acquisition ability which says that, given intact vision, certain strategies will regularly be employed en route to certain language abilities, but also that without this faculty certain alternative (and ultimately specifiable) strategies are available, to achieve the same end. According to this view, it would be wrong to say that alternative strategies lead to 'deficient' language acquisition. It would also be wrong to say that our assumptions about the basic nature of sighted strategies are incorrect.

The second point leads on from this, since Urwin points out that 'developmental delay' may be a grossly misleading term for describing her subjects' performance. Speaking as a linguist who is concerned with language disability and with defining 'delay' versus 'deviance', and so on, I agree very strongly with the drift of this. Once the language system has started to develop, we must beware of over-interpreting certain gaps (e.g. lack of reference to objects out of touch) as evidence for 'language' disability. The relevant question is whether these gaps will eventually lead to language disability (see Elstner, Chapter 3). But first we must know what we want to call 'language disability'. Again, from a linguist's point of view, I would like to emphasize in this connection the following two requirements: (1) the need to distinguish difficulties in the use of language that arise from visual (or any other) handicap from the concept of specific linguistic disability. This might be expressed as communicative versus linguistic disability. The child's ability to implement successful referential acts (see Mulford, Chapter 9) is a case in point. This is certainly not to deny the reality or importance of communicative disability; it is simply to point out that, if linguists are to be involved in assessing blind children's language (a plea that has already, quite properly, been made by other contributors to this volume), we should try to understand the fairly restricted area within which the linguist can be expected to make a professional contribution.

If we accept the distinction between communicative and linguistic disability, then how should we expect the linguist to approach the assessment of the blind child's language? This leads us to the second requirement: (2) establishing the relevant norms of assessment. Candidates, I think, are the following: (a) normal sighted language acquisition - the problem here being that we might expect typically to get what Urwin suggests, i.e. some differences but also some similarities with the blind child. This then brings problems of interpretation (as mentioned already) and a nagging sense that maybe we do not know as much as we thought we did about the sighted child with normal language. (b) The second possible norm is sighted language acquisition in the context of a specific linguistic disability - which might seem so obviously to compound our problems under (a) that it is not worth considering at all. But it is worth mentioning, I think, if only to underline the point that 'specific linguistic disability' is a neutral concept: i.e., where such disability exists (perhaps, say, in the form of some lexical semantic disability), linguists should be able to assess it, regardless of whether it occurs in a blind child, or a deaf child, or a child with mental handicap or with combinations of such handicaps - or, indeed, with no apparent cause for the disability at all. This is important, if the linguist's role is to make contact with intervention; the linguist's assessment must be independent of other (e.g. medical, psychological) terms of assessment, or it may contribute nothing that is new. It is also important in view of McGurk's reminder (McGurk, Chapter 10) that, as far as intervention is concerned, we ought to address ourselves to the problems of the vast majority of blind children, regardless of the fact that, for one reason or another, they may turn out to be unsuitably 'messy' subjects for the purposes of pure research. (c) The congenitally blind adult with normal language provides a third candidate norm, and this is worth considering because it may help us to understand more clearly how to separate out visual handicap from developmental factors; but this norm inevitably suggests a further one, (d) the sighted adult. This is in many ways our starting point. How do linguistically mature congenitally blind adults handle dialogue, for example, in a situation where there is ambiguity of reference, or indeterminacy of the addressee's attention, simply by reason of visual handicap? Do we want to deny congenitally blind adults true linguistic maturity on these grounds? If not, then the difference between the sighted and the congenitally blind adult in such matters should not be ignored when we assess the situation that blind children find themselves in. Or, to put it another way, once we have a clearer picture of the endpoint of the blind child's linguistic development, we stand a better chance of interpreting its midpoint, and so on down. This approach should not replace, but should arguably complement, the approach from comparisons with the sighted child.

Thirdly, Urwin's study of Suzanne, carried on into later stages of language development, clearly suggests that aspects of linguistic development may themselves serve as compensating elements in the communicative system of the blind child. To quote Urwin (I take this from her summary):

> The development of dialogue enabled [Suzanne] to discover new functions for language, such as requesting objects, and played a major role in extending her access to the surrounding context, including the activities and independent perspectives of other people.

So, whether or not language can be said to develop via alternative strategies in the blind child, once developed it may help to compensate for blindness. It is perhaps because of this that we think of blind adults as talking about the same world as sighted adults, even though we know that some of their perceptions might be different. But this in turn raises another comparison that might profitably be studied, namely, the blind adult with normal language ability versus the blind adult with a specific linguistic disability: the question to be asked here is whether language is the only, or the best, means of compensating for blindness.

Finally, I must acknowledge that I have defined the linguist's role quite narrowly in what I have said. I do so simply on the basis of my own experience and what I have learned (and this was a great deal) from the other contributions to this volume. Obviously, I am concerned to discover what should be the appropriate role for the linguist in the assessment of the blind child's language. In what I have outlined here there is, I believe, sufficient work to be done! More importantly, working on lines such as these, linguists might well be able to help significantly with some (but surely not all) aspects of the language problems faced by young blind children.

Chapter 15.

LANGUAGE AND ACTIVE TOUCH: SOME ASPECTS OF READING AND WRITING BY BLIND CHILDREN

Susanna Millar

The relation between language and active touch[1] is arguably one of the most intriguing questions when considering the development of the blind child. Touch and movement, together with tone of voice, provide much of the context necessary for acquiring language. Without this context we expect 'verbalisms' and empty babble. Conversely, we also assume that verbal strategies are particularly important for the blind to mediate a number of other skills. I believe these assumptions to be correct in the main. Nevertheless, I shall argue here almost the opposite case. I shall first present a finding which suggests that even purely verbal associations are not necessarily completely empty of meaning or thought. Secondly, and this is my main argument, I want to make the point that even in such language-based skills as reading and writing, overly verbal strategies can lead to spatial neglect and serious inefficiency.

The Investigation of Semantic Incongruity

The finding which I want to present first provides a corrective to our more usual preconception about 'verbalisms' in the blind. Clearly, totally congenitally blind children cannot know to what quality colour names refer. It is, therefore, often assumed that the use of colour terms by the blind must necessarily be merely empty and meaningless talk of the kind that has come to be known as 'verbalism'. Of course, blind children can and do learn appropriate colour names for objects; but this could be due to rote learning. It is not generally realized, however, that the congenitally totally blind, as I shall show, can also make correct decisions about inappropriate colour-object combinations which they are very unlikely to have learned by rote.

Method

The experimental task which was presented to twelve congenitally totally blind children was to judge whether adjective-noun word pairs were appropriately paired or not. The age range of the children was eight to thirteen years, with a mean age of ten years. Each of the blind children was paired with a sighted child of the same age, sex, and socio-economic status who had achieved the same verbal and digit span scores as his blind cohort. The word pairs were in four 'modality' blocks - auditory, tactual, spatial and visual. All visual terms were colour words. Half the pairs in each block were appropriate adjective-noun combinations, such as *singing bird, hard wood, round ball* and *red rose;* the other half of the word pairs in each block were inappropriate combinations, such as **barking cat,* **soft iron,* **tall dwarf* and **black snow.* Appropriate and inappropriate pairs were interspersed randomly, and care was taken to balance the order of blocks over subjects within each group. The subject's hands rested lightly on two response bars, one designated for appropriate and one for inappropriate word pairs. These were also counter-balanced. The instruction to the subject was to press the relevant response bar as soon as possible when hearing a word pair. Word pairs were spoken at equal rates and a timer-counter was activated at the beginning of each pair. Depressing the response bar stopped the timer-counter so that latencies could be recorded.

Results and Discussion

Overall, errors were negligible. Blind children had an error rate of just under four per cent, and sighted children's error rate was just under two per cent. The youngest blind children did produce more errors on visual and spatial adjectives, both with inappropriate and appropriate pairs. This is hardly surprising, since they will have had less opportunity to learn appropriate pairs. But the older blind children made few errors of any kind. More importantly, error rates produced by the older blind children were very low, even for the inappropriate colour-noun pairs. This means that they were able to come to correct decisions despite the fact that they had never had experience of the relevant perceptual quality.

The most interesting finding came from the analysis of latencies for correct responses (see Figure 15.1). This showed that the blind took significantly longer on inappropriate pairs than the sighted, but only in the visual modality, that is with inappropriate colour-noun combinations ($p < 0.01$). These decisions were also significantly slower than their own decisions on other word pairs, including appropriate colour-noun combinations ($p < 0.01$). This means not only that the blind were not responding by rote to the inappropriate colour-noun pairs, but that they must have thought about them longer. Clearly we need to know far more before we can be certain about the basis on which the blind make such judgments correctly. Presumably, inferences from appropriate pairs that they have learned and from what they know about other qualities that describe objects play a part in this.

Figure 15.1: Mean Latencies for Correct Responses by Blind and Sighted Children to Appropriate (A) and Inappropriate (I) Adjective-Noun Word Pairs Taken from Four Modalities of Perception

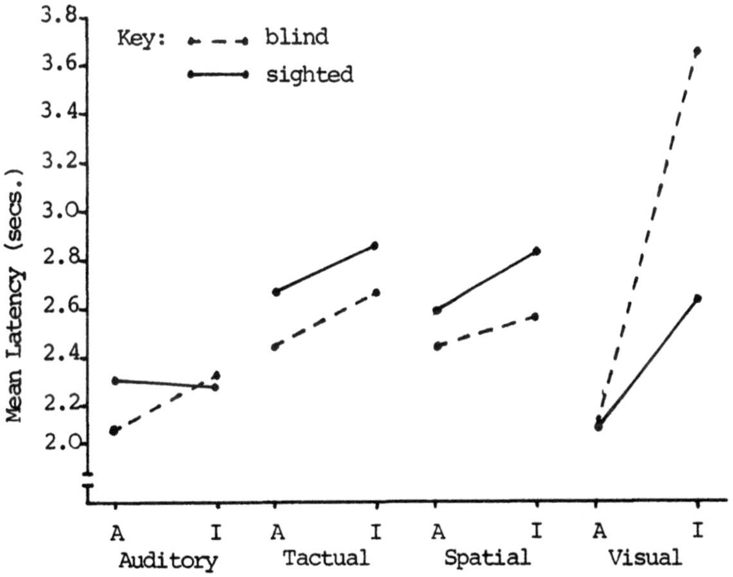

However, whatever the main basis of such decisions may be, the results allow us to reject the notion that purely verbal associations must necessarily be 'empty' in the sense that they are meaningless or cannot be thought about.

LANGUAGE AND BRAILLE READING

The main concern of this chapter is the use of language to mediate other skills, and particularly the fact that verbal strategies can lead to serious inefficiency when they involve a neglect of spatial coding. On the face of it, this seems to be something of a paradox, especially when applied to what is, after all, in the main a linguistic skill - namely reading. Spatial difficulties are rarely considered a problem in this, and there is indeed good evidence that the main difficulties of young sighted children fall in the linguistic field. Many recent formulations have stressed the importance of phonological analysis and coding (Frith, 1980). Deaf children who are very poor at this are typically also very retarded in reading (Conrad, 1979). It is also clear that blind children can remember more Braille letters when they are fast at naming them (Millar, 1975, 1978a). Nevertheless, purely verbal strategies can also have disadvantages in blind reading, and these need to be considered.

Models of Visual Reading

Most models of visual reading would present a picture of the processes involved which, in very simplified form, are graphically represented in Figure 15.2. Two main routes to reading, that is from the visual shapes on the page to the 'internal lexicon', are assumed: a visual route and a phonological route. The main argument has concerned the relationship between these two routes. On the one hand, it is argued that the visual string of letters on the page has to be translated first into sounds, or the phonological values associated with the letter shapes (Route B in Figure 15.2), before the meaning of the word can be accessed in a so-called 'internal lexicon'. On the other hand, it may be also possible to access the meaning in the 'lexicon' directly from the visual configuration (Route A in Figure 15.2) without translating it first into sounds by means of grapheme-phoneme correspondence rules (e.g. Coltheart et al., 1980).

Figure 15.2: Simplified General Visual Reading Model

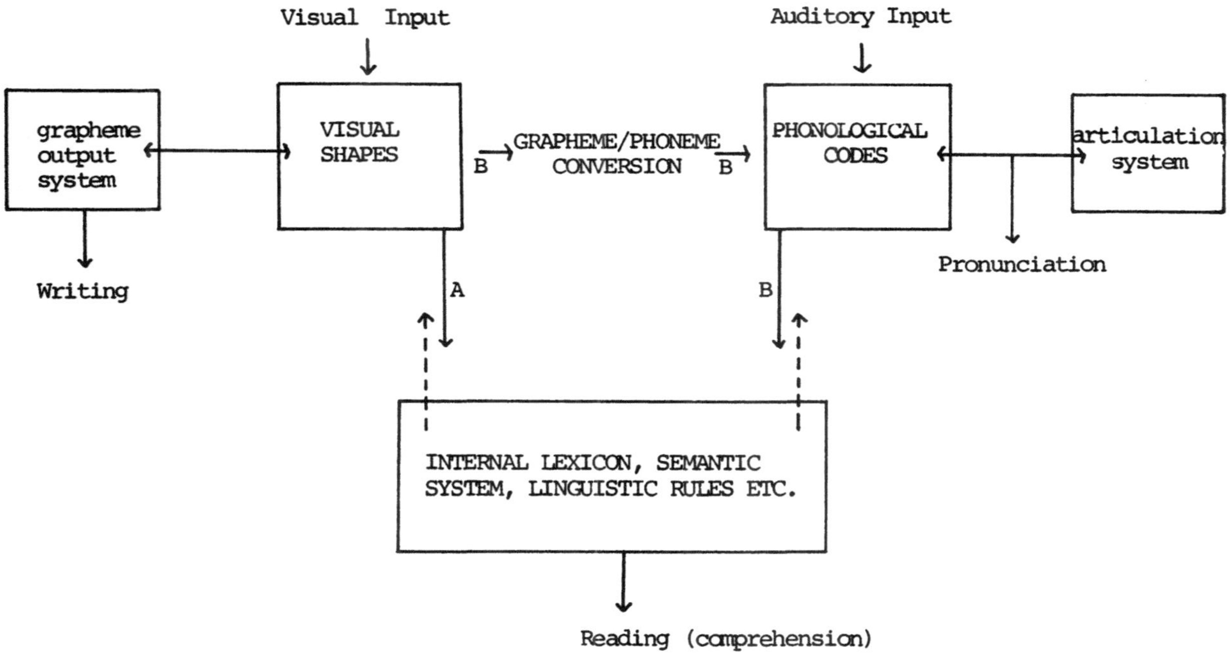

The semantic system also clearly affects the initial coding processes, as indicated by the broken lines in Figure 15.2. However, there seems to be little doubt when considering the visual route, whether it is conceived as direct or complex, that the reader codes the visual information on the page as shapes.

Models of Braille Reading

There are few explicit models of Braille reading. The main differences that are recognized between Braille and visual reading relate to the lack of redundancy in the Braille system, the use of contractions, the fact that it is necessary to read letter by letter rather than in global chunks, and that tactual recognition tends to be more difficult than visual recognition. The majority of the work done on Braille reading relates to the first three of these factors (Foulke, 1982). Clearly, both the lack of redundancy and the use of contractions impose extra burdens, including the learning of extra rules in addition to those necessary for visual reading. In the main, however, the difficulty of tactual recognition has received less attention. It is often blamed on poor tactual 'acuity' for which there is little remedy. Apkarian-Stielau and Loomis (1975) compare tactual perception to 'blurred' vision. Nolan and Kederis (1969) who did much to show up some of the major problems with the Braille system nevertheless assumed that Braille letters are coded as 'outline' shapes, much as they are indeed perceived in vision. However, the evidence that will be reviewed below suggests that the difficulty in the early stages of learning Braille is not due to poor tactual acuity, nor due to problems in associating the Braille letter shape with names, but rather to problems in recognizing the tactual dot patterns of Braille letters as global shapes or forms. In consequence, children sometimes get locked into verbal strategies, such as attempting to label the dots in a pattern by numbers, and failing to pay attention to the spatial relations between the dots in a pattern.

Experimental Findings on the Early Stages of Braille Reading: Non-spatial Coding of Raised Dot Patterns

There is evidence that tactual impressions can be coded in memory, and that such coding differs quite substantially from coding by name or verbal label (Millar, 1975). The paradigm used to demonstrate this was adapted from Conrad (1971). The rationale is that if children code items according to the sound of the name, successive items in a list that all have similar sounding names will be more difficult to remember than successive items which have different sounding names. Similarily, if children code letters according to the felt tactual impression, lists in which successive items are tactually similar will be more difficult to remember than lists in which successive letters are tactually dissimilar.

In order to establish, therefore, whether blind children code letters by their verbal or by their tactual characteristics, the children were tested on lists of Braille letters that were either similar in name-sound, or similar in feel, or dissimilar on both counts. The difference between a subject's scores on lists of similar and dissimilar sounding Braille letters, and between scores on lists of letters with similar or dissimiliar tactual characteristics, showed whether they coded the letters by name or by the tactual impressions. Both forms of coding were found. Moreover, coding by name-sound was associated with an increase of the number of items remembered on the lists of dissimilar items. By contrast, tactual coding, shown by the difference between tactually similar and dissimilar lists, related to the number of remembered dissimilar letters in precisely the opposite direction. Thus, tactual coders remembered less; and the more a child relied on coding by tactual impression rather than by verbal labels, the less he remembered. Nevertheless, even children who relied on tactual coding alone could remember up to three or four items. The strategy is, therefore, not only possible but useful, although clearly different and inferior to verbal coding.

A similar result was found when blind children were tested on Braille letters and raised-dot nonsense patterns (Millar, 1978a). Fast verbal recoding is an advantage. However, the results also suggested that slow naming and a consequent reliance on a relatively poor tactual code was not due to verbal difficulties, but was rather due to the fact that the tactual code is poorly organized. This raised the possibility that the tactual impressions that were remembered, were not, in fact, the physical shapes of patterns in the kind of global form that are so easy to discern visually. Recent findings support this notion.

Braille letters are derived from a small, three

by two vertical by horizontal raised-dot matrix in which the presence or absence of any dot alters the pattern and consequently the letter for which it stands. Each letter of the alphabet also stands for a different word, and prefixes can alter their meaning still further. Not only the pattern of dots, but also their spatial position relative to one another, and relative also to a totally notional external frame, is of importance in determining what verbal label is to be applied to the character. Two dots at the top of the matrix, for example, do not mean the same when they occur at the bottom or in the middle. But while in sighted conditions the references to a top or bottom line for the matrix are visually clearly available, in blind conditions spatial reference presents considerable difficulties. In fact, the evidence from a number of different studies, and using different paradigms, suggests that children do not code the Braille patterns in terms of spatial parameters, let alone as global shapes, in the early stages of learning. The evidence has been surveyed in some detail elsewhere (Millar, 1981) and will consequently only be summarized here where relevant.

An important finding is the poor recall of tactual impressions of Braille letters under certain conditions. The notion, for instance, that tactual patterns are coded as global shapes, as they are indeed visually, would predict that generalization to enlarged size is easy. This is not so. Even when the letters are known in their normal format, and there is no difficulty in discriminating between the enlarged shapes, young Braille readers particularly have problems in recognizing those letters in enlarged format (Millar, 1977a). It has also been found that the number of dots in a shape is more important for discriminating it from another shape than differences in spatial features such as symmetry, or in the spatial relations between dots in a shape (Millar, 1978b). Precisely the opposite would be expected if the raised-dot patterns were coded as global tactual shapes.

On the assumption that Braille patterns are coded as shapes, it could also be expected that the left hand would always be superior in the early stages of reading, since the right hemisphere is involved in spatial perception, and information from the hands tends to go to the contralateral hemisphere (Milner, 1971). Reports on which is the 'better' hand for Braille reading tend, however, to vary with the number of years of Braille experience the subjects have had (Fertsch, 1947; Millar, 1981). Very early in learning there seems to be no hand preference, even when discrimination accuracy is quite good (Millar, 1977b).

The difficulty in coding small raised-dot patterns as global shapes by touch is not confined to the blind, moreover. Blindfolded sighted ten-year-olds were taught to name four Braille letters to a reasonable criterion of accuracy. They were tested on discrimination accuracy which was good; they were then requested to draw the four letters they had learned with the blindfold removed. It was clear from the results that these bright ten-year-olds had little idea of the spatial relations of dots in any of the letters, and even less idea of the shape of the letters (Millar, 1977b). The tactual impression they relied on for naming varied between children, but they clearly did not rely on the actual spatial organization of the patterns. Naming the letters seemed to have been based on some form of 'texture' difference between the letters, which was related to dot density rather than shape. In any case, the difficulty of coding the patterns spatially does explain the rather poor performance with tactual codes found earlier. It also suggests that difficulties in learning the letters in the early stages of Braille stem from a poorly organized spatial code for the letters, rather than from difficulties in naming as such. The apparent paradox that difficulties in the early stages of learning Braille may lie with poor spatial coding, and an over-reliance on verbal coding is strikingly illustrated by the case of a congenitally blind girl who, at almost ten years of age, was found to be completely unable to read Braille.

The Case-Study of Helen

Helen, as she will be called here, was not merely a case of severely retarded reading. The important point is that, although she could not read, she could write stories in Braille and her spelling was as good as that of slightly younger but far more intelligent girls. None of the usual explanations therefore seemed to fit. Helen was a lively, talkative but self-absorbed and rather babyish little girl with an I.Q. in the region of low average on the Williams test (Williams, 1956). However, this low I.Q. clearly did not prevent her from learning to write Braille letters, and indeed all the words for which they stand, as well as many other contractions and rules for their application.

Her learning, however, depended on producing the letters on the 'Perkins' key-board which is used for Braille writing in Britain. In the Braille matrix, the dots in the left column are numbered from one to three and those in the right column from four to six. Any letter can, therefore, be coded verbally by specifying the numbers of the dots it contains. Helen clearly associated the Braille dot numbers with the combination of fingers necessary to produce the letter on the 'Perkins' key-board. Her strategy in writing and spelling was instructive, and very easy to observe, since she called out all she did in a loud voice, without regard to those present, and even when requested not to do so. Any word to be written would first be spelled out by Helen aloud in terms of the dot-number combination of the letters, before she produced the combination on the Perkins Brailler. The strategy, which relied heavily on coding each dot in a letter verbally (by number) was perfectly adequate for writing. For reading it proved useless. Before a dot in a letter on the Braille page can be identified by number, its spatial position at least vis-a-vis the other dots must be recognized. This is precisely what Helen failed to do.

Helen had, of course, been known to be poor at reading for some time, but she had some very good strategies for disguising the extent of this deficit. Her fingers would travel expertly across the page while she recounted with few mistakes the story it contained. But she would still recount the story accurately even if the book were up-side down, or changed surreptitiously. She was clearly relying on memory. When she was first tested on letter naming, however, she showed an error rate of 69 per cent, and scored not a single three-letter word in one minute on test. At the same time, her letter discrimination was highly accurate. In contrast to the error rate at naming, her accuracy on discrimination tests was 77 per cent correct. This makes it necessary to reject the explanation, accepted previously, that Helen had especially poor tactual acuity.

The possibility that Helen might rely on coding 'texture' differences rather than on spatial coding of the shapes to a greater extent than other children was tested in a study which compared her with three other congenitally blind children. Two of the children (A and B in Figure 15.3) were approximately 18 months younger, but with intelligence quotients at a superior level; the third (C in Figure 15.3) was a boy of the same age as Helen, with an average-level I.Q. and reasonably fluent reading for his age. A letter discrimination test was used with a ten-second delay between the presentation of the standard and the test letter. To assess the main coding strategy the children used, three types of interference tasks were interpolated in the ten-second delays. Verbal interference was tested by the repetition of *the..the..the* during delays, although verbal coding was not expected as a basis for discrimination. Spatial interference was provided by having the subjects repetitively feel around two shapes; for texture interference subjects had to feel over two textures during the delay. Figure 15.3 shows the proportion of errors with the different types of interference during delays. It is clear that Helen showed over twice the proportion of errors with texture interference than with shapes, although these also involved feeling across surfaces.

Figure 15.3: The Proportions of Errors for Helen and Blind Subjects A, B and C on Successive Letter Matching with Verbal, Spatial and Texture Interferences.

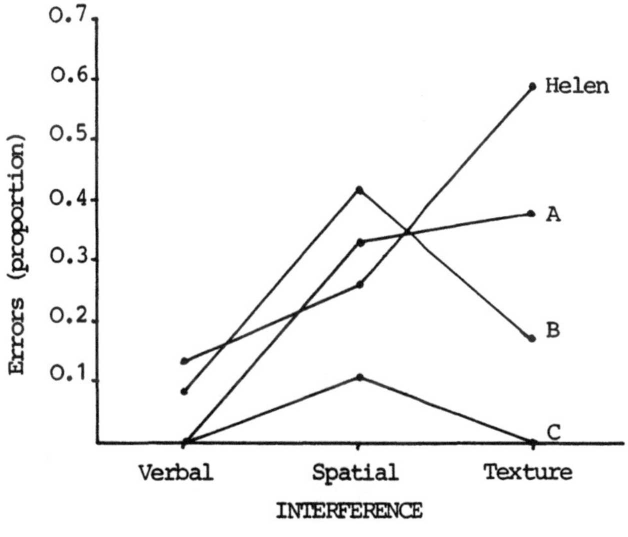

On verbal tests Helen did not differ from the others. For instance, she scored as well on producing and recognizing rhymes as the other three rather more intelligent children. She was well-known for her good verbal memory which, as mentioned above, enabled her to pretend to read. She had also long been known to be poor at spatial tasks, although even here some of her verbally-cued strategies helped her to disguise this at times. More importantly, her retardation in reading had been considered a symptom of poor tactual acuity and general backwardness rather than one of the results of her spatial difficulties. On test, she was found not to have the slightest idea that the Braille dots on the page lined up vertically on each side, and she required a great deal of intensive training before she was able to connect the relative spatial position of the dots with the number labels she was able to employ in spelling and writing. With spatial training she achieved an accuracy of 69 per cent on letter naming after six weeks. It took a further seven months before she achieved any reading age at all on a word speed test. However, her training had to include how to find the left side of her book in order to start reading, despite the fact that she had clearly been taught a very good means of doing so by first finding the spine of the book and working outwards from there. Thus, she was able to say from the outset that the spine of a closed book should be on the left. For Helen, the 'left' meant the side that her left hand was touching.

Verbal versus Spatial Coding

Helen's rather extreme case of dissociation between reading and writing must be explained at least in part by the discrepancy between her spatial and verbal skills, leading to an almost total neglect of spatial coding. The difficulty in teaching her was not so much that she could not learn spatial strategies, but that, left to herself, she would forget to use them and revert to the verbal means which for her were easier. In fact, Helen's case and the findings mentioned earlier, namely that it is difficult to code small tactual dot patterns in terms of spatial references or global form, make very good sense when the conditions of blind exploration are considered. Firstly, when exploring blind, there are no external references to which the dot patterns or the dots in a pattern can be referred. Secondly, the patterns are too small for it to be possible to use self-referent anchors. Thirdly, unless the shape is already known, exploring movements tend to be too rapid and unsystematic to preserve anchor information. When I first started work in this field, I was rather scandalized one day to hear a good Braille teacher admonish a child for moving or rubbing his finger over a letter. He should keep his finger still. Evidently, she had found this useful advice, although it went against all we apparently know about the superiority of active over passive touch. The puzzle is clearer now: the top and sides of a relatively passive finger can provide a spatial frame to which dot positions in a letter can be referred. Fast naming must become easier in that case.

The evidence reviewed so far suggests that difficulties in spatial coding are almost inherent in the tactual perception of dot patterns. Indeed, it now seems rather doubtful that even non-retarded readers code the patterns as outline shapes. The evidence comes from twelve blind children, six of whom could be regarded as retarded readers since their word reading age lagged some two years behind their mental age. They had a mean chronological age of 10;3 years; a mean I.Q. of 101 (Williams test), and a mean word reading age of 8 years. The other six children had a chronological age of 10;1 years, and a mean I.Q. score of 97, while their mean word reading age was 9;11 years and thus commensurate with the level that would be expected at that age. It was argued that if non-retarded readers used outline-shape coding more than retarded readers, it would be expected that presenting the initial letter as an outline shape should speed recognition of shape identity of a second letter. Moreover, presenting the second or test letter as an outline shape should also be better if subjects code the initial letter in terms of its outline shape. However as Figure 15.4 shows quite clearly, errors for both retarded and non-retarded readers were higher in both conditions in which the letter was presented as an outline shape than for matching letters in their normal format. The difference was highly significant ($p < 0.001$) in an analysis of variance with the appropriate factors. Matching by dot patterns was also faster, for both the retarded and non-retarded readers, than matching dot patterns with outline shapes, although there was some indication in the latency data that for the non-retarded readers cuing by outline shape was faster than cuing by dot pattern. The effect was shown by a significant interaction ($p < 0.05$) between retarded versus non-retarded readers and the letter type that had been presented. However, the relation was by no means as large as would be expected according to the hypothesis that the better readers habitually code Braille characters by their outline shape. A much slower process than form recognition seems to underly the recognition of the tactual impression from the page. There is good evidence already (Foulke, 1982) that tactual reading, unlike visual reading, tends to proceed far more as a letter-by-letter sequential process. But the evidence reviewed here suggests that even the letter, as a perceptual form, is not the unit of tactual reading. It is perhaps somewhat surprising that this was the case, even for the non-retarded readers in the above experiment whose ability to name and read words was not in question.

Figure 15.4: The Proportion of Errors and Latencies for Correct Responses in Retarded and Non-retarded Braille Readers in Successive Matching of Braille Letters according to Format.

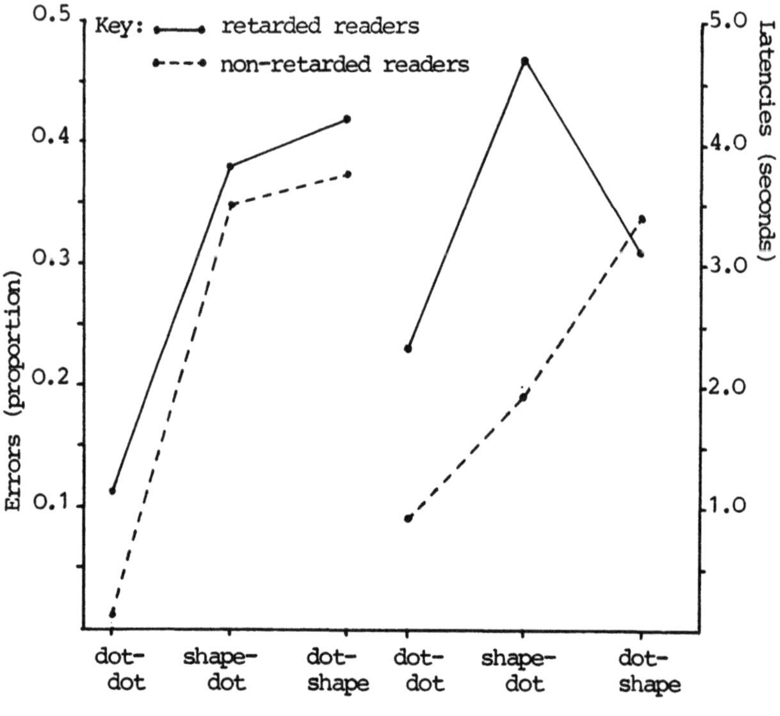

But this finding suggests that there is access to naming and meaning from tactual impressions that are not coded as global shapes. This process itself is not yet well understood.

One further point needs to be made in comparing the use of verbal strategies in tactual versus visual reading. Visual reading and writing provide feedback for each other. Thus visual writing uses movements that follow the same shape as the visually perceived character on the page. Braille writing, on the other hand, is not based on the shape of the Braille letter. On the contrary, it depends on depressing a combination of keys that, at least on the Perkins Brailler used in Great Britain, are arranged horizontally on the keyboard. The Braille letter on the page based on the three by two matrix, on the other hand, has a vertical organization. If Braille readers were to use spatial information to relate reading and writing, therefore, they would have to perform a 90 degree mental rotation, in the opposite direction for the two hands. It seems extremely unlikely that young blind readers can do this, the more so as young blind children tend to have particular difficulties with mental spatial rotation tasks. To relate reading and writing, therefore, the Braille reader, at least at the outset of reading, is again forced to use a verbal mediating strategy. The more obvious strategy, used by most blind children at the outset, is to label the keys on the Brailler with the appropriate dot number. The keys which are depressed by the fore-, middle- and ring-fingers of the left hand are labelled with the numbers one to three, since these produce the left-hand column of dots in a letter; the keys depressed by the corresponding fingers on the right hand are labelled from four to six, since these produce the right-hand column of a Braille letter. Clearly without some means of coding the dots on the page spatially, the dots cannot be identified even by number. But the temptation to rely on verbal strategies as much as possible at the expense of spatial coding, even when that is needed, must be very great.

The Implications for a Model of Braille Reading

The evidence reviewed here on the very early stages of Braille reading suggests that, even in its simplest form, any Braille reading model would have to postulate rather more stages or connections than seem to be absolutely necessary for visual reading.

Whereas, in visual reading, we can accept that even the beginning reader will perceive a string of shapes on the page, this is clearly not possible for Braille. Memory for tactual impressions exists. Evidence from a number of different studies, using converging methods, shows that in the initial stage of reading these tactual impressions are not necessarily organized spatially, let alone as global shapes. Such non-spatial tactual coding, possibly in terms of rather crude 'texture' differences, seems to occur particularly when naming or fast verbal recoding is difficult. But tactual coding does not depend on difficulties in verbal coding. In matching tasks, for instance, tactual coding may be faster (Millar, 1977a) and, therefore, more useful.

Tactual impressions can be associated with names to a limited extent. It was found, for instance, that sighted children could name four Braille letters which they could not draw as shapes (Millar, 1977b). Even when first tested, Helen was able to name some letters, although very few, and not very reliably. Thus, a model must allow for the possibility of connections between the non-spatial tactual impression on the page and naming or meaning. On the other hand, as the evidence from Helen shows, such non-spatial tactual codes are obviously not sufficient for learning to name all the Braille letters, punctuation signs and contractions. Without some spatial analysis of the dots on the page and their relation to each other, it would be impossible even to keep the finger travelling along the letter string without moving to a different line. For letter recognition and word naming, an analysis of the relative spatial position of dots is in fact essential. However, from the evidence of the middle-school-age readers discussed earlier, it seems clear that, even for the non-retarded readers, the unit of reading is not the global letter shape.

Figure 15.5 is an attempt to represent some of the complexity of routes that seem to operate at least at the early stages of reading. Routes labelled A in Figure 15.5 represent the direct route and Routes B the indirect route (via the phonological system) between the shapes on the page and the internal lexicon.

On the basis of the evidence, our - very tentative - Braille reading model needs at least two more types of connection between the tactual impressions on the page and the naming, rule and lexical systems.

Figure 15.5: Simplified Tactual Braille Reading Model

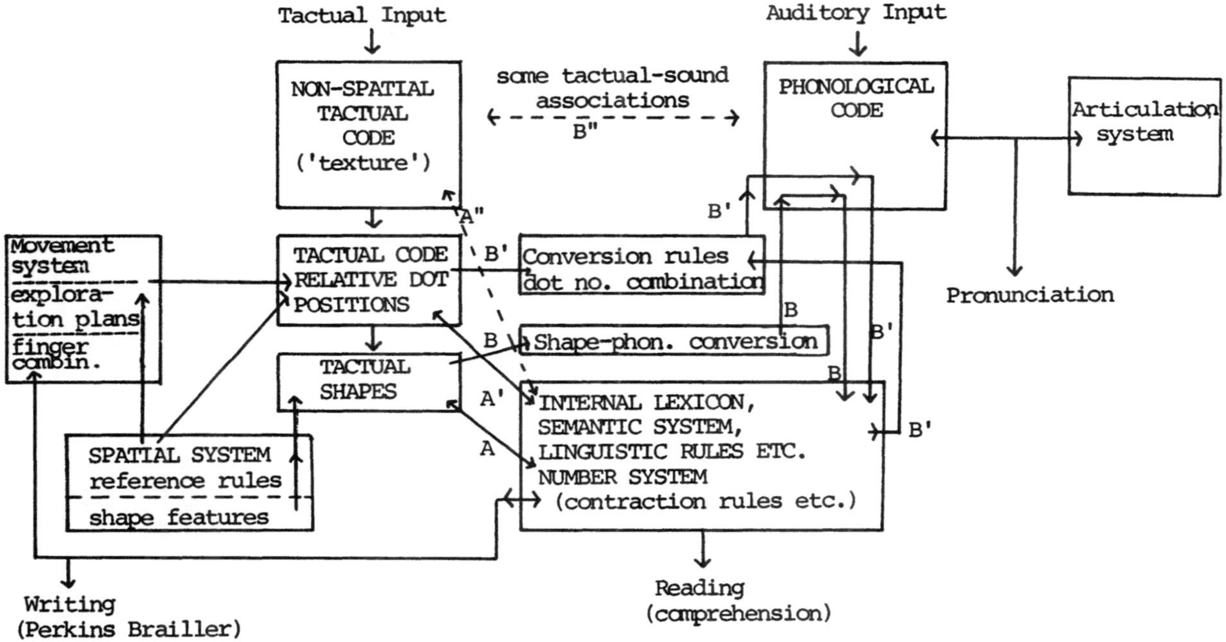

One type of connection must run from the non-spatially coded impression (Routes A" and B" in Figure 15.5) and is here represented by a broken line to show that these have limitations. Another type of connection (Routes A' and B' in Figure 15.5) must be via a code that makes use of some form of spatial analysis of the relations of the dots to each other which is at least sufficient to label each dot in a letter pattern with its number in a matrix. The model also shows that the tactual codes require some input from the spatial system. A dot-numbering system in association with finger combinations is also needed. Most paths are shown as effective in both directions. Indeed, top-down processing in which higher order meaning and context are used is probably more important for Braille than for visual reading.

Presumably, at a somewhat more advanced level of reading when letters or words even may be processed as whole shapes, yet a third connection is needed. As yet relatively little is known about the means of achieving fast and fluent reading in Braille (Foulke, 1982). The point here is that even letter-by-letter sequential processing does not account for the reading process in non-retarded middle school children. For these children the unit of reading seems to depend on a still slower sequential process of identifying the relative spatial positions of each dot and gap within patterns. Many children, other than Helen, interpose a verbal system between the dot pattern on the page and reading for either sound or meaning at this point, namely that of naming the dots in terms of their position number in the Braille matrix. This cannot be done without identifying their relative spatial position, however, which is precisely the point at which Helen failed.

A question that must be asked in connection with this model is whether all these possible routes are obligatory. We do not as yet have an answer to this. The dot numbering system, for instance, may help precisely because the dot positions, although coded spatially, are not organized as spatial wholes or shapes at that point in learning. The numbering system would make it easier to remember the dot combinations not in terms of position, but as digit combinations that can be held in "working memory" (Baddeley, 1976) so that their integration into words and sentences becomes possible. Certainly, if the connection with writing is to be established, a common numbering system between the three by two upright matrix on the page and the horizontally arranged key-board may be important. Interposed also between the dots as tactual impressions on the page and the meaning they bear for the child as letters or words, or contracted parts of words, are quite explicit rules that the Braille reader must learn and master before he can 'perceive' a given pattern correctly. These rules are indeed 'obligatory' for reading beyond the first grade of Braille. However, no child would ever become a fluent Braille reader if all the routes were obligatory. Many of them presumably become so automatic that they drop out with practice. Not all the routes are needed either, for example for comprehension, for appreciating poetry sounds, or for detecting a false tactual pattern in proof-reading. The fact is, however, that fast Braille reading is difficult to achieve. There seem to be two reasons for this: the difficulty of coding small raised-dot patterns in terms of spatial parameters, and the need to incorporate verbal rules and strategies, with a consequent tendency to rely too much on such strategies.

SUMMARY

The main argument in this chapter has been that our preconceptions about the relation between language and active touch in the blind child's thinking and performance can lead us seriously astray. Prima facie, it seems obvious that one of the greatest obstacles to the blind child's comprehension of written as well as spoken language is to have categories of empty concepts, that is words and descriptions which are without meaning because it is impossible that the child should have experienced the referents by touch or by any other remaining sense. Colour words are the most extreme example of this, and so constitute a test case. The fact that the congenitally totally blind can make correct inferences even in understanding these shows that their so-called 'verbalisms' are not as empty as we normally assume. It suggests also that the main obstacle to comprehension does not lie in the absence of experienced qualities.

Almost the converse case was argued about our intuitions on the role of language in mediating other skills, and our assumptions about the information necessarily provided by touch. The advantages of fast verbal recoding for memory, and of verbal strategies in relating Braille reading and writing, for instance, are obvious enough. But, as Helen's extreme dissociation of reading and writing showed, an over-reliance on verbal mediating strategies can become a serious hindrance when it leads to a neglect of the information provided by touch, and particularly to a neglect of the spatial coding of this information. Such a neglect is often difficult to recognize, because we assume that patterns are coded by touch as they are in vision, that is that our finger feels the simple outline shape of a tactual dot pattern in the same way as we can see it on the page. The main problem for reading would then reduce to the difficulty of associating the name or sound with that pattern, with or without conversion rules. However, the fact that we can perceive shape by touch does not necessarily mean that this is what we do feel. On the contrary, the studies reviewed here showed that it is extremely difficult to feel the small raised-dot patterns of which Braille consists as outline shapes. It was shown that they are not even felt as such by children who can read Braille quite well, and that there is an even earlier stage in reading where the tactual impression coded in memory depends on such factors as dot density rather than on the spatial relation between the dots. The findings suggest that there are relationships between the naming and semantic systems and all three forms of tactual coding, although these may differ according to whether tactual impressions are encoded non-spatially, or organized at least in terms of dot position, or when they are involved in fluent reading. In comparison with visual reading, the influence of the naming and of semantic systems thus seems to be more complex and pervasive at all stages of learning to read by touch. Moreover, the very verbal strategies that children may use to compensate for the difficulty of coding the dot patterns spatially can become a hindrance to tactual reading.

NOTES

1. My research work described in this chapter was undertaken with a grant from the Social Science Research Council of Great Britain.

Chapter 16.

THE IMPLICATIONS OF RESEARCH FINDINGS ON BLIND CHILDREN FOR SEMANTIC THEORIES AND FOR INTERVENTION PROGRAMMES

Richard F. Cromer

The mark of a good paper is that it stimulates thoughts in directions that are perhaps rather different from those of immediate concern to the author. The presentation by Susanna Millar in the previous chapter gives us not only a review of her carefully designed experiments on Braille reading by blind children but also an intriguing case history in the great tradition of neurology and neuropsychology. This potent combination provokes a number of thoughts on a variety of related issues, and in this discussion I will focus primarily on two: (1) the need for clearly distinguishing and relating the two different domains of conceptual thought and semantic encoding, and (2) problems that must be considered by those directly concerned with intervention procedures - in this case the teaching of Braille to blind children.

DISTINGUISHING CONCEPTS AND SEMANTICS

Millar's first experimental finding, that blind children are significantly slower on making decisions on incongruous adjective-noun colour-object pairs while nevertheless giving correct replies, clearly demonstrates semantic processing by these children. These colour terms, she claims, are not "empty verbalims" as some of the language of the blind has been occasionally described in the past, but are terms which are actively thought about and responded to. In an earlier chapter, Barbara Landau has already demonstrated that visual terms such as *look* and *see* are not semantically empty. That the terms the blind use might in the past have been thought to be empty verbalisms comes from a lack of differentiation of concepts and semantics (see

Werth, Chapter 8). Many psychologists have used these words as if they were interchangeable, but there is now increasing realization of the need to distinguish clearly between them.

Katherine Nelson (1978) has criticized most models of so-called "semantic memory" for the failure to differentiate between real world knowledge and word meaning. She defines the conceptual level as being what the child learns about the world. By contrast, the semantic level includes both the lexical level (the meaning of words) and knowledge of the relations among words and word meanings. Nelson suggests that in development the lexical level is built up independently of the conceptual level, and that the child must find ways of making appropriate connections between the two. Similarly, Susan Carey (1978) clearly distinguishes what she calls the child's conceptual domain and his lexical or semantic domain. The conceptual domain is the mental representation by which the world is understood. By contrast, the lexical domain is the structured set of words that encodes aspects of the conceptual domain. Each domain has its own identity and structure. This differentiation has often been muddled by psychologists (for example, in the confusion of "semantic memory" with "conceptual memory"), but it is basic in linguistics and anthropology. Sperber (1975), for example, has expressed this distinction by pointing out that semantic knowledge is about categories and not about the world. He considers the sentence *The lion is an animal*, and points out that to know the lion is an animal is not to know anything about lions, not even that they exist, as is shown by the sentence *The unicorn is an animal*. The English speaker knows the sentence *A spinster is an unmarried woman* to be true even if he knows nothing about matrimonial law. As Sperber (1975, p. 91) puts it:

> We might conceive of a machine capable of correctly indicating all the paraphrases, analytic tautologies and contradictions, in short, a machine that would possess all the semantic knowledge on which a language is based, without having, for all that, the least knowledge of the world.

Real world knowledge is termed "encyclopaedic knowledge" by Sperber. Statements of real world knowledge, e.g., *The unicorn does not exist*, are true or false according to the state of the world, and no semantic rules determine their truth value.

During childhood, each domain can develop separately before the mapping of one domain onto the other occurs. Carey (1978) notes, for example, that pre-verbal infants and animals have knowledge of the domain of colour, as can be demonstrated in tests of perceptual matching, in the absence of any corresponding lexical or semantic encoding. This has also been demonstrated for groups who speak languages that only encode limited portions of the colour spectrum. Rosch (1977) has demonstrated that the Dani of Indonesian New Guinea perceive the same focal colours as other human groups even though their language has only two colour terms, *mili* and *mola*.

Since the conceptual and semantic domains are separate, there can at the same time be development within the lexical domain. Thus, the child can be acquiring colour words and semantic knowledge about their use as category words even though he is unable to map these terms correctly onto perceived colour differences. Elsa Bartlett (1978), in a carefully designed study of colour word acquisition in children, found that the children who were the least advanced at naming colours typically produced three or four colour terms without using any of the terms correctly. Young children can often list the names of several colours in response to questions such as *Do you know any colours?* before they know how to map those terms correctly onto the perceptual/conceptual domain. This may help to clarify some aspects of language in the blind. Blind individuals know a great deal about the structure of the lexical domain of colour without ever mapping it onto perceived colours.

The separation of conceptual knowledge from verbal or semantic knowledge has also been demonstrated in cases of brain pathology. For example, Marie-France Beauvois (1981) reports experiments on patients suffering from optic aphasia who will give the wrong name for an object, but correctly mime its use. Shown a picture of a boot, they will correctly pantomime the pulling on of the boot while misnaming the object completely. It would appear that conceptual meaning can be encoded motorically and by images; conceptual meanings exist independently of the semantics of the verbal system and can be encoded by other means.

The important distinction between conceptual and semantic knowledge is implicit in Vygotsky's claim (1962) that language and thought have different roots. Slobin (1978) is studying the language development in children in widely differing language groups in order to explicate the relationship between linguistic and conceptual knowledge in development. One important task for the child is to figure out just which aspects of a particular conceptual notion are encoded in the language of his community.

It is interesting that blind individuals acquire some semantic knowledge before or without conceptual knowledge. It has already been argued that young sighted children do this with colour words, but the process may be highlighted in blind children. What Susanna Millar's experiment so nicely demonstrates is that the language acquired by the blind is not "empty". The words and phrases they use are not learned by rote, but represent meanings and categories that are actively manipulated and thought about. This was particularly clearly demonstrated when it was shown that colour words, for which the blind have no perceptual mappings, were nevertheless responded to correctly in their semantic pairings, and with reaction times indicating active thought processes.

INTERVENTION PROCEDURES AND BRAILLE READING

The main claim of Millar's paper concerns the nature of coding in the reading of Braille. Millar presents evidence that young Braille readers initially use a non-spatial texture coding in which the density of the dots is taken as the crucial differentiating factor for letter identification. She claims that shape coding is superior but that there is little evidence of its use by beginning readers of Braille; Millar therefore suggests the need for directing attention to spatial coding skills instead of relying on verbal strategies, especially in the early stages of teaching Braille reading. The implication for intervention techniques in the teaching of Braille is that shape coding should be actively taught and encouraged. It is worthwhile, therefore, to consider some of the issues that may be of importance in considering intervention procedures with any handicapped group, and to see in what ways these issues specifically affect suggestions for the teaching of Braille reading.

The first consideration concerns whether an observed deficiency is due to a real deficit or whether it is due to an elective strategy of avoiding a non-salient system. Specifically, do the blind suffer from a spatial deficit as a result of their blindness, or do they merely avoid spatial encoding due perhaps to its lessened salience because of the lack of visual input? One way to consider this issue is by analogy to another handicapped group, the deaf. O'Connor and Hermelin have conducted a number of experiments on the ability of deaf children to deal with temporally ordered phenomena. One experimental procedure (Hermelin and O'Connor, 1973) consisted of the presentation of short strings of numbers in a manner that was compatible with either spatial or with temporal encoding. The apparatus consisted of three small windows arranged horizontally. Below these was a single, fourth window. In one condition, three numbers appeared in the upper windows one after the other - one number in each window. These numbers appeared in such a way, however, that they did not occur in a left-to-right order. For example, take the numbers 3, 9, 7 presented one after the other (temporally). These might be presented such that the 7 occurred in the left-hand window, the 3 in the central window, and the 9 in the right-hand window. Thus, spatially, the left-to-right presentation would be 7-3-9, whereas temporally, first-to-last, the numbers would have appeared 3-9-7. After a one-second interval the numbers were exposed one after another in the single window below. This recognition display could show the numbers as they had appeared in temporal order (3-9-7), spatial order (9-7-3) or else randomly (e.g. 9-7-3). The child's task was to judge whether the order of the two presentations was the same or different. The task was the same for a second, similar condition in which the initial presentation was successive, in the lower window, and the recognition task was based on the subsequent three-window display. This three-window display was presented either temporally congruent, spatially congruent, or randomly. Hermelin and O'Connor found that hearing children generally gave temporally ordered recognition responses. Only 3 out of 40 children (7.5 per cent) recognized the left-to-right but not the first-to-last order of the digits. By contrast, 31 out of 57 deaf children (54.5 per cent) recognized the spatially ordered display but not the temporally ordered one. Thus, even when the element of spatial display was eliminated by the use of a single window either for the recognition display or in the second condition for the initial input, more than half of the deaf children failed to recognize the previously presented temporal sequence. These results appear to confirm other findings that deaf children have difficulties with temporally ordered information. However, O'Connor and Hermelin (1973a,b) went on to carry out further experiments that showed that the deaf children were not unable to process temporally ordered information; rather, they use spatial information where they can as a preferred strategy. For example, in one of these experiments (O'Connor and Hermelin, 1973a), 20 hearing and 20 congenitally deaf children viewed material such as photographs of faces presented in five windows. As in the other experiments, the temporal, first-to-last order of the items was incongruent with the spatial, left-to-right order. In another condition 40 deaf and 40 hearing children saw similar items presented successively at the same location. The child's task was the same for both conditions: after viewing the material, the child was shown two temporally adjacent members of the set of five, and he had to tell the experimenter which one had come first. Thus, in this experiment, the children were required to retain only temporal order information. Under these conditions no differences were found between the hearing and deaf children. In other words, when the deaf are instructed to retain only temporally ordered information, they are as efficient as hearing children. This shows that in other experiments, like those mentioned previously, where spatial information is available, the deaf evidence an elective strategy to utilize such information; but they do not have an incapacity to appreciate temporal order.

What about the blind child's use of texture coding rather than spatial coding in the reading of Braille? Millar has presented evidence that Braille dot patterns are not coded as outline shapes. A more comprehensive review of her findings can be found in Millar (1978b). She has shown that better Braille readers make a greater use of spatial coding than the poorer readers, but even here the differences were not as great as would be expected. In any case, it would appear that nothing prevents a blind individual from making use of spatial coding of the Braille letters; rather, he is unlikely to do so unless given special instruction - and, if I understand Millar's position correctly, this is what she is advocating. Further evidence that the blind are not impaired in using spatial coding comes from some findings which are in conflict with those reported by Millar. Millar reasons that since the right hemisphere is responsible for spatial perception, a left-hand advantage for Braille reading should be found if the early learner is coding the material spatially. Her experiments (Millar, 1977a) show no left-hand advantage early in learning. However Hermelin and O'Connor (1971a,b) have reported left-hand superiority for Braille readings not only in adults, but in children. However this discrepancy of results on blind children is eventually resolved, there is evidence of left-hand superiority in adult Braille readers, indicating that spatial encoding is possible, and thus the thrust of Millar's argument - that spatial encoding may need to be actively encouraged - is well taken. It would appear that, in the blind, nothing prevents spatial coding, and therefore one could presumably strengthen its use.

This brings us to a second issue in intervention: is it better to use intervention strategies to strengthen weak or little-used skills, or instead to direct effort to building up compensatory skills? Millar implies that spatial coding is necessary for good Braille reading. Yet she found that even good readers of Braille made significantly more errors in conditions in which letters were presented as outline shapes, indicating continuing use of texture codes. Furthermore, even if younger or poorer Braille readers make greater use of texture coding, they are nevertheless reading, albeit by a non-optimal method. There is some evidence that blind children prefer to use tactual cues rather than spatial ones in cognitive tasks unrelated to Braille reading (see e.g. Cromer, 1973). It would appear that Braille reading can occur whichever type of coding is primarily used. In designing intervention programmes, consideration must therefore be given to the best method which will engage the child in mastering the task. Again, analogies to other fields may be useful. Here, we can consider the kinds of issues raised by research on reading skills and the application of various intervention procedures to dyslexic children.

Studies of adult aphasic patients with acquired reading difficulties have provided some insight into the processes that can be used in that skill. Marshall and Newcombe (1973, 1977) were able to classify patients into groups in terms of which of two basic methods they used on a task requiring them to read single words without context. One method uses a phonemic route in which a word is converted into a sound before it is interpreted. The other method employs a direct semantic route in which the meaning of a word is recovered directly from its visual appearance. The advantage of the phonemic route is that it allows for the pronunciation and reading of new, unfamiliar words. It would thus appear that reading instruction for normal children or intervention programmes with dyslexic children should encourage phonemic coding strategies. The issue is, however, more complex than these findings imply.

Snowling (1980) studied a group of 18 dyslexic children of mean chronological age 12;1 who were substantially behind their peers in reading ability. In this group, the low reading scores could not be attributed to low intelligence, the mean I.Q. being 106. The children in this group were compared to 36 normal readers who were matched in terms of reading age. The task was to make same/different judgments for pronounceable nonsense words presented either auditorially or visually. The four conditions consisted of auditory or visual presentation of the first word coupled with either auditory or visual presentation of the word to be judged as same or different from the first. Both groups did well on the auditory-auditory task. This shows that the dyslexic children had no problems with auditory discrimination. However, there was a significant difference on the visual-auditory task - the task that is most similar to normal reading - with the dyslexic group scoring poorly. Since the groups were matched in terms of reading age, Snowling concluded that the dyslexic readers perform in a qualitatively different manner from normal readers. These dyslexic children evidence a specific impairment in grapheme-phoneme translation; they are not just the low end of a normal distribution of readers.

Jorm (1979) has reviewed evidence on dyslexic children that leads to the same conclusion that these children have difficulty with a phonological route to meaning. He attempts to explain this in terms of a short-term memory deficit. Whatever the true reason for their grapheme-phoneme impairment, suggestions for remediation programmes become apparent. Jorm argues, for example, that because dyslexics can access words visually but have difficulties in using the phonological route, methods of instruction should capitalize on their intact system. Thus, he suggests that the look-say method may be more effective for this group of children than phonic methods that try to teach grapheme-phoneme correspondences. Nevertheless, the great value of the phonemic method is that it allows the reader to access the meaning of unfamiliar and novel words - and this leaves the interventionist with a dilemma: does one use methods of instruction that are directed to the strengths of the individual, as Jorm seems to suggest, or does one use methods addressed to improving a poorly functioning system in that individual, but a system that has overall advantages for him? The best method of instruction may depend on the type and degree of impairment.

Frith (1981), in a review of work on dyslexia, suggests that the kind of intervention programme should depend on the specific handicap in the child. She reviews evidence that dyslexia is a specific deficit and that dyslexic children are not just poor readers at the low end of a scale of reading ability. That is, specific reading deficit (dyslexia) can be distinguished from general reading retardation. Frith cites the epidemiological studies of Rutter and his colleagues (1970, 1975, 1976) who show that this distinction is supported by three kinds of evidence. The first is statistical. Rutter and Yule (1975) point out that there is a hump at the lower end of the normal curve of distribution of reading scores. This hump is accounted for by children with specific reading deficits. The second type of evidence is aetiological. The specific and general groups differ in terms of a number of psychological, neurological and social factors. In particular, the children with specific reading deficits show stronger associations with speech and language delays. The third type of evidence - educational - is the most important in terms of the current claim. It has been found in a follow-up study after four to five years that the effectiveness of remedial teaching is greater for the group with general reading retardation than for the group with specific reading deficit. Frith points out that it is this persistence over time and the relative lack of response to conventional teaching methods that most effectively distinguishes specific reading deficit from general reading retardation. This has important educational implications. As Frith (1981, p. 99) has put it:

> ...it might well turn out that a dyslexic child benefits more from compensatory strategies and a poor reader benefits more from direct methods that strengthen his weakness. Thus the dyslexic might be taught by the development of new skills to replace the deficient ones, while the

poor reader might be taught best by practice in the deficient skill itself.

Before examining the implications this might have for the teaching of Braille reading to blind children, it is worth turning to a third issue in intervention which is related to the direction that intervention might take. Practice in difficult or deficient skills often results in the experience of failure. There may be important motivational reasons for avoiding such failure. Cooper and Griffiths (1978) have made this point in regard to educational programmes for aphasic children. Noting that the language failure of such children is not due to a linguistically deprived environment, they point out that language enrichment and stimulation should not be the sole means of treatment. Children who are subjected to stimulation and demands beyond their abilities may react with disorganized, disturbed, or withdrawn behaviour.

What relevance do these last two issues have to the teaching of Braille reading to blind children? Millar has suggested that beginning Braille readers use a texture code and not a spatial one. Some of her results indicate that even older and better Braille readers continue to use a texture code to a great extent. Millar stresses the importance of spatial code training for Braille reading. Evidence has already been cited that blind individuals do not suffer from a spatial impairment, and thus the first issue raised in regard to intervention programmes for handicapped groups is not very important in the present context. However, the other two issues would seem to require some thought. It must first be adequately demonstrated that spatial coding is necessary for good Braille reading. Second, the finding by Millar that even good Braille readers appear to prefer texture coding needs to be explored. Since with other handicapped groups, intervention forcing a child to use a deficient or non-preferred system has motivational consequences that sometimes outweigh the advantages of such a programme, such issues must be adequately explored with the blind.

Millar's interesting case study and excellent experimental findings have given us pause to ponder a number of interesting issues concerning not only intervention programmes with the blind but with other handicapped groups as well. It is a measure of the worth of her ideas that they extend beyond the particulars of her studies with the blind.

REFERENCES

Affolder, F., Bischofberger, W., Franklin, W. and Stockmann, I. (1980) Perceptual prerequisites for language development. *The Proceedings of the 18th Congress of the International Association of Logopedics and Phoniatrics.* Washington D.C. pp. 163-7

Alich, G. (1960) *Zur Erkennbarkeit von Sprachgestalten beim Ablesen vom Munde.* Doctoral diss. of the University of Bonn, West Germany

Apkarian-Stielau, F. and Loomis, T.H. (1975) A comparism of tactile and blurred visual form perception. *Perception and Psychophysics, 18:* 362-8

Argyle, M. (1980) Die Sprache der Augen. *Der Sprachheilpädagoge, 3:* 66-76

Atkinson, M. (1979) Prerequisites for reference. In E. Ochs and B.B. Schieffelin (eds.) *Developmental Pragmatics.* New York: Academic Press

Baddeley, A.D. (1976) *The psychology of memory.* New York: Harper and Row

Bartlett, E.J. (1978) The acquisition of the meaning of colour terms: a study of lexical development. In R.N. Campbell and P.T. Smith (eds.) *Recent advances in the psychology of language: language development and mother-child interaction.* New York: Plenum Press. pp. 89-108

Bates, E. (1976) *Language and context: the acquisition of pragmatics.* New York: Academic Press

Bates, E., Benigni, L., Bretherton, I., Camaioni, L. and Volterra, V. (1977) *Cognition and communication from 9-13 months: a correlational study.* Program on Cognitive and Perceptual Factors in Human Development Report #12. Institute for the study of Intellectual Behaviour, University of Colorado, Boulder

Bates, E., Camaioni, L. and Volterra, V. (1975) The acquisition of performatives prior to speech. *Merrill Palmer Quarterly, 21:* 205-26. Reprinted in E. Ochs and B.B. Schieffelin (eds.) (1979) *Developmental pragmatics.* New York: Academic Press

Bateson, M.C. (1975) Mother-infant exchanges: the epigenesis of conversational interaction. *Annals of the New York Academy of Sciences, 263:* 101-13

Baumgarten, S. (1979) Zu den Begriffen Sprachstörung, Sprachbehinderung, Sprachschädigung und Sprachauffälligkeit. *Die Sprachheilarbeit, 24:* 67-77

Bayley, N. (1969) *Bayley scales of infant development.* New York: The Psychological Corporation

Beauvois, M.-F. (1981) Optic aphasia: a process of interference between vision and language. Paper presented at the conference, The Neuropsychology of Cognitive Function, The Royal Society, London, 18-19 November 1981

Benesch, F. (1974) Ergebnisse der Erforschung kindlicher Hirnschäden - Konsequenzen für den Bereich der Blindenschule. *Der Blindenfreund, 6:* 141-8

Bernstein, D.K. (1980) *Semantic development in congenitally blind children.* Unpublished doctoral diss., City University of New York

Blank, M. (1981) Verbal communication in hearing and deaf pre-school children. Paper given at the British Psychological Society Conference, Developmental Psychology Section, Manchester, Sept. 1981

Bloom, L. (1973) *One word at a time: the use of single word utterances before syntax.* The Hague: Mouton

Bloom, L., Lightbown, P. and Hood, L. (1975) Structure and variation in child language. *Monographs of the Society for Research in Child Development, 40* (2)

Bowerman, M. (1973) *Early syntactic development: a cross-linguistic study with special reference to Finnish.* Cambridge: Cambridge University Press

Bowerman, M. (1978) The acquisition of word meaning: an investigation into some current conflicts. In N. Waterson and C. Snow (eds.) *The development of communication.* Chichester: Wiley. pp. 263-87

Bracken, H.V. (1969) Mehrfachbehinderung als heilpädagogische Aufgabe. In H. Stutte and H.V. Bracken (eds.) *Vernachlässigte Kinder. Heilpädagogische Forschung, 3. Beiheft.* Marburg: Elwert

Brazelton, T.B., Koslowski, B. and Main, M. (1974) The origins and reciprocity: the early mother-infant interaction. In M. Lewis and L. Rosenblum (eds.) *The effect of the infant on its caregiver.* New York: Wiley. pp. 49-76
Brieland, D.M. (1950) A comparative study of the speech of blind and sighted children. *Speech Monographs, 17/1:* 99-103
Brown, R. (1973) *A first language: the early stages.* Cambridge, Mass.: The University Press
Brown, R. (1977) Introduction. In C.E. Snow and C. Ferguson (eds.) *Talking to children* Cambridge: Cambridge University Press. pp. 1-27
Brown, R. and Hanlon, C. (1970) Derivational complexity and order of acquisition. In J. Hayes (ed.) *Cognition and the development of language.* New York: Wiley. pp. 11-53
Bruner, J.S. (1974/5) From communication to language - a psychological perspective. *Cognition, 3:* 255-87
Bruner, J.S. (1975) The ontogenesis of Speech Acts. *Journal of Child Language, 2:* 1-19
Bruner, J.S. (1978) From communication to language: a psychological perspective. In I. Markova (ed.) *The social context of language.* Chichester: Wiley. pp. 17-48
Burlingham, D. (1961) Some notes on the development of the blind. *Psychoanalytic Study of the Child, 19:* 121-45
Burlingham, D. (1964) Hearing and its role in the development of the blind. *Psychoanalytic Study of the Child, 26:* 95-112
Carey, S. (1978) The child as word learner. In M. Halle, J. Bresnan and G.A. Miller (eds.) *Linguistic theory and psychological reality.* Cambridge, Mass.: MIT Press. pp. 264-93
Carter, A. (1974) *The development of communication in the sensorimotor period: a case study.* Unpublished doctoral diss., University of California, Berkeley
Carter, A. (1978) From sensori-motor vocalizations to words: a case study of the evolution of attention-directing communication in the second year. In A. Lock (ed.) *Action, gesture and symbol: the emergence of language.* London: Academic Press. pp. 309-51
Clahsen, H. (1981) *Der Erwerb der Syntax in der frühen Kindheit.* Inaugural diss., Wuppertal, West Germany

Clark, E.V. (1978) From gesture to word: on the natural history of deixis in language acquisition. In J.S. Bruner and A. Garton (eds.) *Human growth and development: Wolfson College Lectures 1976*. Oxford: The University Press. pp. 85-120

Clark, E.V. (1979) *The ontogenesis of meaning*. Wiesbaden: Adademische Verlagsgesellschaft Athenaion

Clark, E.V. and Clark, H. (1977) *Psychology and Language: an introduction to psycholinguistics*. New York: Harcourt Brace Jovanovich

Clark, R.A. (1978) The transition from action to gesture. In A. Lock (ed.) *Action, gesture and symbol: the emergence of language*. New York: Academic Press. pp. 231-60

Collis, G.M. and Schaffer, H.R. (1975) Synchronization of visual attention in mother-infant pairs. *Journal of Child Psychology, 16:* 315-20

Coltheart, M., Patterson, K. and Marshall, J.C. (eds.) (1980) *Deep dyslexia*. London: Routledge and Kegan Paul

Condon, W.S. and Sander, L.W. (1974) Synchrony demonstrated between movements of the neonate and adult speech. *Child Development, 45:* 456-62

Conrad, R. (1971) The chronology of the development of covert speech in children. *Developmental Psychology, 5:* 398-405

Conrad, R. (1979) *The deaf schoolchild*. New York: Harper and Row

Cooper, J.M. and Griffiths, P. (1978) Treatment and prognosis. In M.A. Wyke (ed.) *Developmental dysphasia*. London and New York: Academic Press. pp. 159-76

Cromer, R.F. (1973) Conservation by the congenitally blind. *British Journal of Psychology, 64:* 241-50

Cross, T. (1977) Mother's speech adjustments: the contribution of selected child listener variables. In C.E. Snow and C. Ferguson (eds.) *Talking to children: language input and acquisition*. Cambridge: Cambridge University Press. pp. 151-88

Crystal, D. (1980) *Introduction to language pathology*. London: Edward Arnold

Cutsforth, T.D. (1932) The unreality of words to the blind. *The Teachers Forum, 4:* 86-9

Cutsforth, T.D. (1951) *The blind in school and society*. New York: American Foundation for the Blind

Dodd, B. (1977) The role of vision in the perception of speech. *Perception, 6:* 31-40

Dodd, B. (1979) Lip reading in infants: attention to speech presented in- and out-of-synchrony. *Cognitive Psychology, 11:* 478-84

Dodd, B. (1980) Interaction of auditory and visual information in speech perception. *British Journal of Psychology, 71:* 541-9

Dodd, B. and Hermelin, B. (1977) Phonological coding by the prelinguistically deaf. *Perception and Psychophysics, 21:* 413-17

Dokecki, P.R. (1966) Verbalism and the blind, a critical view of the concepts and the literature. *Exceptional Children, 32:* 525-30

Donaldson, M. (1978) *Children's minds.* London: Fontana

Dore, J. (1974) A pragmatic description of early language development. *Journal of Psycholinguistic Research, 4:* 423-30

Dore, J. (1975) Holophrases, speech acts and language universals. *Journal of Child Language, 2:* 21-40

Dore, J. (1978) Conditions for the acquisition of speech acts. In I. Markova (ed.) *The social context of language.* Chichester: Wiley. pp. 87-112

Dore, J. (1979) Conversation and preschool language development. In P. Fletcher and M. Garman (eds.) *Language acquisition.* Cambridge: Cambridge University Press. pp. 337-61

Dressler, W.U. and Schaner-Wolles, C. (1981) Patholinguistik als Beitrag der Sprachwissenschaft zur Sprachheilarbeit. *Der Sprachheilpädagoge, 2:* 32-7

Edwards, D. (1973) Sensory-motor intelligence and semantic relations in early child grammar. *Cognition, 2:* 395-434

Elliot, A. (1981) *Child language.* Cambridge: Cambridge University Press

Elstner, W.(1955) Erfahrungen in der Behandlung sprachgestörter blinder Kinder. *Bericht über die Blindenlehrerfortbildungstagung in Innsbruck 1955.* Wien: Verlag des Bundes-Blindenerziehungsinstitutes. pp. 26-34

Elstner, W. (1966) Sprachstörungen bei blinden Kindern. *Der Blindenfreund, 86:* 33-41

Elstner, W. (1971) Blindheit und Sprachstörungen. *Heilpädagogische Forschung, 2:* 225-52.

Elstner, W. (1972) Rhythmische Erziehung sprachgeschädigter Kinder. In W. Orthmann (ed.) *Schulische Betreuung sprachbehinderter Kinder.* Berlin: Marhold. pp. 59-94

Erber, N.P. (1974) Visual perception of speech by deaf children: recent developments and

continuing needs. *Journal of Speech and Hearing Disorders, 39:* 178-85
Ewertsen, H.W. and Nielsen, H.B. (1971) A comparative analysis of the audiovisual, auditive and visual perception of speech. *Acta Otolarying, 72:* 201-5
Ferrier, L. (1978) Some observations of error in context. In N. Waterson and C.E. Snow (eds.) *The development of communication.* Chichester: Wiley. pp. 471-84
Fertsch, P. (1947) Hand dominance in reading Braille. *American Journal of Psychology, 60:* 335-49
Fisher, C.G. (1968) Confusions among visually perceived consonants. *Journal of Speech and Hearing Research, 11:* 796-804
Fiske, D. (1978) *Strategies for personality research, the observation versus interpretation of behavior.* San Francisco: Jossey-Bass
Fladeland Waterhouse, S.V. (1930) Some psychological effects of blindness as indicated by speech disorders. *Journal of Expression, 4*
Fodor, J.A. (1981) The present status of the innateness controversy. In J.A. Fodor (ed.) *Representations.* Cambridge, Mass.: MIT Press
Foulke, E. (1982) Reading Braille. In U. Schiff and E. Foulke (eds.) *Tactual perception: a sourcebook.* Cambridge: Cambridge University Press
Fraiberg, S. (1968) Parallel and divergent patterns in blind and sighted infants. *Psychoanalytic Study of the Child, 23:* 264-300
Fraiberg, S. (1974) Blind infants and their mothers: an examination of the sign system. In M. Lewis and A. Rosenblum (eds.) *The effects of the infant on its caregiver.* New York: Wiley and Sons. pp. 215-32
Fraiberg, S. (1977) *Insights from the blind: comparative studies of blind and sighted infants.* New York: Basic Books, and London: Souvenir Press
Fraiberg, S. and Adelson, E. (1975) Self-representation in language and play: observations of blind children. In E. Lenneberg and E. Lenneberg (eds.) *The foundations of language development: multi-disciplinary approach,* Vol. 2. New York: Academic Press. pp. 177-92
Frith, U. (1980) *Cognitive processes in spelling.* London: Academic Press
Frith, U. (1981) Experimental approaches to developmental dyslexia: an introduction. *Psychological Research, 43:* 97-109

Führing, M., Lettmayer, O., Elstner, W. and Lang, H. (1981) *Die Sprachfehler des Kindes und ihre Beseitigung*. Wien: Österreichischer Bundesverlag. 8th edition

Furth, H. (1966) *Thinking without language*. New York: Free Press

George, F. (1970) *Models of thinking*. (Advances in Psychology: 1) London: George Allen and Unwin

Göllesz, V. (1972) Über die Lippenartikulation der von Geburt an Blinden. *Papers in Interdisciplinary Speech Research*. Proceedings of the Speech Symposium, Szeged, 1971. Budapest: Akadéiai Kiadó. pp. 85-91

Graham, M.D. (1968) *Multiply impaired blind children: a national problem*. New York: American Foundation for the Blind

Greenfield, P. and Smith, J. (1976) *The structure of communication in early language development*. New York: Academic Press

Grice, H.P. (1975) The logic of conversation. In P. Cole and J.L. Morgan (eds.) *Syntax and semantics 3: speech acts*. New York: Academic Press. pp. 41-58

Halliday, M.A.K. (1973) *Explorations in the functions of language*. London: Arnold

Halliday, M.A.K. (1975a) Learning how to mean. In E.H. Lenneberg and E. Lenneberg (eds.) *Foundations of language development: a multidisciplinary approach*, Vol. 1. New York: Academic Press

Halliday, M.A.K. (1975b) *Learning how to mean*. London: Arnold

Halliday, M.A.K. (1979) One child's protolanguage. In M. Bullowa (ed.) *Before speech: the beginnings of interpersonal communication*. Cambridge: Cambridge University Press

Harley, R. (1963) *Verbalism among blind children*. New York: American Foundation for the Blind

Hartlage, L.C. (1976) Development of spatial concepts in visually deprived children. *Perceptual and Motor Skills, 42*: 255-8

Häusler, R. (1968) *Sprachbehinderungen an Sonderschulen für Sehbehinderte und Blinde*. Unpublished dissertation at the Institut für Hör,- Sprach- und Sehgeschädigtenlehrer in the Pädagogische Hochschule and University of Heidelberg

Hermelin, B. and O'Connor, N. (1971a) Functional asymmetry in the reading of Braille. *Neuropsychologia, 9*: 431-5

Hermelin, B. and O'Connor, N. (1971b) Right and left handed reading of Braille. *Nature, 231*: 470

Hermelin, B. and O'Connor, N. (1973) Ordering in recognition memory after ambiguous initial or recognition displays. *Canadian Journal of Psychology, 27:* 191-9

Herron, C.A. (1974) *A study of relational prepositions and their comprehension by blind and sighted children.* Honours thesis, Princeton University, USA.

Hess, M. (1959) *Die Sprachprüfung in der logopädischen Praxis.* Freiburg, Schweiz: Universitätsverlag

Hockett, C.F. (1960) The origin of speech. *Scientific American, 203:* 89-96

Homburg, G. (1981) Methodische Überlegungen zur therapeutischen Arbeit mit dysgrammatisch sprechenden Kindern. *Die Sprachheilarbeit, 26:* 267-81

Ihssen, W.B. (1977) Die Bedeutung von Linguistik, Psycholinguistik und Soziolinguistik für die Sprachbehindertenpädagogik. *Die Sprachheilarbeit, 22:* 165-76

Ihssen, W.B. (1978) Linguistik, Kindersprachforschung und Pathologie der Kindersprache. *Linguistische Berichte, 55:* 62-70

Ingram, D. (1976) *Phonological disability in children.* London: Edward Arnold

Jakobson, R. (1941) *Kindersprache, Aphasie und allgemeine Lautgesetze.* Frankfurt a.M.: Suhrkamp, 1969. Translated as *Child language, aphasia and phonological universals.* The Hague: Mouton, 1968

Jorm, A.F. (1979) The cognitive and neurological basis of developmental dyslexia: a theoretical framework and review. *Cognition, 7:* 19-33

Karmiloff-Smith, A. (1979) Language development after five. In P.J. Fletcher and M. Garman (eds.) *Language acquisition.* Cambridge: Cambridge University Press. pp. 307-23

Kaye, K. (1977) Towards the origin of dialogue. In H.R. Schaffer (ed.) *Studies of mother-infant interaction.* London: Academic Press

Keenan, E.O. and Schieffelin, B.B. (1976) Topic as a discourse notion: a study of topic in the conversations of children and adults. In Ch.N. Li (ed.) *Subject and topic.* New York: Academic Press. pp. 335-84

Kephart, J.G., Kephart, C.P. and Schwarz, G.G. (1974) A journey into the world of the blind child. *Exceptional Children, 40*: 421-7

Kiphart, E. (1972) Sensomotorische Entwicklungshilfen. *Der Blindenfreund, 92:* 52-60

Kostjutschek, N.S. (1974) *Die Entwicklung der Sprache bei blinden Kindern.* Institut für Defektologie der Akademie der Pädagogischen Wissenschaften, Moscow

Kruse, E. (1980) Zentrale Sprachentwicklungsstörungen - Differentialdiagnose und Therapie. *Die Sprachheilarbeit, 25/6:* 205-12

Kubiak, I. (1979) Spracherziehung bei 3- bis 5-jährigen Kinder mit HSR. *Die Sonderschule, 24/6:* 362-71

Labov, W. and Fanshel, D. (1977) *Therapeutic discourse.* New York: Academic Press

Landau, B. (1982) *Language learning in blind children: relationships between perception and language.* Unpublished doctoral diss., University of Pennsylvania

Landau, B. and Gleitman, L.R. (in prep.) *Language development and the language of perception in blind babies.* Manuscript, University of Pennsylvania

Landau, B., Gleitman, H. and Spelke, E. (1981) Spatial inference and geometric representation in a child blind from birth. *Science, 213:* 1275-8

Leech, G. (1971) *Meaning and the English verb.* London: Longman

Leischner, A. (1967) Die Sprachstörungen im Kindesalter. *Zeitschrift für Kinderheilkunde, 100:* 137-59

Lenneberg, E.H. (1967) *Biological foundations of language.* New York: Wiley

Leopold, W. (1949) *Speech development of a bilingual child, Vol. 3, Grammar and general problems.* Evanston: Northwestern University Press

Lewis, M. and Rosenblum, L.A. (eds.) (1977) *Interaction, conversation and the development of language.* New York: Wiley

Liberman, A.M., Cooper, F.S., Shankweiler, D.P. and Studdert Kennedy, M. (1967) Perception of the speech code. *Psychological Review, 74:* 431-61

Linck, H.A. and Haberkamp, H. (1976) Sprachentwicklungsbehinderung - Sprachentwicklungsverzögerung, Versuch einer Abgrenzung. *Folia Phoniatrica, 28:* 141-60

Locke, J. (1690) An essay concerning human understanding. Reprinted in *The Empiricists.* New York: Anchor Press, 1974

Lopata, D.J. and Pasnak, R. (1976) Accelerated conservation acquisition and IQ gains by blind children. *Genetic Psychology Monographs, 93:* 3-25

Lux, G. (1933) Eine Untersuchung über die nachteilige Wirkung des Ausfalls der optischen

Perzeption auf die Sprache des Blinden. *Der Blindenfreund, 53:* 166-70
Lyons, J. (1975) Deixis as a source of reference. In E.L. Keenan (ed.) *Formal semantics of natural language.* Cambridge: Cambridge University Press. pp. 61-83
MacDonald, J. and McGurk, H. (1978) Visual influences on speech perception processes. *Perception and Psychophysics, 24:* 253-7
McGurk, H. and Buchanan, L. (1981) *Bimodal speech perception: vision and hearing.* Unpublished paper, University of Surrey
McGurk, H. and MacDonald, J. (1976) Hearing lips and seeing voices. *Nature, 264:* 746-8
McGurk, H. and MacDonald, J. (1977) *Hearing lips and seeing voices: a new illusion.* Paper to the Annual Conference of the British Psychological Society, University of Exeter
McShane, J. (1980) *Learning to talk.* Cambridge: Cambridge University Press
McTear, M. (1978) Review of Snow and Ferguson (eds.) Talking to children. *Journal of Child Language, 5:* 521-30
Mansfeld, F. (1952) Die Lehre Arnold Gehlens von den Kreisprozessen und ihre Bedeutung für das Blindenwesen. *Der Blindenfreund, 72/2:* 35-51
Marshall, J.C. and Newcombe, F. (1973) Patterns of paralexia: a psycholinguistic approach. *Journal of Psycholinguistic Research, 2:* 175-99
Marshall, J.C. and Newcombe, F. (1977) Variability and constraint in acquired dyslexia. In H. Whitaker and H.A. Whitaker (eds.) *Studies in neurolinguistics, Vol. 3.* New York: Academic Press. pp. 257-86
Maxfield, K.E. (1928) *The blind child and his reading.* New York: American Foundation for the Blind
Menyuk, P. (1964) Comparison of grammar of children with functionally deviant and normal speech. *Journal of Speech and Hearing Research, 7:* 107-21
Menyuk, P. (1969) *Sentences children use.* Cambridge, Mass.: MIT Press
Millar, S. (1975) Effects of tactual and phonological similarity on the recall of Braille letters by blind children. *British Journal of Psychology, 66:* 193-201
Millar, S. (1977a) Early stages of tactual matching. *Perception, 6:* 333-43
Millar, S. (1977b) Tactual and name matching by blind children. *British Journal of Psychology, 68:* 377-83

Millar, S. (1978a) Short-term serial tactual recall: effects on grouping tactually probed recall of Braille letters and nonsense shapes by blind children. *British Journal of Psychology, 69:* 17-24

Millar, S. (1978b) Aspects of memory for information from touch and movement. In G. Gordon (ed.) *Active touch.* Oxford: Pergamon Press. pp. 215-27

Millar, S. (1981) Crossmodal and intersensory perception and the blind. In R.D. Walk and H.L. Pick Jr. (eds.) *Intersensory perception and sensory integration.* London: Plenum Press

Miller, G. (1967) Information and memory. In G. Miller (ed.) *The psychology of communication.* Harmondsworth: Penguin Press. pp. 3-13

Miller, G. and Johnson-Laird, P. (1976) *Language and perception.* Cambridge: Cambridge University Press

Miller, G. and Nicely, P.E. (1955) An analysis of perceptual confusions among some English consonants. *Journal of the Acoustical Society of America, 27:* 338-52

Miller, M. (1976) Zur Logik der frühkindlichen Sprachentwicklung. Stuttgart: Klett

Miller, M. and Weissenborn, J. (1979) Pragmatische Voraussetzungen für den Erwerb lokaler Referenz. In K. Martens (ed.) *Kindliche Kommunikation.* Frankfurt: Suhrkamp. pp. 61-75

Mills, A.E. (1978) *Visual information and imitation in child language.* Paper to the Child Language Seminar, York, England

Mills, A.E. (to appear) The acquisition of German. In D.I. Slobin (ed.) *The crosslinguistic study of language acquisition.* Hillsdale, New Jersey: Erlbaum

Mills, A.E. and Thiem, R. (1980) Auditory-visual fusions and illusions in speech perception. *Linguistische Berichte, 68/80:* 85-108

Milner, B. (1971) Interhemispheric differences in the localization of psychological processes in man. *British Medical Bulletin, 27:* 272

Miner, L.E. (1963) A study of the incidence of speech deviations among visually handicapped children. *New Outlook for the Blind, 57:* 10-14

Mulford, R.C. (1981) *Talking without seeing: some problems of semantic development in blind children.* Unpublished doctoral diss., Stanford University

Murphy, C. and Messer, D. (1977) Mother, infants, and the pointing gesture. In H.R. Schaffer (ed.)

Studies in mother-infant interaction. London: Academic Press
Neilson, I. (1981) *Visual development in the 'blind' child.* Paper given at the British Psychological Society Conference, Developmental Psychology Section, Manchester, Sept. 1981
Nelson, K. (1973) Structure and strategy in learning to talk. *Monographs of the Society for Research in Child Development, 38* (Serial No. 149)
Nelson, K. (1978) Semantic development and the development of semantic memory. In K.E. Nelson (ed.) *Children's language, Vol. 1.* New York: Gardner Press. pp. 39-80
Nolan, C.Y. (1960) On the unreality of words to the blind. *New Outlook for the Blind, 54:* 100-2
Nolan, C.Y. and Kederis, C.J. (1969) *Perceptual factors in Braille word recognition.* New York: American Foundation for the Blind
Norris, M., Spaulding, P.J. and Brodie, F.H. (1957) *Blindness in children.* Chicago: University of Chicago Press
Ochs, E., Schieffelin, B.B. and Platt, M.L. (1979) Propositions across utterances and speakers. In E. Ochs and B.B. Schieffelin (eds.) *Developmental pragmatics.* New York: Academic Press. pp. 251-68
O'Connor, N. and Hermelin, B. (1973a) Short-term memory for the order of pictures and syllables by deaf and hearing children. *Neuropsychologia, 11:* 437-42
O'Connor, N. and Hermelin, B. (1973b) The spatial or temporal organization of short-term memory. *Quarterly Journal of Experimental Psychology, 25:* 335-43
O'Connor, N. and Hermelin, B. (1978) *Seeing and hearing and space and time.* London: Academic Press
Oléron, P. (1950) *Recherches sur le développement mental de sourds muets.* Paris
Oller, D.K. and Kelly, C.A. (1974) Phonological substitution processes of a hard-of-hearing child. *Journal of Speech and Hearing Disorders, 39:* 65-74
O'Neill, J.J. (1954) Contributions of the visual components of oral symbols to speech comprehension. *Journal of Speech and Hearing Disorders, 19:* 429-39
Ortony, A. (ed.) (1979) *Metaphor and thought.* Cambridge: Cambridge University Press
Pavlovitch, M. (1920) *Le langage enfantin: acquisition du serbe et du français par un enfant*

serbe. Paris: Champion
Pechmann, T. and Deutsch, W. (1980) From gesture to word and gesture. *Papers and Reports on Child Language Development, 19:* 113-20
Peuser, G. (1978) *Aphasie. Eine Einführung in die Patholinguistik*. Munich: Fink
Piaget, J. (1951) *Play, dreams and imitation.* London: Routledge and Kegan-Paul
Piaget, J. (1953) *The origins of intelligence in the child*. London: Routledge and Kegan-Paul
Piaget, J. (1955) *The child's construction of reality*. London: Routledge and Kegan-Paul
Piaget, J. and Inhelder, B. (1969) *The psychology of the child*. London: Routledge and Kegan-Paul
Provence, S. and Lipton, R. (1962) *Infants in institutions*. New York: International Universities Press
Rieder, K. (1980) Angewandte Sprachwissenschaft und Sprachheilpädagogik. *Der Sprachheilpädagoge, 4:* 2-10
Rogow, S.M. (1972) Language acquisition and the blind retarded child: a study of impaired communication. *Education of the Visually Handicapped:* 36-40
Rogow, S.M. (1973) Speech development and the blind multi-impaired child. *Education of the Visually Handicapped:* 105-9
Ronjat, J. (1913) *Le développement du langage observé chez un enfant bilingue*. Paris: Champion
Rosch, E. (1977) Linguistic relativity. In P.N. Johnson-Laird and P.C. Wason (eds.) *Thinking: readings in cognitive science*. Cambridge: Cambridge University Press. pp. 501-19
Ross, J.R. (1972) Act. In D. Davidson and G. Harman (eds.) *The semantics of natural language*. Dordrecht: D. Reidel. pp. 70-126
Rowland, C.M. (1980) *Communicative strategies of visually impaired infants and their mothers*. Unpublished doctoral diss., University of Oklahoma
Rowland, C.M. (1981) Communicative strategies of visually impaired infants and their mothers: descriptive data. In B. Urban (ed.) *Proceedings of the 18th Congress of the International Association of Logopedics and Phoniatrics*. American Speech- Language and Hearing Association. pp. 87-92
Rutter, M., Tizard, J. and Whitmore, K. (eds.) (1970) *Education, health and behaviour*. London: Longman
Rutter, M., Tizard, J., Yule, W., Graham, P. and Whitmore, K. (1976) Research report: Isle of

Wight studies 1964-1974. *Psychological Medicine, 6:* 313-32
Rutter, M. and Yule, W. (1975) The concept of specific reading retardation. *Journal of Child Psychology and Psychiatry, 16:* 181-97
Sachs, H., Schegloff, E. and Jefferson, G. (1974) A simplest systematics for the organisation of turntaking for conversation. *Language, 50:* 696-735
Sachs, J. (1977) Talking about there and then. *Papers and Reports on Child Language Development, 13:* 56-63
Sackett, G.P. (1979) The lag sequential analysis of contingency and cyclicity in behavioral interaction research. In J.D. Osofsky (ed.) *Handbook of infant development.* New York: Wiley
Sackett, G.P. (1980) Lag sequential analysis as a data reduction technique in social interaction research. In D.B. Sawin, R.C. Hawkins, L.O. Walker and J.H. Penticuff (eds.) *Exceptional Infant, Vol. 4: psychosocial risks in infant-environment transactions.* New York: Brunner-Mazel. pp. 300-40
Schaffer, H.R. (ed.) (1977) *Studies in mother-infant interaction.* London: Academic Press
Schiefelbusch, R.L. and Lloyd, L.L. (eds.) (1978) *Language perspectives, retardation and intervention.* Baltimore: University Park Press
Scholz, H.-J. (1970) Von der Notwendigkeit linguodiagnostischer Verfahren für die Zeit der Sprachentwicklung. *Die Sprachheilarbeit, 15/4:* 97-103
Scupin, E. and Scupin, G. (1907) *Bubis erste Kindheit, Vol 1.* Leipzig: Th. Griebens Verlag
Semzowa, M.I. (1961) Besonderheiten der Erkenntnistätigkeit blinder Kinder im jüngeren Schulalter. *Die Sonderschule, 6/6:* 336-40 and *7/1:* 29-38
Semzowa, M.I. and Solnzewa, L.I. (1966) Die psychologisch-pädagogische Untersuchung blinder Schulanfänger. *Die Sonderschule, 11/5:* 279-83 and *11/6:* 344-51
Sinclair-de Zwart (1969) Developmental psycholinguistics. In D. Elkind and J.H. Flavell (eds.) *Studies in cognitive development.* Oxford: Oxford University Press. pp. 315-36
Sinclair-de Zwart (1970) The transition from sensory motor behaviour to symbolic activity. *Interchange, 1:* 119-26
Slobin, D.I. (1973) Cognitive prerequisites for the development of grammar. In C. Ferguson and D.I. Slobin (eds.) *Studies in child language development.* New York: Holt, Rinehart and Winston. pp. 175-276

Slobin, D.I. (1978) *Universal and particular in the acquisition of language.* Paper presented at the workshop-conference "Language acquisition: state of the art", University of Pennsylvania, May 19-22, 1978

Smith, M., Chethik, M. and Adelson, E. (1969) Differential assessment of "blindisms". *American Journal of Orthopsychiatry, 39/5:* 807-17

Smith, N.V. (1973) *The acquisition of phonology.* Cambridge: Cambridge University Press

Snow, C. (1977a) Mother's speech research: from input to interaction. In C. Snow and C. Ferguson (eds.) *Talking to children: language, input and acquisition.* Cambridge: Cambridge University Press. pp. 1-27

Snow, C. (1977b) The development of conversation between mothers and babies. *Journal of Child Language, 4/1:* 1-22

Snowling, M.J. (1980) The development of grapheme-phoneme correspondence in normal and dyslexic readers. *Journal of Experimental Child Psychology, 29:* 294-305

Solnzewa, L.I. (1975) Die Besonderheiten in der Entwicklung des blinden Vorschulkindes. *Die Sonderschule, 20/5:* 304-8

Solnzewa, L.I. (1977) Die Besonderheiten der psychischen Entwicklung blinder Kinder. *Die Sonderschule, 22/2:* 104-10

Solnzewa, L.I. (1980) Kompensation der Blindheit im Kleinkindalter. *Die Sonderschule, 25/1:* 34-9

Solnzewa, L.I. (1981) Kompensation der Blindheit in der frühen Kindheit. *Die Sonderschule, 26/4:* 228-34

Sperber, D. (1975) *Rethinking symbolism.* Cambridge: Cambridge University Press. (Originally published in French in 1974.)

Stern, D.N. (1974) Mother and infant at play: the dyadic interaction involving facial, vocal and gaze behaviors. In M. Lewis and L. Rosenblum (eds.) *The effect of the infant on its caregiver.* New York: Wiley. pp. 187-214

Stern, D.N., Jaffe, J., Beebe, R. and Bennett, S.L. (1975) Vocalizing in unison and in alternation: two modes of communication within the mother-infant dyad. *Annals of the New York Academy of Sciences, 263:* 89-99

Stillman, R.S. (ed.) (1978) *The Callier-Azusa Scale.* Dallas, Texas: Callier Center for Communication Disorders

Stinchfield, S.M. (1928) *Speech pathology.* Mogrilia, Mass.: Expression Company

Sumby, W.H. and Pollack, J. (1954) Visual contribution to speech intelligibility in noise. *Journal of the Acoustical Society of America, 26:* 212-15
Summerfield, Q. (1979) Use of visual information for phonetic perception. *Phonetica, 36:* 314-31
Tervoort, B. (1972) The understanding of passive sentences by normal, deaf and hard-of-hearing children. In *Proceedings of the VIth Congress of Applied Linguistics.* Heidelberg
Tervoort, B. (1981) *Mother-deaf child interaction.* Unpublished paper, University of Amsterdam
Thimm, W. (1977) Soziale Rahmenbedingungen der Sondererziehung und Rehabilitation Sehgeschädigter. *Der Blindenfreund, 97/3/4:* 74-83
Trevarthen, C. (1974) Conversation with a two-month-old. *New Scientist, 62:* 230
Trevarthen, C. and Hubley, P. (1978) Secondary intersubjectivity: confidence, confiding and acts of meaning in the first year. In A. Lock (ed.) *Action, gesture and symbol: the emergence of language.* London: Academic Press. pp. 183-231
Tronick, E.D., Als, H. and Brazelton, T.B. (1977) Mutuality in mother-infant interactions. *Journal of Communication, 27:* 74-9
Urwin, C. (1978a) *The development of communication between blind infants and their parents: some ways into language.* Unpublished doctoral diss., University of Cambridge, England.
Urwin, C. (1978b) Early language development in blind children. *British Psychological Society Occasional Papers, 2/2:* 73-87
Urwin, C. (1978c) The development of communication between blind infants and their parents. In A. Lock (ed.) *Action, gesture, symbol: the emergence of language.* London: Academic Press. pp. 79-108
Urwin, C. (1979) Preverbal communication and early language development in blind children. In *Papers and Reports on Child Language Development, 17:* 119-28
van der Geest, T. (1977) Some interactional aspects of language acquisition. In C. Snow and C. Ferguson (eds.) *Talking to children.* Cambridge: Cambridge University Press. pp. 89-107
van der Geest, T. (1978) Mother-child interaction and their researchers. *Grazer linguistische Studien, 10:* 46-69
van der Geest, T. (1981) Psychologische aspecten van taalwetenschappelijk onderzoek. In M. Steehouder (ed.) *Taalbeheersingsonderzoek.* VIOT. pp. 200-12

van der Geest, T. and Heckhausen, J. (1981) Kommunikative Anpassung zwischen Kindern verschiedenen Alters und verschiedener Muttersprache. *Zeitschrift für Entwicklungspsychologie und Pädagogische Psychologie, 13:* 83-105

Vygotsky, L.S. (1962) *Thought and language.* Cambridge, Mass.: MIT Press, and New York: Wiley. (Originally published in Russian in 1934)

Walden, B.E., Prosek, R.A., Montgomery, A.A., Scherr, C.K. and Jones, C.J. (1977) Effects of training on the visual recognition of consonants. *Journal of Speech and Hearing Research, 20:* 130-45

Walkerdine, V. and Corran, G. (1979) *Cognitive development: a mathematical experience?* Paper presented at the British Psychological Society Conference, Developmental Section on Social Cognition, Southampton, Sept. 1979

Walkerdine, V. and Sinha, C. (1978) The internal triangle: language, reasoning and the social context. In I. Markova (ed.) *The social context of language.* Chichester: Wiley. pp. 151-76

Warren, D.H. (1977) *Blindness and early childhood development.* New York: American Foundation for the Blind.

Wason, P.C. and Johnson-Laird, P.N. (1972) *Psychology of reasoning: structure and content.* London: Batsford

Werth, P. (1981) The concept of 'relevance' in conversational analysis. In P. Werth (ed.) *Conversation and discourse: structure and interpretation.* London: Croom Helm. pp. 129-54

Wexler, K. and Culicover, P. (1980) *Formal principles of language acquisition.* Cambridge, Mass. MIT Press

White, R.W. (1959) Motivation re-considered: the concept of competence. *Psychological Review, 66:* 297-333

Williams, M. (1956) *Williams intelligence test for children with defective vision.* Reading: N.F.E.R. Publishing Company

Wills, D.M. (1970) Vulnerable periods in the early development of blind children. *Psychoanalytic Study of the Child, 25:* 461-80

Wills, D.M. (1978) Early speech development in blind children. *The Psychoanalytic Study of the Child, 34:* 85-117

Wilson, D. and Sperber, D. (1981) On Grice's theory of conversation. In P. Werth (ed.) *Conversation and discourse: structure and interpretation.* London: Croom Helm. pp. 155-178

Wode, H. (1977) Four early stages in the development of L1 negation. *Journal of Child Language, 4:* 87-102
Wode, H. (1981) *Learning a second language. I. An integrated view of language acquisition.* Tübingen: Narr
Wood, M. (1970) *Problems in the development and home care of preschool blind children.* Unpublished doctoral diss., University of Nottingham, England
Woodward, M.F. and Barber, C.G. (1960) Phoneme perception in lipreading. *Journal of Speech and Hearing Research, 3:* 212-22
Wundt, W. (1911) *Völkerpsychologie Bd. I: Die Sprache.* Leipzig: Engelman. 3rd ed.
Young, E.H. and Hawk, S.S. (1955) *Moto-kinesthetic speech training.* Stanford, California: Stanford University Press

AUTHOR INDEX

SUBJECT INDEX

For Product Safety Concerns and Information please contact our EU representative GPSR@taylorandfrancis.com
Taylor & Francis Verlag GmbH, Kaufingerstraße 24, 80331 München, Germany

www.ingramcontent.com/pod-product-compliance
Ingram Content Group UK Ltd.
Pitfield, Milton Keynes, MK11 3LW, UK
UKHW022156190926
475702UK00003B/50

* 9 7 8 1 0 4 1 1 9 9 7 1 7 *